Corruption, Development and Institutional Design

This is IEA Conference Volume No. 145

Corruption, Development and Institutional Design

Edited by

János Kornai
Harvard University, USA and the Collegium and the Central European University, Budapest, Hungary

László Mátyás
Central European University, Budapest, Hungary

and

Gérard Roland
University of California, Berkeley, USA

palgrave
macmillan

in association with the
INTERNATIONAL ECONOMIC ASSOCIATION

First published 2009 by
PALGRAVE MACMILLAN

Palgrave Macmillan in the UK is an imprint of Macmillan Publishers Limited, registered in England, company number 785998, of Houndmills, Basingstoke, Hampshire RG21 6XS.

Palgrave Macmillan in the US is a division of St Martin's Press LLC, 175 Fifth Avenue, New York, NY 10010.

Palgrave Macmillan is the global academic imprint of the above companies and has companies and representatives throughout the world.

ISBN-13: 978–0–230–54699–8 hardback
ISBN-10: 0–230–54699–4 hardback

This book is printed on paper suitable for recycling and made from fully managed and sustained forest sources. Logging, pulping and manufacturing processes are expected to conform to the environmental regulations of the country of origin.

A catalogue record for this book is available from the British Library.

A catalog record for this book is available from the Library of Congress.

10 9 8 7 6 5 4 3 2 1
18 17 16 15 14 13 12 11 10 09

Printed and bound in Great Britain by
CPI Antony Rowe, Chippenham and Eastbourne

Contents

List of Tables and Figures

Tables

Figures

The International Economic Association

A non-profit organization with purely scientific aims, the International Economic Association (IEA) was founded in 1950. It is a federation of some sixty national economic associations in all parts of the world. Its basic purpose is the development of economics as an intellectual discipline, recognising a diversity of problems, systems and values in the world and taking note of methodological diversities.

The IEA has, since its creation, sought to fulfil that purpose by promoting mutual understanding among economists through the organization of scientific meetings and common research programmes, and by means of publications on problems of fundamental as well as of current importance. Deriving from its long concern to assure professional contacts between East and West and North and South, the IEA pays special attention to issues of economies in systemic transition and in the course of development. During its fifty years of existence, it has organized more than a hundred round-table conferences for specialists on topics ranging from fundamental theories to methods and tools of analysis and major problems of the present-day world. Participation in round tables is at the invitation of a specialist programme committee, but fourteen triennial World Congresses have regularly attracted the participation of individual economists from all over the world.

The Association is governed by a Council, composed of representatives of all member associations, and by a fifteen-member Executive Committee which is elected by the Council. The Executive Committee (2002–2005) at the time of the Marrakech Congress was:

President:	Professor János Kornai, Hungary
Vice-President:	Professor Bina Agarwal, India
Treasurer:	Professor Jacob Frenkel, Israel
Past President:	Professor Robert Solow, USA
President-elect:	Professor Guillermo Calvo, Argentina
Other members:	Professor Maria Augusztinovics, Hungary
	Professor Eliana Cardoso, Brazil
	Professor Duardo Engel, Chile
	Professor Heba Handoussa, Egypt
	Professor Michael Hoel, Norway
	Professor Jean-Jacques Laffont, France
	Professor Andreu Mas Colell, Spain

Sir Austin Robinson was an active Adviser on the publication of IEA Conference proceedings from 1954 until his final short illness in 1993.

The Association has also been fortunate in having secured many outstanding economists to serve as President:

Gottfried Haberler (1950–53), Howard S. Ellis (1953–56), Erik Lindahl (1956–59), E.A.G. Robinson (1959–62), Ugo Papi (1962–65), Paul A. Samuelson (1965–68). Erik Lundberg (1968–71), Fritz Machlup (1971–74), Edmund Malinvaud (1974–77), Shigeto Tsuru (1977–80), Victor L. Urquidi (1980–83), Kenneth J. Arrow (1983–86), Amartya Sen (1986–89), Anthony B. Atkinson (1989–1992), Michael Bruno (1992–95), Jacques Drèze (1995–99), Robert M. Solow (1999–2002) and Janos Kornai (2002–05).

The activities of the Association are mainly funded from the subscriptions of members and grants from a number of organizations. Support from UNESCO since the Association was founded, and from its International Social Science Council, is gratefully acknowledged.

Preface and Acknowledgements

The Fourteenth World Congress of the International Congress of the International Economic Association (IEA) was held between 29 August and 2 September 2005 at the Palais des Congrés in Marrakech. The Congress is deeply grateful to the patron of the Congress, His Majesty Mohammed VI, whose support made the event possible and the Congress was inaugurated by a letter from His Majesty, read by the adviser to the King. M. Abdelaziz Meziane Belfik.

The Congress programme consisted of six invited lectures, nine invited sessions, and 52 contributed papers in addition to the Presidential address. The programme focused on the following main themes: New Trends in Economics; Understanding the great Changes in the World; and Economic Reform in Morocco.

The preparation of the Congress was the responsibility of the IEA President, János Kornai, ably assisted by an international programme committee, co-chaired by Gérard Roland and László Mátyás. The full list of the Programme Committee is as follows:

B. Agarwal, Institute of Economic Growth, India
M. Augusztinovics, Institute of Economics. Academy of Sciences, Hungary
Péter Benczúr, MNB, National Bank, Hungary
Guillermo Calvo, University of Maryland, USA
F. Canova, Pombeu Fabra, Barcelona, Spain
E. Cardoso, Brazil
M. Chafiki, Mohammed V University, Rabat and Ministry of Privatization, Morocco
A. Dnes, University of Hull, UK
V. Costancio, Bank of Portugal, Lisbon, Portugal
E. Engel, Yale University, New Haven, USA
B. Field, University of Massachusetts, USA
J.-P. Fitoussi, OFCE, Paris, France
J. Frenkel, Merrill Lynch, London, UK
S. Gaechter, University of St. Gallen, Switzerland
H. Handoussa, ERF, Cairo, Egypt
M. Hoel, University of Oslo, Norway
F. Kubler, University of Mannheim, Germany
Wu Jinglian, Peking University and Chinese Academy of Social Sciences, China
S. Jurajda, CERGE-EI, Czech Republic

M. Kaser, University of Oxford, UK
G. Kézdi, Central European University, Hungary
J. Krishnakumar, University of Geneva, Switzerland
P. Lane, University of Dublin, Ireland
B. Lockwood, Warwick University, UK
A. Mas Collel, University Pompeu Fabri, Barcelona
U. Pagano, University of Siena, Italy
G. della Paolera, The American University of Paris, France
F.K. Padoa Schioppa, Rome, Italy
P. Pestieau, CORE, Belgium
A. Ratfai, CEU, Hungary
P. Rey, University of Toulouse, France
L. Simon, University of California, Berkeley, USA
R. Solow, MIT, Boston, USA
E. Somanathan, Indian Statistical Institute, India
K. Suzumura, Hitotsubashi University, Japan
A. Vercelli, University of Sienna, Italy

We owe a debt of gratitude to the Local Organizing Committee, particularly Fathallah Oualalou, Minister of Finance and Privatization and Mohammed Chafiki, Chairman of the Local Organizing Committee. The other members were: Mustapha Arrifi, Mohamed Benchekroun, Amina Chemlal, Laila Essadki, Omar Faraj, Hakim Firadi, Mohamed Fadel Mokhtari, Mohamed Ouchen, Mohamed Rguigue, Hicham Zakani.

The organization also involved much work for the administrative staff. We would like to thank the Secretary-General, Jean-Paul Fitoussi. In Paris, Véronique de Labarre and Marie David, in Berkeley, Carol Smallfield and in Budapest, Katalin Szabó worked tirelessly. Finally, we are deeply indebted to all those who helped the dissemination of the Congress achievements. We extend sincere thanks to the scholars who contributed papers, to the IEA Chief Editor, Michael Kaser, to IEA editor, Maureen Hadfield and the publisher Amanda Hamilton, Palgrave Macmillan. The Congress proceedings are published in two volumes edited by János Kornai, László Mátyás and Gérard Roland.

We are grateful to the many institutions who supported the Congress financially, the Ministry of Finance and Privatization, Royal Air Maroc, Maroc Telecom, the Banque Centrale Populaire and Caisse de Dépôt et de Gestion. Generous grants were also awarded by Banca d'Italia, the Bank for International Settlements, the European Central Bank, the Ford Foundation, the Inter Ammerican Development Bank and UNESCO/ISSC.

List of Contributors

Luis A. Andrés, World Bank, Washington DC, USA

Steve Boucher, University of California, Davis, USA

Alessandra Casarico, Università Bocconi, Milan, Italy

Carlo Devillanova, Università Bocconi, Milan, Italy

C. Simon Fan, Lingnan University, China

José Luis Guasch, World Bank, Washington DC, USA

Richard Green, University of Southampton, UK

János Kornai, Harvard University, USA, Collegium and Central European University, Budapest, Hungary

Jana Kunicová, California Institute of Technology, USA

László Mátyás, University of Budapest, Hungary

Claude Ménard, Université de Paris, Panthéon Sorbonne, France

Mustapha Nabli, World Bank, Washington DC, USA

Klara Sabirianova Peter, Georgia State University, USA

Gérard Roland, University of California, Berkeley, USA

Susan Rose-Ackerman, Yale University, USA

Carlos Silva-Jáuregui, World Bank, Washington DC, USA

Oded Stark, University of Klagenfurt, Austria; University of Bonn, Germany; University of Vienna, Austria; Warsaw University, Poland; Warsaw School of Economics, Poland

Stephane Straub, World Bank, Washington DC, USA

Jan Svejnar, University of Michigan, USA

J. Edward Taylor, University of California, Davis, USA

Silke Uebelmesser, University of Munich, Germany

Evgeny Yakovlev, Centre for Economic, Financial and International Research, Moscow, Russian Federation

Ekaterina Zhuravskaya, Centre for Economic, Financial and International Research, Moscow, Russian Federation; Centre for Economic Policy Research, UK

List of Abbreviations and Acronyms

BEEPS	Business Environment and Enterprise Performance Surveys
BETTA	British Electricity Trading and Transmission Arrangements
BG	British Gas
BOO	Build, own, operate
BOT	Build, operate, transfer
BT	British Telecommunications
CEFIR	Centre for Economic and Financial Research
CEPR	Centre for Economic Policy Research
CIS	Commonwealth of Independent States
CLPR	Closed list proportional representation
CORRWB	Control of corruption index (World Bank)
CPI	Corruption perception index
DGFT	Director General of Fair Trading
DPI	Database on political institutions (World Bank)
ENHRUM	Encuesta Nacional a Hogares Rurales de Mexico (Mexico National Rural Household Survey)
EU	European Union
FGLS	Feasible generalized least square
GDP	Gross Domestic Product
GLS	Generalized least square
GMM	Generalized method of moments
IMF	International Monetary Fund
INEGI	Instituto Nacional de Estadistica, Geografía e Información (National Institute of Statistics, Geography and Information)
IRR-WACC	Internal rate of return-weighted average cost of capital
ITU	International Telecommunication Union
LAC	Latin American country
MMC	Monopolies and Mergers Commission
NGC	National Grid Company
NETA	New Electricity Trading Arrangements
NIE	Northern Ireland Electricity
OFT	Office of Fair Trading
OLADE	Latin American Organization of Energy
OLPR	Open list proportional representation
PR	Proportional representation
RECs	Regional Electricity Companies
RPI	Retail Prices Index
SOE	State-owned enterprises
TI	Transparency International

Introduction: Great Changes in the World and in Economics – Corruption, Development and Institutional Design

János Kornai, László Mátyás and Gérard Roland

The Fourteenth World Congress of the International Economic Association took place in Marrakech between 29 August and 2 September 2005. The main themes of the Congress were 'New Trends in Economics' and 'Understanding the Great Changes in the World'. These two volumes present the reader with the presidential address by János Kornai, many of the distinguished invited lectures (by Yingyi Qian and Jinglian Wu, Timur Kuran, Edmund Phelps and Philippe Aghion) and many papers presented at the different invited sessions organized by Masa Aoki (Mechanisms of Institutional Change), Herbert Gintis (The Implications of Experimental Economics For Economic Theory), Mustafa Nabli (Is Democracy a Binding Constraint for Economic Growth in the Middle East and North Africa Region?), Susan Rose-Ackerman (Trust and Distrust in Post-socialist Transition), Jan Svejnar (15 Years of Post-Socialist Transition), Oded Stark (The New Economics of the Brain Drain: Analytics, Empirics and Policy) and Claude Ménard (Institutional Design and Economic Performance).

There have been many changes both in the world and in economics around the turn of the millennium. A fundamental change has been the end of the cold war and the post-socialist transition in Central and Eastern Europe, China and Vietnam. Countries like China and India have engaged on an impressive growth path. Globalization has continued to unravel with goods, capital and people moving more freely around the globe. With 9/11 and the Iraq war, but also Chechnya, Kosovo, Afghanistan and the continued conflict in the Middle East, new concerns have arisen about fault lines of conflict in the twenty-first century. Simultaneously, the spread of democracy continues throughout the world. Spectacular advances in information technology which are affecting the technology of production and the organization of firms as well as communication channels in general are also triggering social and cultural change that we are only beginning to grasp. Many other profound changes have also been taking place. The world in 2007 is completely different from the world even twenty or thirty years before.

Several of these important changes in the world have been concomitant to changes in economics. This is not surprising. Some of the changes in economics have been brought about by important changes in the world.

The large-scale economic transition from socialism to capitalism has contributed in a significant way to placing institutional economics firmly in the mainstream. The large output fall and strong subsequent variation in macroeconomic performance across countries came quite unexpectedly to the mainstream of the profession who thought that liberalization, stabilization and privatization should put these economies on a virtuous growth path. Economists started taking seriously the idea that the dismal performance of the Russian economy and of most of the Former Soviet Union economies in the 1990s could be attributed to institutional failure. The transition experience convinced a large part of the economics profession of the importance of institutions as the underpinning of a successful market economy. The Marrakech Congress is a good reflection of the current strength of institutional economics as the invited sessions and various of the distinguished lectures related to institutional issues. The themes of the Congress also reflect an attempt to enrich the analysis of institutions by looking at *systems of institutions*, that is, by studying the different institutions forming an economic system (political, legal, cultural, social,...) and analysing the interactions between institutions. Another important change in economics is the increasing success of behavioural economics. The standard model of rationality is being put into question as several of its core components are contradicted by a large body of work in psychology. Models of behavioural economics or of economics and psychology are introducing change to the standard assumptions of *Homo Oeconomicus* and deriving new predictions about economic behaviour. More and more evidence is produced by experimental economics about individual and group behaviour, testing standard assumptions about rationality but also about game theory. The results of these experiments lead to the formulation of new assumptions and behavioural models. These are only some of the visible examples of changes in economics but, of course, many other changes have also been taking place in many different fields.

The two main themes – 'Understanding the Great Changes in the World' and 'New Trends in Economics' – are the *leitmotifs* of both volumes containing selected papers from the Marrakech Congress. Each chapter reflects either one or both of the main themes. Most chapters in the present volume deal with three important issues: corruption, development and institutional design.

Corruption, rent-seeking and governance are obviously important issues in research on institutions. Jana Kunicova and Susan Rose-Ackerman analyse the effect of political institutions on corruption. They distinguish between three types of electoral rules: 1. plurality, 2. proportional representation (PR) with open lists and 3. PR with closed lists. They argue that under PR, there are more collective-action problems for voters and opposition parties to solve in monitoring incumbents. Indeed, voting districts are smaller under the plurality rule and this gives voters greater incentive to monitor politicians. Further, opposition politicians have more incentive to monitor incumbents under the plurality rule because there is clear alternation of governments, whereas under PR there is usually a coalition government with changing alliances. On top of that, the closed PR list shelters corrupt politicians from punishment by the electorate. These hypotheses are confirmed by cross-country regressions which also show that presidential countries are more corrupt, as are those countries with a federal structure.

In Russia, President Putin has tried to fight corruption while increasing the centralization of government. Evgeny Yakovlev and Ekaterina Zhuravskaya evaluate the changes that have taken place between the Yeltsin and Putin administrations. They focus in particular on state capture, that is, the successful influential activities of oligarchs within the state apparatus. As a consequence, firms without political influence stagnated and their overall productivity, sales and investment declined. This had a negative effect on tax collection and on regional small business. What has changed since Putin's selective crackdown on the oligarchs? They find no significant change in measures of capture and on the negative economic effects of capture. Similarly, in 1999 a law was passed to restrict tax breaks to enterprises – one of the most popular forms of preferential treatment for enterprises. They find that the reduction in tax breaks was offset by an increase in preferential subsidies and loans. They also concluded that enterprises belonging to the federal government became the most powerful lobbyists.

Mustafa Nabli and Carlos Silva-Jauregui analyse the relationship between democracy and its deficit in the Middle East and North Africa (MENA) region. There is no question that democracy lagged behind in the MENA region. There is a persistent democracy gap. Contrary to what can be observed in the rest of the world, there is no correlation in the MENA region between the level of income and progress in democracy. The rich oil-exporting countries in particular have among the lowest democracy scores. Per capita income growth in the MENA region has also been low, though not as low as in Sub-Saharan Africa. However, the general literature on the link between democracy and growth is hardly conclusive and many of its results are either fragile or conditional. While there may have been little democratic progress in MENA countries there has been good progress in human development, in particular in education and health. The authors discuss a battery of governance indicators and conditions needed for good governance under democracy. Countries like Iraq, Lebanon and Syria that are more fragmented had the worst initial conditions for good governance. Oil-producing countries usually had worse governance indicators. The authors were sceptical that good governance might result from non-democratic regimes. On the other hand, obstacles to reform were numerous and political-economy factors would tend to favour the status quo. One must aim for reforms such as greater economic openness, less clientelism, improvements in the legal framework that would create a virtuous circle in favour of democratic progress.

The transition countries were obviously those that experienced the greatest institutional change with varying results. Klara Sabirianova Peter,

Jan Svejnar and Katherine Terrell compare the experience of the Czech Republic and Russia in terms of economic convergence and catching up with the technological frontier, where the latter is measured by the estimated efficiency of the top third of foreign firms operating in a country. They found the distance from this frontier larger for domestic firms in Russia compared to the Czech republic, but that it did not decrease and even increased during some periods. They also tested for the spillover effects from foreign direct investment. They found that in industries with a greater share of foreign firms, domestic firms were falling behind more than in sectors with a smaller foreign presence. However, in the Czech Republic this effect weakened over time. Interestingly, they also find positive spillovers but in only foreign firms.

Entrepreneurship is a key factor for the successful performance of an economy. It is a topic that has been under-researched by economists. Simeon Djankov, Yingyi Qian, Gérard Roland and Ekaterina Zhuravskaya present the results of a pilot study of Chinese entrepreneurs as part of a broader international research initiative on the topic. They surveyed entrepreneurs and non-entrepreneurs sharing the same age, gender and education distribution. They found that, controlling for these characteristics, entrepreneurs were more willing to accept a risk-neutral gamble. The major difference they found in terms of family background was that entrepreneurs had nearly three times more entrepreneurs in their family or among their childhood friends. They were more driven by greed and had different labour–leisure preferences from non-entrepreneurs. These variables were highly significant in different regressions. Entrepreneurs were also more optimistic about the business environment than non-entrepreneurs.

Oded Stark organized a session on immigration policies for the Congress. This is an increasingly important policy issue in most continents. In a joint chapter with Steve Boucher and Edward Taylor, evidence is provided in favour of the 'brain gain' effect. Using data from Mexico, they found that villages with migrants have a higher average level of schooling than other villages. Moreover, the emigrating workers, in general, have higher skills than the domestic workers. However, these findings were valid for migration within Mexico. Migration from rural Mexico to the USA does not show positive effects on schooling in the villages of migrants. In a chapter with Simon Fan, the phenomenon of 'educated unemployment' is analysed, that is, voluntary unemployment by highly skilled workers who prefer to wait and search for a job offer from a foreign country rather than settling for a domestic job. They showed that besides the brain drain usually mentioned in relation to highly skilled workers there is a 'brain gain' related to the incentives of individuals to acquire higher education. This brain gain may have negative effects in the short run – the phenomenon of 'educated unemployment' – but in the long run the brain gain and the higher level of human capital in the economy can generate sufficient positive externalities to bring about an economic takeoff. In a joint chapter with Alessandra Casarico and Silke Uebelmesser, the choice of the optimal immigration policy is analysed in a situation where there is asymmetric information about the skill of migrant workers and where the destination country can tax migrants. They find that there is a dynamic trade-off between selecting high-skill migrant workers, who will pay more taxes and incentives of potential migrants to invest in skill acquisition. A relatively open immigration policy of a destination country may affect positively the incentives to invest in skill acquisition in the home country and thus benefit the home country despite a brain drain effect. Another chapter by the same authors together with Carlo Devillanova generates the same effect in a framework where agents are homogeneous and migration policies are set in a non-cooperative way.

Complementarities between institutions was a key factor in understanding regulatory issues. Claude Ménard analyses the case of water utilities. In the 1980s, economists recommended privatization of utilities in order to reduce or eliminate politicized intervention. Other axes of reform were (i) to dismantle monopolies as much as possible in order to induce competition; (ii) to allocate exploitation rights via competitive auctions; and (iii) to establish a monitoring framework and an optimal design for a regulation system. In line with the Washington consensus, there was a belief that a 'one size fits all' approach to this problem would be fruitful. However, institutionalist thinking emphasizes the importance of the institutional endowments and the cross-country differences in human resources available to implement recommended reforms. Institutional endowments are critical because regulation is a governance issue. In the case of water utilities, since water must be provided to all citizens, depolitization may not be avoided and must try to design the best regulation system that fits local conditions of developing countries.

Regulations and institutional design are also the object of the chapter by Luis Andrés, José Luis Guasch and Stephane Straub who focus on the performance of infrastructure companies. Using data on more than one thousand concessions in Latin America between 1980 and 2000 they examine the impact of aggregate measures of regulatory quality on the divergence between the internal rate of return and the average cost of capital. There is a significant impact of overall regulatory quality. Similarly, the presence of independent regulators has a negative impact on contract renegotiation and regulators appear to act as a barrier against opportunistic behaviour by governments, especially in environments of weaker governance. They find that price-cap schemes lead to more contract renegotiation. Also, autonomous regulatory bodies are associated with reductions in the number of employees.

Finally, Richard Green analyses the evolution of the energy sector in the UK which has changed greatly since the privatization policies of the early 1980s. He emphasizes the strong learning component associated with institutional changes. Efforts to introduce competition in the privatized gas industry did not work immediately. British Gas initially behaved like a price-discriminating monopoly and kept out entry by not committing to a price schedule for the use of its pipelines and by giving itself the opportunity to renegotiate with customers who would be targeted by competitors. A rule had to be imposed restricting it from buying more than 90 per cent of gas supplies. Even so, competition initially remained marginal at best. The firm had to be split into parts, a process that took a few years. Many changes were also operated to the setup of regulatory institutions to avoid collusive tendencies (regulatory boards instead of individual regulators) but also excessive rigidities. It was found that important gains could be achieved by transparency in regulation.

Other topics that were the object of invited sessions were published in the first Congress volume. These two volumes should be seen as a whole. All in all, we hope that the selection of chapters in these volumes will give the readers a snapshot of recent trends in economics and how they reflect important changes taking place in the world.

Part 1

Political Environment

1
Electoral Rules and Constitutional Structures as Constraints on Corruption

*Jana Kunicová and Susan Rose-Ackerman**

1 Introduction

Elections serve two functions in representative democracies. First, they select political actors who enact public policies in the light of constituents' preferences. Second, they permit citizens to hold their representatives accountable and to punish them if they enrich themselves in corrupt or self-serving ways. In other words, elections provide both *incentives* for politicians to enact certain kinds of policies and *constraints* on politicians' malfeasance. In this chapter, we focus on the second of these two functions and investigate how different electoral systems constrain corrupt rent-seeking, holding constant other political, economic and social factors.

We study three stylized categories of electoral rules: plurality/majoritarian systems with single-member districts (PLURALITY), and two kinds of proportional representation (PR) systems: closed- and open-list (CLPR and OLPR). Under a closed-list system, party leaders rank candidates, and voters only cast votes for parties. Under an open list, voters both select a party and rank candidates given the party's selection of candidates. In contrast to PR systems, voters under PLURALITY rule both cast their ballots for specific candidates and elect a single representative from their district of residence.

The control of corrupt political rent-seeking depends both on the locus of rents and on whether any actors have both the incentives and the ability to monitor those politicians with access to rents. We argue that PLURALITY and PR systems differ in two ways. First, the locus of corrupt opportunities differs. Under PR, the party leadership can more effectively concentrate corrupt opportunities in its own hands, so individual legislators have relatively fewer rent-seeking opportunities. Under PLURALITY rule, party leadership does not have as much power over the individual legislators as in PR systems, so the

* This chapter is a shortened version of Kunicová and Rose-Ackerman (2005). Readers are referred to that paper for more extensive citations to the literature and more details on the results reported here.

locus of rents in PLURALITY is more evenly divided between the party leadership and individual legislators. Second, under PLURALITY, the monitoring of rent seekers is likely to be more stringent than the monitoring of rent seekers under PR.

Although our primary focus is on the methods by which the legislature is chosen, we also recognize that a complete model should include other institutional features of a political system such as the level of individual freedom, presidentialism/parliamentarism, federalism, bicameralism, and the strength of parties. We examine the interaction between presidentialism and electoral rules and include other institutional variables, most notably federalism and individual freedom and rights, as controls in our empirical work.

Our research stands at the intersection of two broad literatures: one examining electoral rules and their effects, and the other attempting to explain political corruption. Electoral rules have been shown to affect the incentives of political actors to organize and hence the number of political parties, as well as the way in which parties and politicians compete for votes, producing individualistic personalistic versus party-centered systems. Theoretical arguments conclude that, in established democracies with national parties, PLURALITY rule tends to produce two major parties; in contrast, PR produces several competing parties. In addition, electoral rules are believed to affect party discipline: where politicians have incentives to cultivate a personal vote, party discipline will be low. We build on these stepping stones. We argue that electoral rules help determine the interaction between voters and organized political actors as well as the dynamic among and within political parties. As a result, electoral rules affect the incentives and ability of voters and opposition politicians to organize and to monitor the corruption of incumbents.

The chapter is organized as follows. Section 2 clarifies what we mean by corrupt political rent-seeking and distinguishes between this type of corruption and pork-barrel spending. Then in Section 3 we present our basic theoretical argument about the link between electoral rules and corrupt rent-seeking followed by Section 4 where we add presidentialism to this framework. We state our hypotheses in Section 5, describe the data and methods used to test them in Section 6, and in Section 7 present the results of the regression analysis. We conclude in Section 8 with a discussion placing our results in the context of recent contributions to the literature.

2 Defining corruption

Corruption is an elusive phenomenon that is difficult to capture in a single crisp definition. Researchers have made numerous attempts to do so, but each has its own problems (Lancaster and Montinola 1997). Our own approach views corruption as both a moral and a legal category. We emphasize the institutional roots of corruption under the presumption that changes in institutional structures will change the incentives for self-dealing. We focus on the corrupt rent-seeking of elected officials (as opposed to appointed bureaucrats) in systems that hold periodic elections with a reasonable amount of political competition and uncertainty of electoral outcome. We define such corruption as *the misuse of public office for private financial gain by an elected official*, a formulation which is now standard in systematic comparative studies (Rose-Ackerman, 1999). Thus, our topic covers activities that lead to the personal financial enrichment of politicians, not cases in which politicians themselves make pay-offs to get political support. Our normative view of representative democracy holds that elected officials should act as the agents of those who have elected them. Thus, by 'misuse' we mean deviation from the public official's role as an agent of voters. Voters and politicians participate in a principal–agent relationship in which voters entrust their elected politicians with various control rights over public resources. Politicians are expected to act on behalf of voters and in their best interests in exchange for political support. Corrupt rent-seeking occurs if politicians deviate from this ideal and renege on these obligations in favour of their personal financial interest. An important corollary here is that a corrupt politician, if exposed, will be punished by voters in the next poll – precisely because of having reneged on his or her implicit principal–agent agreement with voters. Corrupt rent-seeking is an illicit and covert activity. Furthering the interests of one's constituents is not corrupt under this definition although it may have undesirable consequences for the system as a whole.

An important complication arises if corrupt rent-seeking goes hand-in-hand with actions that favour one's constituents. One could imagine a scenario in which a politician accepts secret kickbacks from a company that, in turn, promises to build a factory in the politician's home district, or that is selected as a contractor on a public works project in the district. These actions might be in the interest of the politician's electoral base compared with the case of no factory or no public works project. Notice that this example fuses two different acts with electoral implications that go in opposite directions. 'Bringing home the bacon' in the form of job creation and public works in one's district surely carries an electoral premium, but illicit payments may reduce the constituency benefits of the project. We assume that if a representative's corrupt rent-seeking becomes publicly known, it decreases his or her popularity and chances for re-election. The acceptance of kickbacks and bribes is considered corruption under our definition; engaging in pork-barrel politics is an analytically distinct form of activity that is rewarded rather than punished by the electorate.

3 Theoretical framework: monitoring corrupt political rent-seeking

Electoral rules affect the probability of detection by shaping the incentives and ability of political actors to monitor corrupt political rent-seeking.

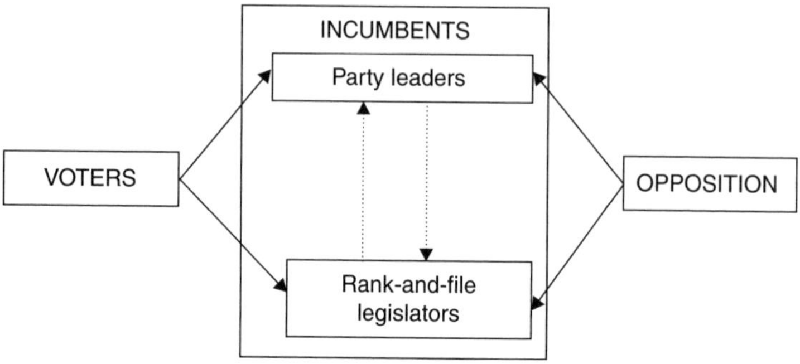

Figure 1.1 Monitoring corrupt political rent-seeking

Figure 1.1 depicts the oversight relations that are shaped by the electoral rules. It includes four types of actors. The first are the incumbent party leaders; the second are the individual rank-and-file legislators who are not in the leadership; the third are political opponents, either individuals or parties; and the fourth are the voters themselves. The incumbents – party leaders and/or individual legislators – have opportunities to extract corrupt rents. However, they are monitored by the political opposition and by voters, and perhaps, by each other.

We specify the objective functions of these political actors as follows. First, incumbent politicians, both leaders and rank-and-file, care about individual wealth and re-election. They would like to maximize rents without being detected, because detection is associated with costs, both monetary (such as legal fees or even a prison term) and political (decrease in probability of re-election). Second, opposition candidates care about winning office. Their chances of winning increase as the chance of the incumbents' re-election decreases, so the opposition benefits from revelations of corruption involving incumbents. Finally, voters prefer honest elected officials to those who enrich themselves through pay-offs. Voters' utility decreases when public resources are diverted for private gain. This is, of course, the reason why we assume that a corruption scandal lowers the incumbent's chance of re-election. We posit that even if bribes are paid in connection with projects that benefit voters, voters do not view corruption as a necessary cost of such projects; they prefer honestly provided 'pork' to projects whose costs have been inflated by corruption. Thus, corrupt pay-offs to politicians are not, in our framework, passed through to voters.

The first salient difference between voting systems is the locus of control over corrupt rents, that is, the *opportunities* for private gain. Under CLPR the party leaders are very powerful vis-à-vis the rank and file because they determine a candidate's ranking on the list. Thus the leadership faces most of the opportunities for private gain and can determine how the spoils are divided.

The rank-and-file party members in the legislature face few individualized corrupt opportunities. The situation is similar under OLPR, except that the leadership itself may be more divided and unstable. Individual members can challenge the leadership by threatening to campaign against them through direct appeals to voters.

Compare the situation under PLURALITY rule. Here, individual incumbents may gain power within the party because of the strength of their local power base or their strategic position within the legislature. Such incumbents may be able to demand a share of the rents of political power in the form of corrupt pay-offs and/or in 'pork-barrel' projects for their districts. Of course, under some conditions individual members have little bargaining power because the leadership can replace them with other members in its efforts to form a majority coalition. However, at other times the majority party may have a slim margin overall or face difficulties getting sufficient votes on a particular issue. A member might also be a pivotal vote on a key committee or have enough of an independent following to launch an attack on the leadership. Individual members can then use their bargaining power vis-à-vis the leadership to get benefits so long as the threat to defect is credible. The legislators' own preferences for pay-offs or pork will be a function of the oversight by voters, the media, and citizens groups, on the one hand, and challengers, on the other.

This discussion suggests that in terms of uncovering corrupt rent-seeking, monitoring the leadership is relatively more important under PR, and monitoring the rank and file is relatively more important under PLURALITY rule. Of course, leaders may be able to garner corrupt rents under PLURALITY rule as well. Our claim is only that individual legislators have more opportunities for rent extraction under PLURALITY than under CLPR. Thus, in PR systems, especially closed-list ones, the opportunities for rent extraction are vested mainly in party leaders. In PLURALITY they are divided between the party leaders and individual representatives.

Monitoring incentives and abilities

Now consider the *incentives* and *ability* of political actors to engage in monitoring. The oversight relations that interest us are mainly voters' and political opponents' monitoring of both party leaders and individual politicians. We are not concerned with the overall level of oversight, but with the way the electoral system affects monitoring at the margin. In addition, we assume both that monitoring is costly and that hiding one's malfeasance is a difficult and imperfect process.

Monitoring by voters

As a normative matter, rank-and-file politicians need to be more closely monitored by voters under PLURALITY rule than under CLPR because the rank-and-file incumbents have more control over rents under PLURALITY rule. As a positive matter, we argue that this is what we would expect to happen.

Voters' ability to monitor the relevant actors depends on the voters' ability, first, to observe malfeasance if it occurs and, second, to organize for oversight. Assume that corrupt rent-seeking imposes costs on citizens in terms of inflated budgets, low-value public projects, etc. Hence, if voters can identify corrupt politicians, they will punish them by voting against them at the next election. Persson and Tabellini (2000) argue that voting over individual candidates, as in a PLURALITY rule system, creates a direct link between individual performance and re-election. This, in turn, gives incumbents an incentive to avoid corruption (Persson, Tabellini and Trebbi, 2003).

However, so far, this argument does not distinguish well between voting systems. In CLPR systems, the leadership is also known to the voters. Because it is precisely the leadership that needs to be monitored under CLPR, voters can identify those politicians most subject to corrupt incentives for personal enrichment. Of course, it is not sufficient to identify those who might be corrupt. In addition, voters must be able to assess whether the politicians are actually engaging in malfeasance. They need to monitor the rank and file under PLURALITY and the leadership under CLPR.

Such monitoring should be easier in 'small' districts. By 'small' we do not mean district magnitude (the number of representatives elected per district), but rather the voting population of the district. Correcting for other factors, such as geographical size, voters in a district with a small population are more likely to have direct contact with their representative and hence more information about the candidates they elect. In addition, as we argue below, they will have more incentives to organize for oversight. Yet it is not obvious that electoral systems are systematically related to the geographic size of districts. Many PR systems have nation-wide districts, whereas PLURALITY systems are usually partitioned into geographically compact districts. However, the total population size of the country surely plays a role as well in determining the size of districts: Large countries such as USA or India are likely to have more populous districts than Luxembourg or Slovenia. To test the relative impact of these factors, we regressed the average district size in a country on the PLURALITY dummy and national population. The coefficients on both the PLURALITY dummy and population are highly significant with the expected signs: PLURALITY systems are indeed associated with the size of the district, controlling for the effect of the total population of the country. Given this empirical regularity and holding the freedom of press constant, we would expect that information about individual kickbacks to politicians would be less readily available to voters in CLPR systems with large districts than in PLURALITY systems with smaller districts.

The second argument concerns the incentives of voters to organize to provide oversight. Free-rider problems are ubiquitous in political life, and the monitoring of corruption is no exception. In general, collective action problems among voters should be less severe in small groups than they are in large groups. This suggests that citizens in smaller districts, measured by number of voters, ought to find it easier to overcome free-rider problems than those in larger districts. Holding other factors constant, PLURALITY rule produces districts with smaller numbers of voters than PR. Thus, overcoming free-rider problems may be easier in such systems.

Our discussion of monitoring by voters has so far left out OLPR systems. There, as with CLPR, the leadership controls the rents. Yet OLPR shares one feature with PLURALITY rule: voters can cast their votes for particular candidates, albeit within a party. However, the first feature of PLURALITY systems – relatively small single-member districts – is absent in OLPR systems. This disables grass-root monitoring by voters who, in addition, are likely to face considerable collective action problems. Furthermore, individual candidates are likely to have little say over their party's rent-extraction activities. On balance, then, OLPR systems fall in between CLPR and PLURALITY systems.

However, under any electoral system, one may doubt the importance of monitoring by voters in constraining politicians' corrupt behaviour. After all, even relatively small districts might be large enough for collective action problems to arise. However, although this type of monitoring is neither a sufficient nor a perfectly efficient constraint on corrupt political rent-seeking, we believe that at the margin it will affect whether or not politicians engage in malfeasance. We claim that information about a politician's lifestyle is likely to be more easily accessible in smaller districts. Of course, in addition to direct contact with their representative, voters are informed through media and active anti-corruption law enforcement. Although these factors account for many uncovered corruption cases, we have no reason to believe that the type of electoral system affects the freedom of press or of the effectiveness of the prosecutorial system. In this sense, media freedom and judicial/prosecutorial competence are outside of our theoretical framework although in our empirical specifications we do control for these alternative revelation mechanisms.

Monitoring by political opponents

Because voters face collective action problems even in 'small' districts, the second piece of the puzzle is particularly important. This is the competitiveness of the political system and its impact on the monitoring of incumbents by their political opponents. As we noted above, challengers have a direct incentive to uncover the malfeasance of incumbents because they increase their probability of winning office once the incumbent is discredited. They can do this under PR systems by investigating the integrity of party leaders and under PLURALITY rule at the district level as well. We argue, however, that it is less likely that the opposition will effectively monitor incumbents under PR. Our claim concerns the adverse effects of multiple parties and coalition politics on monitoring.

Under PLURALITY rule, coalition governments are unlikely unless many regional parties exist. Because the election is an all-or-nothing affair, the stakes are high for the challenger. This gives the party out of power an incentive to undermine the incumbent's integrity. Under PR, coalitions are common, and in many countries parties do not sort themselves into two stable blocs. Instead, a party currently in opposition may expect to form a coalition with one or more of the incumbent parties sometime in the future. If this is so, opposition politicians may want to form a coalition with a party currently in power. If so, they have little incentive to expose the corruption of politicians whom they might need to collaborate with in the future.

The lack of a clear alternation between fixed groups of parties deters inter-party monitoring. Furthermore, if a politician uncovers a scandal under PLURALITY rule with two parties, the benefits flow to him and his party. Under PR, even if the party that uncovers the scandal is especially rewarded at the polls for its vigilance and integrity, the scandal provides marginal benefits for all opposition parties. This could produce a race in which opposition parties compete to reveal a scandal, but under plausible conditions, everyone may keep quiet if the cost of uncovering malfeasance is high and/or if the scandalmonger is punished by being excluded from future coalitions.

In short, the impact of competitive politics on the monitoring of corrupt rent-seekers may actually fall as the number of parties increases. The number of parties is a poor proxy for the intensity of competition, at least with respect to the control of corrupt self-enrichment by politicians.

Comparison of electoral systems

Table 1.1 summarizes our arguments about the oversight relations under three types of electoral system, holding other factors constant. The table presents our claims about the *relative* incentives and ability of political actors to monitor rent-extraction by politicians. Thus an entry that reads 'strong' means stronger relative to the other electoral systems listed.

PLURALITY rule scores the highest of the three stylized electoral systems on both incentives and the ability of political actors to monitor rent-extraction. Districts with small numbers of voters somewhat mitigate the collective-action problems of voters and make it easier for them to observe the behaviour of individual legislators – likely participants in most corrupt deals in such systems. At the opposite extreme, under CLPR, collective action problems are likely to be more serious, and voters find it difficult to observe the behaviour of party leaders – the primary locus of corrupt deals in CLPR. Furthermore, PLURALITY rule will produce opposition parties with higher incentives to unveil the corrupt rent-seeking of incumbents than in multiple party regimes. Because OLPR systems share features of both CLPR and PLURALITY systems, they occupy an 'intermediate' category in monitoring corrupt self-enrichment.

Table 1.1 Relative incentives and the ability to monitor corrupt political rent-seeking

	Voters → Incumbents Mechanism: Accountability; Collective action		*Opposition → Incumbents Mechanisms: Duverger's Law, Coalition formation*	
	Incentives	*Ability*	*Incentives*	*Ability*
PLURALITY *Main locus of rents:* individual reps.& party leaders	STRONG	STRONG	STRONG	STRONG
OLPR Main locus of rents: Party leaders	INTERMEDIATE	INTERMEDIATE	WEAK	WEAK
CLPR *Main locus of rents:* Party leaders	WEAK	WEAK	WEAK	WEAK

The table omits one monitoring possibility included in Figure 1.1 – intraparty oversight. This can involve both rank-and-file monitoring of leaders and leadership monitoring of the rank and file. Such monitoring is unlikely to be a sufficient constraint on corrupt rent-seeking under any electoral system. The basic problem is collusion. If there is little outside monitoring by voters, opponents, or other aspects of civil society, leaders can collude with the rank and file to share corrupt rents. Internal party whistle-blowers can arise, but without external monitors, this is likely to be a risky role to play even under PLURALITY rule.

To conclude, we predict that PLURALITY rule voting will do a better job at controlling corrupt political rent-seeking than PR, especially CLPR. The cost of PLURALITY rule may be a political system that focuses on providing benefits to narrow ranges of constituents in key districts, but that is simply the consequence of the more individualized nature of politics. Under PLURALITY rule, corrupt opportunities for personal gain will be concentrated in just those political actors who are best able to be monitored by voters, and the two-party system that frequently results will give opponents an incentive to uncover scandals at any level.

4 Presidential and parliamentary systems

Opportunities for corruption are enhanced by centralized control over government. Then those with power can, if they wish, create rent-seeking opportunities with little oversight inside government. In particular, a president who controls the executive branch has rent-creating possibilities that can be used for personal gain. In a presidential system, the leaders of the legislative parties are less powerful than under a parliamentary system (Shugart, 1998; Mainwaring, 1995). They must negotiate with the president to pass legislation and do not control the rents that arise within the executive.

Because of the president's undivided power over many sources of rents, diverting them for personal gain is likely to be easier than in a more collegial system of cabinet government. The president can also create additional rents through executive action. In spite of the legislature's incentive to monitor the president, his fixed-term office gives him considerable leeway subject only to the threat of impeachment. The legislature has no instrument similar to the vote of no confidence in parliamentary systems. Of course, legislatures do try to restrict presidential freedom, but their control is less direct than that exercised by a parliament over the Cabinet in a parliamentary system. In addition, in most presidential systems, US-style checks and balances are absent, and presidents tend to have extensive legislative and non-legislative powers. This is not inherent in the nature of presidential systems but is an empirical reality. Using a large cross-section of countries, Kunicová (2005) shows not only that presidentialism *per se* is associated with higher corruption, but also that the more extensive the president's powers, the greater the corruption. Thus, monitoring of the executive by the legislature is, in principle and in practice, more difficult in presidential systems than in parliamentary ones.

Presidents frequently need to cooperate with the legislature to get policy initiatives passed. A corrupt president may seek to enact statutes that incorporate rent-generating opportunities that can be exploited for personal gain. To pass such laws, however, the president needs to bargain with the legislature. In such cases, electoral rules affect the strength of legislative parties and their bargaining power in dealings with the President.

Theoretical claims about electoral rules and party strength have two prongs. First, as discussed above, parties are stronger under CLPR than under PLURALITY rule. Second, parties are weaker in presidential systems than in parliamentary systems because in the former they do not need to organize themselves to form a government (Mainwaring, 1995; Shugart, 1998). Taken together, these arguments imply that parties will be weakest in presidential systems with PLURALITY-rule legislatures and strongest in parliamentary systems operating under CLPR. The other two possibilities fall somewhere between the extremes.

The relation to the expected level of corrupt rent-seeking is complex. On the one hand, we expect presidential systems to generate more opportunities for corrupt enrichment than parliamentary systems that use similar voting rules for the legislature. On the other hand, we expect that CLPR systems will have greater levels of corrupt rent-seeking than PLURALITY systems. The combination of CLPR and presidentialism is likely to create unfortunate synergies.

Under CLPR, the president can form an alliance with the party leaders to share rents at relatively low transaction costs because the rank and file does not have to be included. Even if the parties are somewhat weaker than under a parliamentary system, they still control their members. In contrast, if a president faces a PLURALITY-rule legislature whose parties are weak, he may have to bargain with a multitude of individual members in order to form an alliance. Any alliance will be difficult to form in the first place because of the number of legislators involved. Furthermore, it may be difficult to sustain if marginal members threaten to defect. Even rank-and-file members of a party that is nominally allied with the president have an incentive to be 'integrity entrepreneurs' to enhance their own reputations. This discussion suggests that the greater opportunities for corrupt rent-seeking created by presidentialism should be especially evident in CLPR systems. OLPR ought to be an intermediate case.

To complete the argument, consider the possibility of monitoring by voters and opposition politicians. These groups have an incentive to monitor the president, but their ability is limited. For voters, the situation is similar to that of their monitoring of party leaders – the collective action problems are large in nation-wide districts and evidence of corruption is hidden in public contracts and individualized decisions that are hard to monitor. In contrast, legislators from parties different from the president's do have an incentive to monitor, and if they control the legislature, they may have the power to enact laws that constrain the president. The issue is then whether the role of opposition parties ought to differ between PR and PLURALITY systems. The problem for a corrupt president is not simply to get a majority behind the corrupt initiative, but also to ensure that minority legislators do not blow the whistle to enhance their own political standing with the voters. It appears that what matters in presidential bargaining with the legislature is not the number of parties that the president needs to work with, but the extent to which these parties are capable of voting as unified blocs. In this sense, CLPR seems to be most conducive to corrupt deals.

5 Hypotheses

From our discussion above, we derive the following two hypotheses:

H1 *Existence of a relationship between electoral rules and corruption. Ceteris paribus*, we expect CLPR systems to be the most corrupt, followed by OLPR, and then PLURALITY systems.

H2 *Interaction effects. Ceteris paribus*, presidential PR systems are expected to be more corrupt than their parliamentary counterparts. We predict that CLPR presidential systems will be especially corrupt relative to other types of government structures.

6 Data, measurement and econometric methods

Our empirical tests use cross-country data that characterize countries in terms of the level of corruption and the legislative selection mechanism. To this basic data we add information on whether a separately elected president exists and include other background political and economic variables.

Corruption data

Corruption is necessarily difficult to define, systematically observe and measure. However, several indices attempt to capture the abuse of political and bureaucratic power across countries. We rely on the Control of Corruption Index (*CORRWB*), also known as *GRAFT*, compiled by the World Bank (Kaufmann, Kraay, and Zoido-Lobaton, 1999). This index includes estimates for 124 countries using data similar to that used by Transparency International (TI) which has published its annual *CPI* ranking of countries since 1995 (Lambsdorff, 2005). Both TI and the World Bank aggregate surveys of perceived corruption across countries based on the views of business people, risk analysts, investigative journalists and the general public. Specifically, the focus is on kickbacks in public procurement, the embezzlement of public funds, and the bribery of public officials. Although the two indices are highly correlated, we prefer *CORRWB* because it covers a larger number of countries and is a 'second-generation index' in terms of aggregation methodology. It uses an unobserved components model to aggregate up to thirty surveys in 1997–8. This model expresses the observed data as a linear function of unobserved corruption plus a disturbance term capturing perception errors and sampling variation in the indicator. The model allows one to compute the variance of this disturbance term, which is a measure of how informative the index is. The point estimate of control of corruption is the mean of the conditional distribution of *CORRWB* given the observed data and ranges between −2.5 (most corrupt) and +2.5 (least corrupt). The variance of this conditional distribution provides an estimate of the precision of the *CORRWB* indicator for each country.

The indices measure overall perceptions of public-sector corruption in a country, but our interest is only in rent-seeking corruption by politicians. Ideally, we would prefer a more precise measure of political, as opposed to bureaucratic, corruption. Unfortunately, only one of the component surveys, the Gallup International, distinguishes between political and administrative corruption, and it has very limited country coverage. However, as reported in the TI *CPI Framework Document*, the correlation between the assessments of political and bureaucratic corruption is 0.88. Transparency International considers this a justification for 'blending political and bureaucratic corruption, because there is no strong evidence that countries differ in prevalence of one type of corruption over another' and claims that 'the extent of political corruption is well-represented by these data' (Lambsdorff, 1998). The same argument can also be made for *CORRWB*, because it shares the same substantive characteristics as the *CPI*. Furthermore, the survey respondents are mostly people who would be particularly familiar with high-level corruption, most of which will involve top political actors even if it occurs within the executive branch.

Institutional data

Our theoretical model concentrates on the distinction between three broad and stylized electoral rules: *PLURALITY*, *CLPR* and *OLPR*. The electoral system variables are derived from the World Bank's Database on Political Institutions (DPI 2a) as described in Beck *et al.* (1999). We also check the robustness of our results by using a measure of party-centrism developed by Seddon, Gaviria, Panizza, and Stein (2003) and by substituting for our dummies the proportion of lower-house seats elected by *CLPR*.

The original dummy variables *PLURALITY* and *CLPR* and *OLPR*, taken from DPI 2a for a cross-section of countries in 1997, have a non-empty intersection. In most cases, this reflects the fact that some bicameral systems use PR for one house and *PLURALITY* for another, or that there are mixed electoral rules in a unicameral legislature. We create mutually exclusive categories, *PLURALITY*, *CLPR*, and *OLPR*, by considering which electoral rule elects the majority of representatives in the Lower House. To see if the group of 'hybrid' electoral systems is different from the 'pure' ones, we construct two dummy variables, *PRMIXED* and *PLUMIXED*. The former takes the value one when a system that we have characterized as PR also has plurality elements. The latter takes the value one whenever a system labelled as *PLURALITY* has some PR features. There are fourteen countries in each of these categories.

We consider two alternatives to our main explanatory variables. First, we employ the index of particularism (*PARTICULARISM*). It is designed to be an 'indicator of the degree to which individual politicians can further their careers by appealing to narrow geographic constituencies, on the one hand, or party constituencies, on the other' (Seddon, Gaviria, Panizza, and Stein, 2003). The index is based on the seminal work by Shugart and Carey (1992).

The second alternative to simple electoral system dummies is CLSHARE, a variable that, first, distinguishes between systems where CLPR dominates and all others, and, second, reflects the strength of CLPR in those systems where it is the dominant rule. Thus the variable is 0 for all systems we classify as *PLURALITY* and *OLPR* and takes on values greater than .5 and less than or equal to one for countries in our CLPR category, that is, those that elect at least half of their legislatures using CLPR. It is obtained by interacting *PLIST* from Persson, Tabellini, and Trebbi (2003) with the *CLPR* dummy. Thus, for those that have a share of CLPR that is less than half, for example, Albania and Armenia, CLSHARE takes the value of zero.

To test for interaction effects between electoral rules and presidentialism, we employ a presidential dummy (*PRESIDENT*). *PRESIDENT* is derived from

DPI 2a and takes the value 1 if the system has a directly elected president independent of the legislature and 0 otherwise. We interact *PRESIDENT* with the electoral rules dummies to obtain mutually exclusive categories *CLPRES, OLPRES, PLPRES, CLPARL, OLPARL,* and *PLPARL.*

Control variables

We control for other institutional and background conditions. Theoretical work on federalism is inconclusive. On the one hand, a more decentralized system might make monitoring easier for voters. On the other hand, local politicians may be able to wield monopoly power over voters, especially in systems with a history of local political or economic fiefdoms. Recent empirical work has found that, on balance, federal systems are more corrupt than unitary systems (Treisman, 2000). Thus, we include federal structure as a control variable. The dummy (*FEDERAL*) is taken from DPI 2a; it has the value 1 if there are autonomous regions with extensive taxing, spending, and regulatory authority.

To control for economic development, we use the log of averaged GDP per capita (*GDP*), 1995–7 (World Bank, 2001). We also control for other aspects of the political system that may influence the level of corruption – such as political rights and liberties. Freedom House (*FREEDOM*) provides a measure of these factors (consult http://www.freedomhouse.org/research/freeworld/2000/methodology.htm). Its index is a composite of several aspects of personal and economic freedom, including freedom of the press, an aspect of public life that is particularly relevant to the control of corruption. We averaged the years 1992/3 to 2000/1; the index takes values from 1 (free) to 7 (least free). Because we are only interested in democracies, we exclude from our sample those countries that score 5.5 or higher on this index even if some of these countries have formal electoral institutions.

Although we consider GDP per capita and the Freedom House index to be the most important background controls, we also experimented with a larger set of economic, cultural and social variables that were shown to influence corruption by other studies. These results are reported in Kunicová and Rose-Ackerman (2005); the addition of these variables did not change the results.

Econometric methods

Each country's $CORRWB_i$ index has a different conditional variance, which makes our data set heteroscedastic by definition. Because standard errors are reported for each country estimate, we employ weighted least squares (WLS) to correct for this problem, using the inverse of the standard error of $CORRWB_i$ as analytic weights. To check the robustness of our results, we also ran all our models using OLS with White-corrected standard errors. The results we report below were not materially affected (see Kunicová and Rose-Ackerman, 2005).

In testing H1, we use *PLURALITY* as an excluded category and examine the coefficients on *CLPR* and *OLPR* as well as the marginal impact of introducing mixed electoral elements; significant negative coefficients on *CLPR* and *OLPR* mean that these systems lead to more corruption than *PLURALITY*. *CLPR* includes many more cases than *OLPR*. Therefore, we test whether a potentially insignificant coefficient on *OLPR* means that *OLPR* is closer to *PLURALITY* than *CLPR*, or that there are simply not enough cases to determine its effect.

Testing H2 requires employing 'interaction terms' between electoral rules and presidentialism. However, because we are dealing with categorical variables, we simply divide our sample of countries into six mutually exclusive categories (*CLPRES, OLPRES, PLPRES, CLPARL, OLPARL*, and *PLPARL*) and use plurality-parliamentary systems (*PLPARL*) as a benchmark group that should be least corrupt according to our theory.

Finally, although we used WLS and OLS with robust standard errors to correct for heteroscedasticity, further regression diagnostics are warranted to identify influential observations and outlying cases. For each of our three hypotheses, we select a representative model and examine influential observations that influence the intercept (studentized residuals), regression coefficient, or the model as a whole.

7 Empirical results

The empirical results are mostly consistent with our theoretical claims. Regression diagnostics demonstrate that the results are not unduly influenced by influential observations or outlying cases.

H1: the relationship between electoral rules and corruption

Table 1.2 reports the results of the four models that we used to test H1. Model 1 is a benchmark regression without any institutional structure. It shows that *GDP* and *FREEDOM* alone explain 68 per cent of variation in *CORRWB* on a sample of 93 countries. Adding electoral rules, presidentialism, and federalism explains an additional 8 per cent of variance. Most importantly, *CLPR, PRESIDENT*, and *FEDERAL* all have negative coefficients significant at a 10 per cent level or better. The coefficient on *OLPR* also has the right sign, is smaller than the coefficient on *CLPR*, but just misses significance. However, a post-estimation test reveals that we cannot distinguish it from *CLPR*. Therefore, on the basis of Model 2 we can only claim that PR systems are more corrupt than *PLURALITY*. In addition, mixed systems that add some degree of 'PR-ness' to *PLURALITY* are also significantly more corrupt than pure *PLURALITY* systems. In fact, the coefficient is similar to that on *CLPR*, suggesting that the anti-corruption benefits of *PLURALITY* rule only hold in relatively pure cases. In contrast, the other type of mixed system cannot be distinguished from a full-scale PR regime.

Table 1.2 H1: Electoral rules and corruption

	Model 1 *Coeff*	*Model 2* *Coeff*	*Model 3* *Coeff*	*Model 4* *Coeff*
CLPR		***−0.39		
		(0.14)		
OLPR		−0.29		
		(0.18)		
PLU-MIXED		***−0.44		
		(0.16)		
PR-MIXED		−0.08		
		(0.15)		
PRESIDENT		***−0.33	*−0.25	*−0.23
		(0.12)	(0.12)	(0.14)
FEDERAL		*−0.32	***−0.42	***−0.43
		(0.17)	(0.14)	(0.16)
PARTICULARISM			**0.21	
			(0.09)	
C-PARTICULARISM			−0.30	
			(0.26)	
CLSHARE				*−0.31
				(0.15)
GDP	***0.59	***0.54	***0.47	***0.64
	(0.07)	(0.07)	(0.07)	(0.08)
FREEDOM	***−0.20	***−0.22	***−0.27	***−0.17
	*(0.06)	(0.05)	(0.06)	(0.06)
Intercept	***−4.31	***−3.28	***−2.8	***−4.44
	(0.72)	(0.69)	(0.77)	(0.86)
Adj. R-sq.	0.68	0.76	0.78	0.80
Obs.	93	93	93	67

Notes: Dependent variable: *CORRWB*. Estimation: weighted least squares. Weights: inverse of standard errors of *CORRWB*.
Significance: *** for $p < .01$; ** for $.05 > p \geq .01$; * for $.10 > p \geq .05$ (2-tailed tests).

Model 3 tests the robustness of our results, replacing our electoral rule dummies by an interval measure of individual-versus-party-centrism of the electoral system, proxied by the index of particularism (*PARTICULARISM*). We find *PARTICULARISM* to be positively significant which is what we expect because it is inversely related to 'PR-ness'. In comparison to our attempt to distinguish different types of systems along one basic dimension – electoral rules, the *PARTICULARISM* variable includes many more features of electoral systems that make them more party-centred. Because the aggregation method of the *PARTICULARISM* index requires many judgments that make the index difficult to interpret, we prefer our electoral dummies that provide a simple, more transparent measure of electoral structure. The additional control variable, *C-PARTICULARISM*, measures the proportion of elected legislators considered in the *PARTICULARISM* index (see Seddon, Gaviria, Panizza, and Stein, 2003). We are encouraged that an alternative effort to measure the power of political parties across electoral systems produces consistent results.

Finally, Model 4 replaced the electoral dummies with *CLSHARE*. This also proves to be a good proxy for the electoral system dummies used in Model 2. Its main drawback is the fall in the number of data points from 97 to 67. Running Model 2 with the countries in Model 4 produced consistent results. Thus it appears that not much additional value is added by using *CLSHARE* instead of the dummies.

On balance, these results strongly suggest that PR, federalism, and presidentialism increase corruption holding other factors constant. What can be said about the magnitude of these effects? Model 2 allows the following numeric experiments. If we compare a country using plurality rule to one with *CLPR*, the World Bank corruption control index would be .39 higher in the former; this is about .41 of *CORRWB*'s standard deviation. For the sake of comparison, this is about the same effect as an increase in *GDP* per capita to about 49 per cent of its current level. Although this hypothetical experiment needs to be taken with several grains of salt, it does suggest that the relative magnitude of the effect of electoral rules on corruption is rather large when compared to the effect of economic development. Yet the effect of electoral rules seems to be smaller than that of other institutional factors such as federalism and presidentialism.

Interaction between presidentialism and electoral rules

Table 1.3 reports the results obtained by interacting presidentialism with electoral rules. The most important result here is that presidentialism interacts with PR to produce a particularly corruption-prone political system. Model 1 uses *PLPARL* (that is, Westminster democracy) as a benchmark category, which we expect to be the least corrupt. The tests confirm our predictions. All five remaining categories (*CLPRES, OLPRES, PLPRES, CLPARL,* and *OLPARL*) have negative signs. Only *CLPRES*, however, is statistically significant, together with *PLUMIX*, federalism and the background controls. Post-estimation tests show that all coefficients, except *OLPRES*, are different from *CLPRES*. However, the coefficients on *CLPARL* and *OLPARL* are not statistically different from each other. Therefore, in Model 2, we use all parliamentary systems as a benchmark category. Post-estimation tests once again reveal that we cannot distinguish the coefficients on *CLPRES* and *OLPRES*. *PLPRES* is different from *CLPRES* (the difference is significant at 0.01 level), but it is not significantly different from the base case. Similar to H1, the same results hold when we include a large set of controls. These results suggest that the real problem is not the voting system viewed in isolation but is, instead, the interaction between proportional representation and presidentialism. The voting system produces powerful party leaders who are difficult to monitor and permits corrupt interactions to occur between them

Table 1.3 H2: The interaction effects: electoral rules and presidentialism

	Model 1 *Coeff*	*Model 2* *Coeff*
CLPRES	***−0.67	***−0.58
	(0.16)	(0.13)
OLPRES	−0.26	−0.18
	(0.36)	(0.35)
PLPRES	−0.22	−0.17
	(0.15)	(0.14)
CLPARL	−0.17	
	(0.19)	
OLPARL	−0.14	
	(0.19)	
PLUMIXED	**−0.39	**−0.33
	(0.15)	(0.14)
PRMIXED	−0.12	−0.14
	(0.15)	(0.14)
FEDERAL	*−0.30	*−0.30
	(0.17)	(0.17)
GDP	***0.53	***0.52
	(0.07)	(0.07)
FREEDOM	***−0.21	***−0.20
	(0.05)	(0.04)
Intercept	***−3.33	***−3.44
	(0.70)	(0.68)
Adj. R-sq.	0.75	0.75
Obs.	94	94

Notes: Dependent variable: *CORRWB*. Estimation: weighted least squares. Weights: inverse of standard errors of *CORRWB*. Significance: *** for $p < .01$; ** for $.05 > p \geq .01$; * for $.10 > p \geq .05$ (2-tailed tests of significance).

and directly elected presidents in systems with weak popular and political control.

8 Discussion and conclusions

The choice of electoral rules can influence the level of political corruption. Under our theoretical framework, PR systems are more susceptible to corruption relative to *PLURALITY* systems because PR leads to more severe collective action problems for voters and opposition parties in monitoring corrupt incumbents. Closed party lists weaken the link between re-election and performing well in office. We have also hypothesized the existence of interaction effects between electoral rules and presidentialism. Our empirical findings support our theoretical hypothesis that PR systems, especially in conjunction with presidentialism, are associated with higher levels of corruption. The most important route by which CLPR seems to produce high levels of corruption is through its interaction with presidentialism.

How do our findings compare to those of other scholars who have explored related questions empirically? Lijphart (1999) argues theoretically that consensus democracy (a term that subsumes PR systems) should constrain corruption, but empirically he finds consensus democracies to be *more* corrupt. However, the coefficients are not significant in his bivariate regression covering 36 countries. Our findings, with significant coefficients in the same direction, are based on a much larger sample and include relevant controls. Thus, we reject Lijphart's hypothesis with more force than his own empirical findings. However, it may well be that 'consensus democracy' is simply an overly aggregated measure. For example, although PR systems are more consensual than plurality systems, presidential systems are less consensual than parliamentary ones. Lijphart's theory would predict that presidential systems ought to be more corrupt, which we indeed find. Finally, we show that federal or decentralized systems are more corrupt, which again goes against Lijphart's expectations.

A more recent empirical study of political institutions and corruption by Persson and Tabellini (2003) has both better country coverage and more econometric sophistication than Lijphart's work. Although we reach a similar basic finding concerning the greater corruption of PR systems, we make the opposite predictions about presidentialism. Persson and Tabellini expect presidential systems to be less corrupt due to their competitive nature and to checks and balances, but they cannot confirm this prediction empirically, except on a subset of old democracies. US-style checks and balances may indeed have a constraining effect on corruption, especially in well-established democracies, but we argue that checks and balances are not a representative, let alone fundamental, feature of presidential systems. Once new and fragile democracies are included in the sample, presidentialism becomes a significant predictor of higher corruption levels, controlling for major economic, political and social background factors. Theoretically, we have traced this relationship back to more fundamental and prevalent characteristics of presidentialism, such as fixed terms in office and legislative bargaining patterns, and we argue that these make presidential systems structurally more susceptible to corruption.

Our work further differs from Persson and Tabellini (2000, 2003) in our treatment of proportionality and mixed systems. Persson and Tabellini argue theoretically that the channels through which proportionality leads to higher corruption are the percentage of representatives elected on party lists and district magnitude. Their findings suggest that the systems that constrain corruption best are those that *both* have no representatives elected on party lists and have large districts. Of course, in practice, such systems do not exist. The analytical problem here is that district magnitude and the percentage of legislators elected on party lists are not independent variables but rather move together in opposite directions as the system moves from proportional to majoritarian.

Our findings about mixed systems help one to understand these two contradictory tendencies. We show that adding some PR to plurality systems substantially increases corruption (PLU-MIXED), while adding some plurality to PR systems has no effect (PR-MIXED) (Table 1.2 Model 2). PLU-MIXED systems increase the proportion of politicians elected on party lists, which is bad for corruption control because, we argue, it increases the power of party leaders and raises monitoring costs. PR-MIXED systems lower the percentage of members elected on party lists while retaining high district magnitudes. Compared to pure PLURALITY systems, this should be good for corruption control according to Persson and Tabellini, but it has no effect according to our results.

Clearly, from the point of view of proposing reforms, more work should be done on the causal variables to discover if any of them can be treated as separate foci of reform in an otherwise unchanged electoral system. The results reported here are essentially reduced form econometric results that demonstrate an association that is consistent with our underlying story. An empirical exploration of the underlying causal mechanisms is a logical next step in this line of research and should help sort out the conflicting causal stories.

We have treated electoral systems and other aspects of government structure as exogenous and studied their impact on corruption. However, in practice, electoral rules are themselves chosen by political actors who may be concerned to limit or restrict corruption. In most cases, today's corrupt individuals did not design the structure of government under which they operate. Nevertheless, one can ask if the empirical regularities we find could have been self-consciously produced by politicians who are more or less concerned with their ability to extract rents from the state. The fact that all democracies have not converged on a single equilibrium constitutional form and set of electoral rules suggests either that the goals of political actors differ or, as is likely, that the functions served by government institutions go far beyond the control (or encouragement) of corruption. For example, although the empirical analysis dealt with corruption, we raised the possibility that there may be a trade-off between systems that provide targeted benefits to narrow constituencies and those that foster corruption. The design of constitutional structures and electoral rules is a balancing act that has produced a wide range of solutions.

References

Beck, T., G. Clarke, A. Groff, P. Keefer, and P. Walsh (1999) 'New Tools and New Tests in Comparative Political Economy: The Database of Political Institutions', World Bank (mimeo).

Kaufmann, D., A. Kraay, and P. Zoido-Lobaton (1999) 'Aggregating Governance Indicators', World Bank Working Paper 2195, Washington, DC.

Kunicová, J. (2005) 'Corruption: Another Peril of Presidentialism', California Institute of Technology (mimeo).

Kunicová, J. and S. Rose-Ackerman (2005) 'Electoral Rules and Constitutional Structures as Constraints on Corruption', *British Journal of Political Science*, vol. 33, no. 10, pp. 1567–85.

Lambsdorff, J. G. (1998) 'The Transparency International Corruption Perception Index: 4th edition', http://www.uni-goettingen.de/~uwvw.

Lancaster, T. D. and G. Montinola (2001) 'Comparative Political Corruption: Issues of Operationalization and Measurement', *Studies in Comparative International Development*, vol. 36, no. 3, pp. 3–28.

Lijphart, A. (1999) *Patterns of Democracy: Government Forms and Performance in Thirty-Six Countries* (New Haven, CT: Yale University Press).

Mainwaring, S. (1995) 'Presidentialism, Multipartism, and Democracy', *Comparative Political Studies,* vol. 26, no. 2, pp. 198–228.

Persson, T. and G. E. Tabellini (2000) *Political Economics: Explaining Economic Policy* (Cambridge, MA: MIT Press).

Persson, T. and G. E. Tabellini (2003) *The Economic Effects of Constitutions* (Cambridge, MA: MIT Press).

Persson, T., G. E. Tabellini, and F. Trebbi (2003) 'Electoral Rules and Corruption', *Journal of the European Economic Association*, vol. 1, no. 4, pp. 958–89.

Rose-Ackerman, S. (1999) *Corruption and Government: Causes, Consequences, and Reform* (New York: Cambridge University Press).

Seddon, J., A. Gaviria, U. Panizza, and E. Stein (2003) 'Political Particularism Around the World', *World Bank Economic Review*, vol. 17, no. 1, pp. 133–43.

Shugart, M. S. (1998) 'The Inverse Relationship Between Party Strength and Executive Strength: A Theory of Politicians' Constitutional Choices', *British Journal of Political Science,* vol. 28, no. 1, pp. 1–29.

Shugart, M. S. and Carey, J. M. (1992) *Presidents and Assemblies: Constitutional Design and Electoral Dynamics* (New York: Cambridge University Press).

Treisman, D. (2000) 'The Causes of Corruption: A Cross-National Study', *Journal of Public Economics*, vol. 76, no. 3, pp. 399–457.

World Bank (2001) *World Development Indicators* (Washington, DC: The World Bank) CD-ROM.

2
State Capture: From Yeltsin to Putin

Evgeny Yakovlev and Ekaterina Zhuravskaya

1 Introduction

In this chapter we attempt to assess the results of Putin's centralization and anti-corruption measures on the overall level of state capture in the Russian regions as well as on the balance of power between different interest groups. We proceed by, first, describing the results of previous research on state capture in Russia's regions during Yeltsin in Section 2 and, then, analysing the changes in the nature and the level of state capture during Putin's administration in Section 3. Section 4 concludes.

2 State capture during Yeltsin's governance[1]

After the collapse of the Soviet Union a new force emerged in Russia, which was to affect the country's economy and politics. The name of this force was oligarchy. A large-scale privatization of state assets at the beginning of the 1990s, which led to a growth in income inequality, was combined with weak legal and political institutions, a legacy from communist times. The fragility of democratic institutions and the state's poor accountability to the public made the governments in Russia easily susceptible to 'capture' by the new wealth. Politically powerful firms influenced the very rules of the game in the economy: they created obstacles to the emergence and development of competitive businesses and changed the direction and speed of economic reform. The 1999 BEEPS survey confirmed that state capture was deeply rooted in the economic and political processes of the country: in the composite index of state capture among 20 transition countries Russia ranked fourth.

At the same time, decentralization brought Russian regions a greater autonomy and the opportunity to pursue their own economic policies. Regional economic policies and, in particular, their susceptibility to capture varied significantly depending on industrial concentration, level of education, voter awareness, etc. The study by Slinko, Yakovlev and Zhuravskaya (2005) creates a measure of state capture in the Russian regions based on Russian legislation during the period 1992–2000, and evaluates the effects of capture on politically influenced firms. The authors show that politically powerful firms benefit greatly from their political influence. Compared to firms without political influence, powerful firms' sales and employment grew faster; they invested more and received greater profits, and besides, their performance picked up with the growth of capture.

Although there is no evidence that capture had a significant impact on aggregate economic growth, the study shows that the rest of the economy suffered from state capture by powerful elites:

- firms without political influence stagnated, and their productivity, sales and investments declined with the increase in capture;
- regional small businesses deteriorated, their share of employment and retail turnover went down with the growth in capture;
- regional budgets were negatively affected as tax collection decreased and arrears to the budgets increased with an increase in the level of state capture.

Many different interest groups competed for influence over the state institutions at the regional level. Which has been the most effective captor of the Russia's regional states? Studies which have looked at this question are scarce mainly due to the lack of enterprise-level data related to politics. According to these studies, a firm's political power is determined by a firm's size, both in terms of cash (and ability to bribe) and employment (social significance),[3] as well as ownership structure. Frye (2002) shows that Russian state-owned firms were engaged in state capture at least as much as private firms. Since the state did not exercise tight control over state-owned firms, these firms' managers appropriated both control and cash flows for their private benefit. Yakovlev and Zhuravskaya (2004) showed that enterprises, which belonged to foreign or regional private owners, were more likely to be captors whereas enterprises owned by federal private oligarchs were less likely to be captors. They also showed that enterprises, which were members of larger financial-industrial groups or members of groups that had engaged in loans-for-share schemes were more effective captors. As for industrial structure, the World Bank study (2000) shows that enterprises, operating in natural resource sectors, extract more rents and so are more likely to be captors.

3 State capture under Putin

All empirical studies of state capture so far have examined the phenomenon during the first eight years of Russian capitalism, that is, during President Yeltsin's term in power. It is widely accepted, however, that there has been a big shift in the relationship between the state and business during President Putin's first and second terms. A number of the richest and most famous Russian businessmen found themselves behind bars or in exile abroad. Further, the process of centralization, which might eventually reduce local capture, has been initiated. Do these factors lead to a decrease of capture and redistribution of power to new winners?

3.1 Data, methodology, and measures

Our analysis uses an extended version of the data on preferential treatments of large firms by regional legislation from Slinko, Yakovlev and Zhuravskaya (2005). For the analysis, we supplement these data with the data on firm-ownership structure from Guriev and Rachinsky (2005). These two data sets are described in detail below. Basic financial and other statistical data on enterprises come from the GNOZIS data set which covers more than 30,000 large and medium-sized firms between 1992 and 2003. The compilation of data from all of these sources results in a data set with 301 firms in 72 Russian regions. Region-level statistics come from Goskomstat, Russia's official statistical agency (http://www.gks.ru/catalog/default.asp). For the most part, Goskomstat's regional series are available for 1996–2000, but some (for example retail turnover) start in 1992.

The preferential treatment data

The database from Slinko (2005) contains all preferential treatment between 1992 and 2000 given by regional legislators and regulators to 978 firms in Russia. Firms were chosen on the basis of being among the five largest firms at least once between 1992 and 2000 in any Russian region. An enterprise was said to be treated preferentially if it received any of the following benefits: tax breaks, investment credits, subsidies, subsidized loans and loans with a regional budget guarantee, official delays in tax payments, subsidized licensing, free grants of state property, or a special 'open economic zone' status for their territory. The number of regional laws and regulations that granted distinct preferential treatments to each firm in the sample for every year collected. The source of the information about preferential treatments is the comprehensive database of Russia's regional legislation 'Consultant Plus' (www.consultant.ru/Software/Systems/RegLaw).

We extend these data by adding observations for up to 2003 and a sub-sample of firms that were among the five largest in terms of sales in 72 regions for the period from 2001 to 2003. In total, the resulting data set contains preferential treatments for 1065 firms for the years from 1992 to 2003.

Ownership data set from Guriev and Rachinsky (2005)

Ownership data that we start with are described by Guriev and Rachinsky (2005) as follows:

> The [ ] project identified the structure of control for about 1,700 large firms in 45 sectors of Russian economy...[ ] The sectors were selected based on their size in order for the survey to cover as large a portion of the economy

as possible...[ ] The next stage was to target the largest establishments and firms within the sectors. In industry, for example, our firms represented 35 per cent of employment and 85 per cent of sales for the selected sectors. Finally, economists and business journalists interviewed investment banks, consultancies, business advisers, information agencies and other institutions. They identified the main controlling owners of each firm and the portion of the firm they owned as well as any subsidiaries owned by the firms. This in turn generated new sets of firms to be investigated – subsidiaries and corporate owners. A chain would step downward when a firm owned no subsidiaries and would step upward when an 'ultimate owner' or 'controlling party' was identified. The data were checked and supplemented with publicly accessible information. (p. 132)

We follow the methodology described in Slinko, Yakovlev and Zhuravskaya (2005). Thus, state capture is measured as the concentration of preferential treatments in the region; and a firm's political influence is measured as a share of preferential treatments given to the firm in the total number of preferential treatments in the region. Figures 2.1a and 2.1b present the level of state capture (average across time concentration of preferential treatments) in Russian regions during President Yeltsin's second term and Putin's first term in power.

3.2 Has the overall level of state capture decreased under Putin?

In contrast to Yeltsin's time, which was notorious for the accumulation of power in the hands of oligarchs, Putin's presidency has been characterized by open fights with the most famous of them: Berezovsky, Gusinsky, Khodorkovsky, and Lebedev. In addition, Putin attempted a centralization process, restricting autonomy of regional political elites and moved political and economic power from the regions to the federal centre.[4] A new tax law, which restricted the use of individual tax breaks, was adopted, as well as a number of other laws, aimed at easing the burden of business regulation.[5] A new anti-corruption campaign was launched and governors considered the most corrupt, such as Rutskoy in Kursk region and Nazdratenko in Primorsky region, were not permitted to run for re-election. The governor of Yaroslavl region, Lisitsin, was under criminal investigation in the autumn of 2004 because of pursuing illegal paternalistic policies towards regional business.

Considering the initiatives described above, one might expect a significant decrease in the level of capture in the regions and in its negative effect on the regional economies. However, various polls and President Putin himself in his annual address to the Federal assembly in 2003 drew attention to the spreading corruption in various government bodies.[6] Similarly, our data show no significant change in the level of capture in the regions: the level of state capture grew gradually during Yeltsin's first term and remained almost unchanged during Yeltsin's second term and Putin's first term (see Figure 2.2). The measure of state capture in the first four years of Putin's

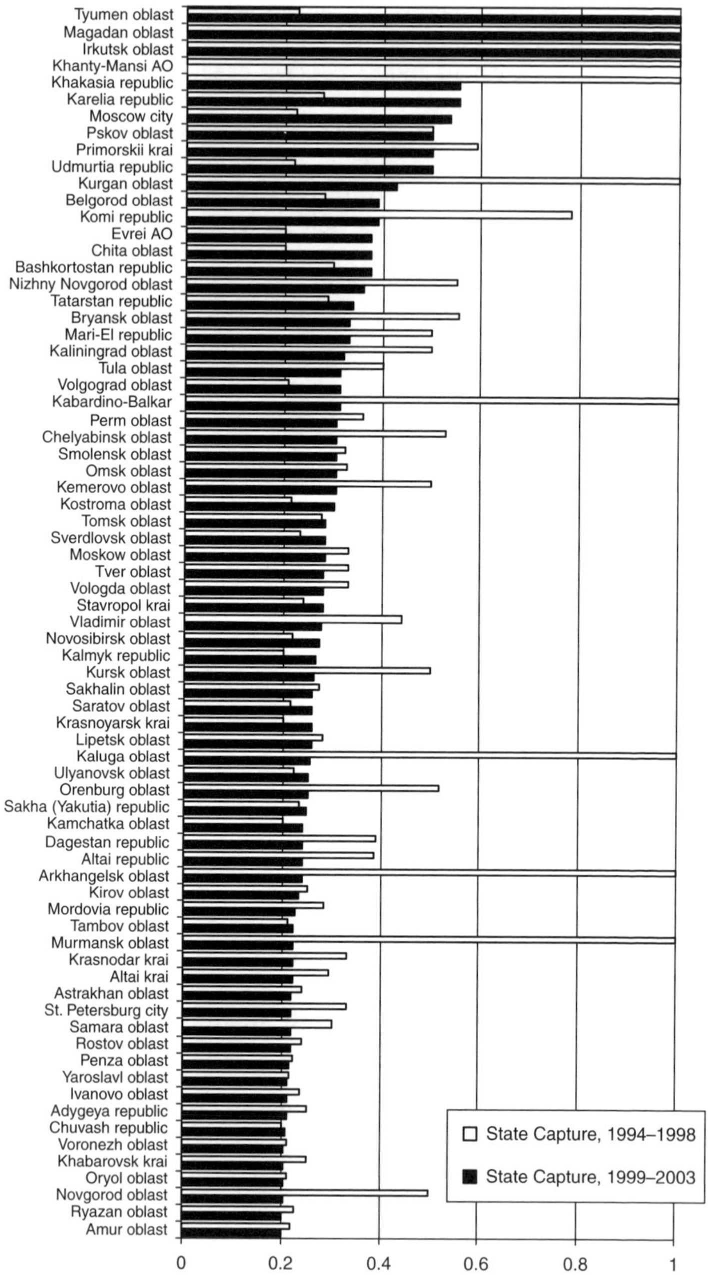

Figure 2.1 Mean concentration of preferential treatment by region under President Yeltsin's terms (1994–1998) and President Putin's first term (1999–2003)
Source: Slinko, Yakovlev and Zhuravskaya (2005).

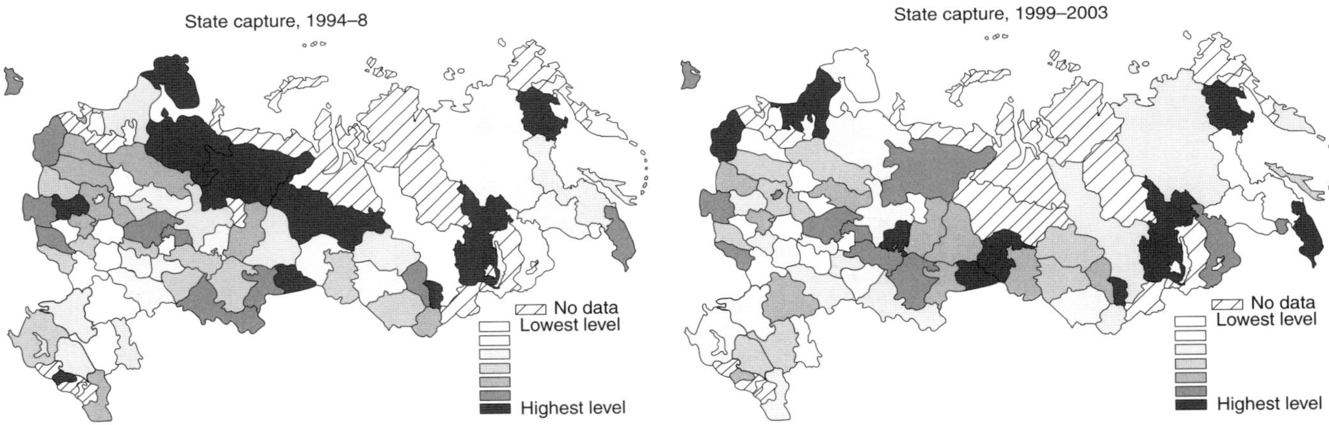

Figure 2.2 Regional distribution of average concentration of preferential treatment in President Yeltsin's and President Putin's terms, 1994–2003

Table 2.1 Correlation between state capture (2000–2003) and other corruption indexes

	no. of PTs 2000–3	*PTC,* 1996–9	*no. of PTs* 1996–9	*State capture (INDEM&TI),* 2000	*Business capture (INDEM&TI),* 2000	*Administrative corruption (INDEM&TI),* 2000
PTC, 2000–3	−0.37**	0.25**	−0.09	0.14	0.30*	0.43**
no. of PTs, 2000–3		−0.3**	0.48**	−0.10	−0.13	−0.24

Note: * significant at 10%; ** significant at 5%.
Source: authors' calculations.

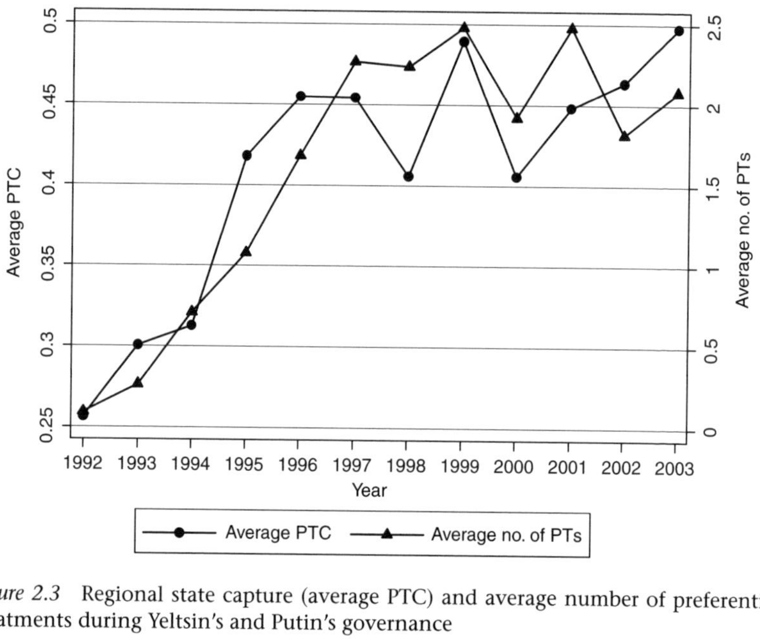

Figure 2.3 Regional state capture (average PTC) and average number of preferential treatments during Yeltsin's and Putin's governance
Source: Slinko, Yakovlev and Zhuravskaya (2005).

presidency was strongly correlated with the measure in Yeltsin's second term and with alternative corruption measures (see Table 2.1).[7]

Just as in Yeltsin's time, the regional state capture under Putin's administration negatively affected small business development as well as the growth of large and medium-size firms with no political power. Output of small businesses and regional retail turnover was significantly reduced with an increase in state capture (see Figure 2.3). Growth in profitability, productivity, sales, employment and investment of firms without political

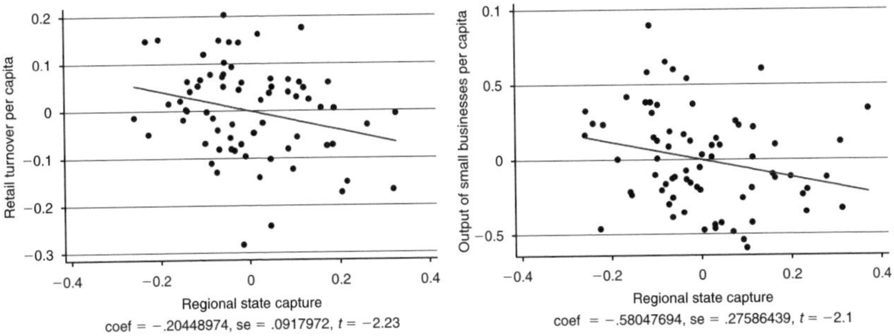

Figure 2.4 State capture and small business growth

Note: Charts present residual correlation of indicators of regional performance and state capture after accounting for the following control variables: the total number of preferential treatments in a region, initial level of the dependent variable, initial level of regional education (with the share of labour force that attained higher education), dummy for a republic status of the region. Number of preferential treatments is instrumented by its initial level. The specification used is between-effects, i.e., regressions on averages across time.

connections also significantly slowed down in high capture environments (see Figure 2.4).

3.3 What was the effect of tax reform aimed at restricting possibilities for preferential treatment of specific enterprises?

Using the available data we present an example of the effect of a partial reform aimed at fighting corruption. At the end of 1999, a tax law restricting tax breaks given to individual firms was enacted. Tax breaks were the most popular type of preferential treatment, constituting one-third of the total number of preferential treatments in Russia's regions. Nevertheless, the law has not resulted in any considerable change of either the number or concentration of preferential treatments provided by the regions to firms. The law has only led to a change in the type of preferential treatment given out: as Figure 2.5 shows, the share of tax breaks significantly decreased, whereas the share of subsidies, subsidized budget loans, budget guaranties of credits and subsidized energy prices have significantly increased after the enactment of this law.

3.4 Who has received preferential treatments?

The question that we address here is whether Putin's measures, in particular his attacks on oligarchs and consolidation of power in the hands of the federal centre, have led to real redistribution of political power, the rise of new financial-industrial groups and the fall of previous favourites. We address this question by looking at firms' characteristics, such as size of firms and industrial structure.

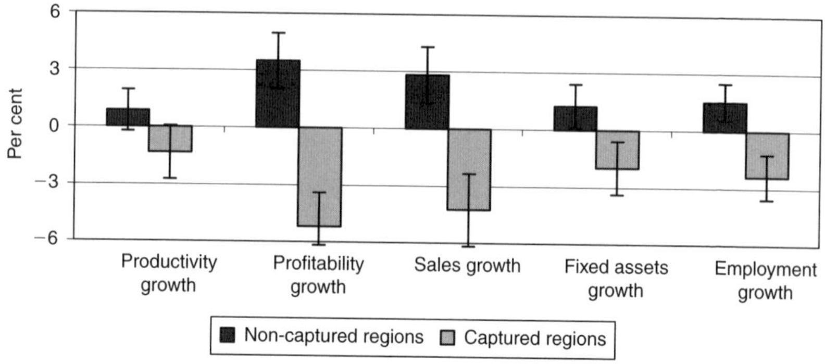

Figure 2.5 State capture and performance of firms with no political power
Note: In the figure the 'captured' and 'non-captured' regions are defined as regions in the top and bottom thirds of the distribution with respect to the value of the average residual preferential treatment concentration after accounting for the following control variables. We control for the total number of preferential treatments in a region, initial level of the dependent variable, initial level of regional education (with the share of labour force that attained higher education), dummy for republic, dummy for state enterprise. Columns indicate residual performance indicators after accounting for the same set of control variables. Black bars indicate 95% confidence intervals. In all corresponding regressions number of preferential treatments is instrumented by its initial level.

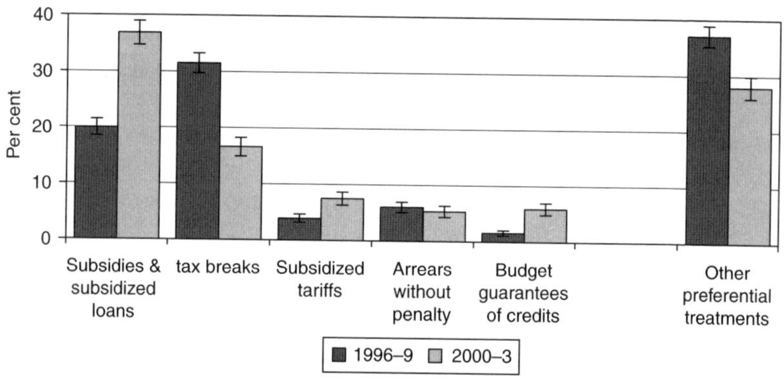

Figure 2.6 Distribution of preferential treatments by type
Note: The figure presents distribution of preferential by types. Columns indicate share of preferential treatment of this type in total number of preferential treatments. Error bars indicate standard errors.

Theory predicts concentration of political power in the hands of the biggest and richest enterprises. The means of bargaining with politicians are both employment, which is of great political benefit to politicians, and rents that enterprises can use to bribe politicians. Under Yeltsin, firms with higher employment, output and capital, firms in extraction industries, and firms that belonged to larger financial-industrial groups were more likely to exert

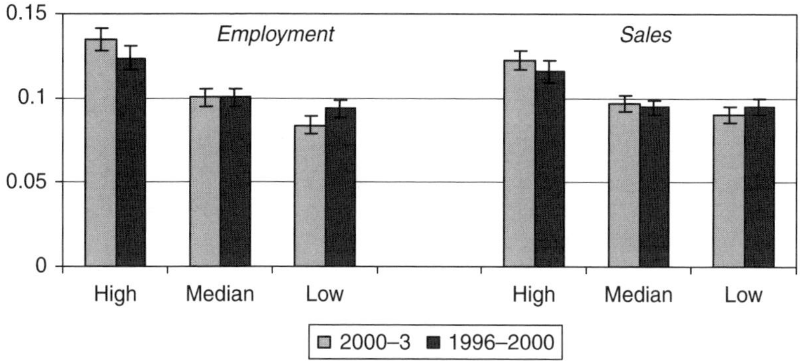

Figure 2.7 Firm's size and political power

Note: The figure presents mean values of preferential treatment share by groups with high, median, and low employment and sales. Firms with high, median, and low employment and sales are defined as firms in the top, median, and bottom thirds of the distribution with respect to the average level of firm's employment or sales share in employment or sales of the five biggest regional firms, respectively. Error bars indicate standard errors.

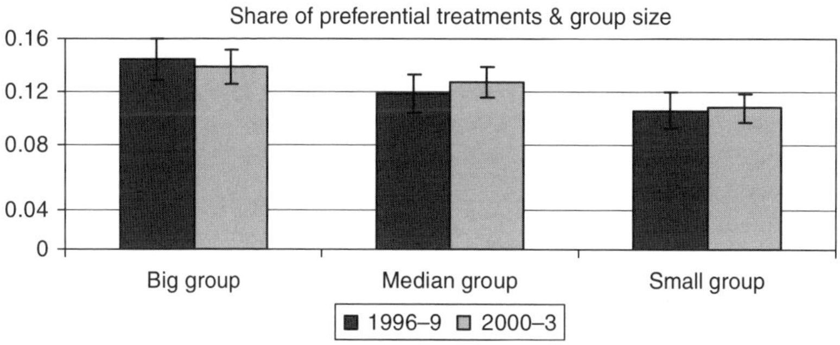

Figure 2.8 Financial-industrial group's size and firm's political power

Note: The figure presents mean values of preferential treatment share by groups of firms which belong to big/median/small group. Firms which belong to big/median/small group are defined as firms in the top/median/bottom thirds of the distribution with respect to the group size, respectively. Error bars indicate standard errors.

political influence. Things have not changed under Putin. Figures 2.7 and 2.8 show that firms with bigger output and employment relative to other firms in the regions received more preferential treatment. Figure 2.7 shows that firms that belong to a bigger financial-industrial group are also likely to be successful captors. Finally, Figure 2.9 shows that the average political influence of firms in extraction industries is greater than influence of firms from all other industries, except the machine-building and electricity industries.

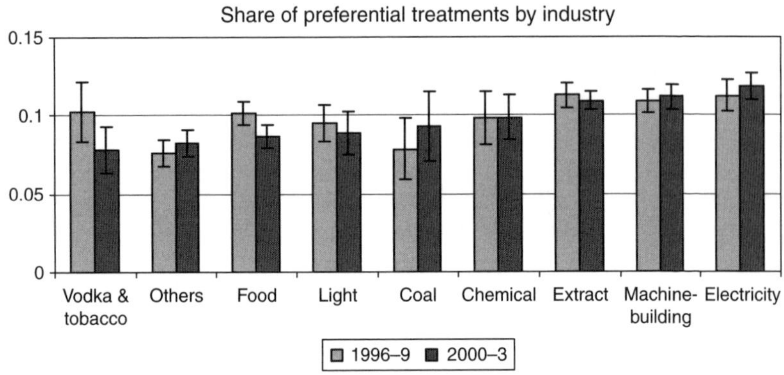

Figure 2.9 Industry structure and firm's political power

Note: The figure presents mean values of preferential treatment share of firms from different industries. Error bars indicate standard errors.

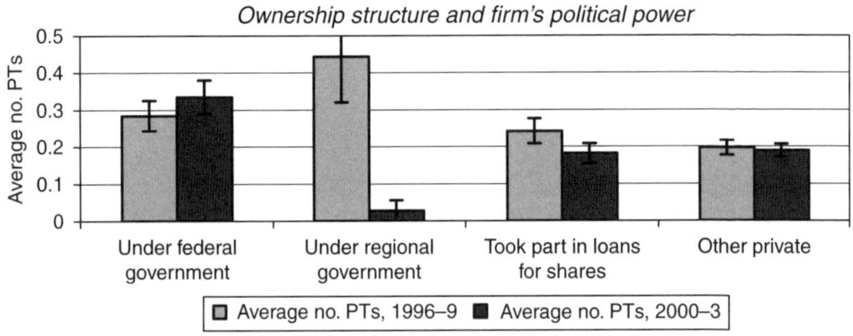

Figure 2.10 Ownership structure and firm's political power

Note: The figure presents mean values of preferential treatments of firms with different ownership. Error bars indicate standard errors.

Concentration of political power in the centre during Putin's administration can be traced in the data: enterprises that belong to the federal government were the most effective lobbyists during Putin's governance, whereas private enterprises whose owners had previously been engaged in notorious 'loans-for-shares' schemes and enterprises that belonged to regional governments lost political power. Under Putin's governance only one group, enterprises in federal ownership, received significantly more preferential treatment (see Figure 2.10).

4 Conclusions

To summarize, our study shows that there have been no significant changes in the overall level of state capture at the regional level in Russia between

Yeltsin's and Putin's time in power, despite all the attempts of Putin's administration to centralize governance. We provide illustrations of how firms and regional officials managed to circumvent the partial reforms aimed at reducing corruption at the regional level. There was, however, an important change in the nature of most influential groups between Yeltsin's and Putin's time. We showed that there was a shift in the allocation of bargaining power within regions to firms in federal government ownership from private firms in general and in particular from private firms that belonged to the largest national industrial groups as well as from the firms owned by the regional government. Firms that belong to the federal government have become the most politically powerful lobbyists at regional level.

Notes

1. The phenomenon of shaping institutions by powerful businesses is called state capture. See Olson (1965, 1982); Stigler (1971) for pioneer works. For empirical work on state capture in transition countries, see Hellman, Jones Kanufmann and Schankerman (2000), Hellman and Schankerman (2000), Hellman, Jones and Kaufmann (2003), Hellman and Kaufmann (2003), Hellman (1998), Slinko, Yakovlev and Zhuravskaya (2005) and Yakovlev and Zhuravskaya (2003).
2. BEEPS are Business Environment and Enterprise Performance Surveys, conducted jointly by the World Bank and the European Bank for Reconstruction and Development in transition countries in 1999 and 2002. See http://info.worldbank.org/governance/beeps/ for description, Data and research.
3. For theoretical prediction, see Shleifer and Vishni (1994); for evidence from Russian regions, see Slinko, Yakovlev and Zhuravskaya (2005) and Yakovlev and Zhuravskaya (2003).
4. Seven large federal districts were created which took away some regional autonomy.
5. See CEFIR study 'Monitoring the Administrative Barriers to Small Business Development in Russia' (2003).
6. According to ROMIR polling agency (www.romir.ru), people put unsuccessful anti-corruption measures as the second biggest failure of President Putin.
7. The State Capture Measure in Yeltsin's governance also correlate with alternative corruption indexes. See Slinko, Yakovlev and Zhuravskaya (2005).

References

Anderson, J., J.S. Hellman, G. Jones, B. Moore, H. Muller, S. Pradhan, R. Ryterman and H. Sutch (2000) 'Anticorruption in Transition: a Contribution to the Policy Debate' *World Bank report*, no. 20925 vol. 1.

Frye, T. (2002) 'Capture or Exchange? Business Lobbying in Russia', *Europe–Asia Studies*, vol. 54, no. 7, pp. 1017–36.

Guriev, S. and A. Rachinsky (2005) 'The Role of Oligarchs in Russian Capitalism', *Journal of Economic Perspectives* vol. 19, pp. 131–50.

Hellman, J.S. (1998) 'Winners Take All: The Politics of Partial Reform in Postcommunist Nations', *World Politics*, vol. 50, no. 2, pp. 203–34.

Hellman, J.S. and D. Kaufmann (2003) 'The Inequality of Influence', *World Bank* (mimeo).

Hellman, J.S. and M. Schankerman (2000) 'Intervention, Corruption and Capture', *Economics of Transition*, vol. 8, no. 3, pp. 545–76.

Hellman, J.S., G. Jones and D. Kaufmann (2003) 'Seize the State, Seize the Day: State Capture, Corruption and Influence in Transition', *Journal of Comparative Economics*, vol. 31, no. 4, pp. 751–73.

Hellman, J.S., G. Jones, D. Kaufmann and M. Schankerman (2000) 'Measuring Governance, Corruption, and State Capture? How Firms and Bureaucrats Shape the Business Environment in Transition Economies', *World Bank Policy Research Working Paper*, no. 2312.

Olson, M. (1965) *The Logic of Collective Action* (Cambridge, MA: Harvard University Press).

Olson, M. (1982) *The Rise and Decline of Nations: Economic Growth, Stagflation, and Social Rigidities* (New Haven and London: Yale University Press).

Shleifer, A. and R. Vishny (1994) 'Politicians and Firms', *Quarterly Journal of Economics*, vol. 109, no. 4, pp. 995–1025.

Slinko, I., E. Yakovlev and E. Zhuravskaya (2005) 'Laws for Sale: Evidence from Russia', *American Law and Economics Review*, vol. 7, no. 1, pp. 284–318.

Stigler, G.J. (1971) 'The Economic Theory of Regulation', *Bell Journal of Economics and Management Science*, pp. 3–21.

Yakovlev, E. and E. Zhuravskaya (2004) 'State Capture and Controlling Owners of Firms', World Bank (background paper for the Country Economic Memorandum for Russia).

3

Democracy for Better Governance and Higher Economic Growth in the MENA Region?*

Mustapha K. Nabli and Carlos Silva-Jáuregui

1 Introduction

Democracy is valued in itself. The extent to which a citizen is able to live in an open society and participate in its democratic process directly affects his/her wellbeing. But democracy can also affect welfare indirectly through its effects on other aspects of the social and economic interactions that influence the wellbeing of people. Democracy can often positively affect the relative rights of social groups, such as gender-specific groups or minorities. In the economic area democracy may affect the distribution of income, with democracies, for instance, tending to pay higher wages and improve human capital. It may also affect the volatility of incomes, with democracies tending to produce fewer recessions and affect the economic rate of growth. Nobel Prize Laureate Amartya Sen observes that famines never occurred under democratic regimes.

To the extent that democratic development reinforces and is reinforced by these various positive effects, democracy will generally gain more acceptance, and opposition to it will weaken. But what happens if there are trade-offs between democratic development and any of these positive social and economic effects? What happens in cases where a democratic process brings into power a government which is able to pursue policies which undermine gender equality or the rights of a minority group? What happens in

* The views expressed in this chapter are entirely those of its authors, and should not be attributed to the World Bank or its Board of Directors. We are grateful for the many insights, comments and ideas contributed by Hasan Abuyoub and Samir Makdisi, as co-panelists, and Mouna Cherkaoui, Jean-Paul Fitoussi, Heba Handoussa, Janos Kornai, Timur Kuran, and Gérard Roland. We thank Daron Acemoglu for sharing the transformed Freedom House Political Rights Index data. We would also like to thank Ibrahim Elbadawi, Phillip Keefer, Paloma Anos-Casero, Farrukh Iqbal and Robert Beschel for helpful comments and suggestions, and to Paul Dyer and Claudia Nassif for their effective research assistance.

situations where democratic development leads for some reason to a reduction in incomes or a reduction in the rate of economic growth? In these situations, individuals and society may still value democracy despite the trade-offs. Society may introduce checks and balances and develop institutional mechanisms within the democratic process to reduce or eliminate the likelihood of a negative outcome.

In view of the complexity of the issues related to democratic development the objective of this chapter is to discuss only one topic: does democracy tend to induce higher or lower economic growth? The aim is to help to understand the links between democracy and economic growth. But it should be made clear that any finding which suggests that democracy leads to less growth would not lead to any presumption that democracy should be sacrificed for the sake of growth. This is a choice that needs to be made by any society (through the democratic process preferably!) given its special circumstances. On the other hand a positive link would reinforce the strength of argument for democracy.

The chapter focuses more specifically on the Middle East and North Africa Region (MENA)[1] given the recent emphasis on democratic development. Actually democracy has risen dramatically on the agenda for and in MENA region countries. It has become an explicit objective of foreign policy for the USA as well as the G8. Whether it is *the* primary objective and whether it is being pursued effectively are issues which are subject to much heated debate. But there is no doubt that promoting democracy is high on the agenda of both the USA and the European Union in the context of its European Neighbourhood Policy. Equally, if not more important is the increased domestic pressure for change from within the region. Civil society at large has been demanding more political openness over the last few years. This has been more eloquently and forcefully expressed in the United Nations Development Programme (UNDP) Arab Human Development Reports.

The reasons for the recent call for democratic change are varied and complex. For foreign players, these may be connected to possible or presumed links between the lack of democracy and 'terrorism',[2] or between democracy and 'security of borders'. For domestic actors, the reason may simply be that the people of the region aspire to greater empowerment and freedom after decades, if not centuries, of political oppression. But this chapter will not delve into those issues. Nor will we look into the determinants of democratic development. For instance, there is a large literature and much debate about whether economic growth fosters democratization as first advanced by Lipset (1959). Most recently Friedman (2005) argued that over the long run a rising living standard fosters openness, tolerance and democracy, while recognizing that in the short run economic growth makes more secure whatever political structure may be in place; and economic stagnation and crisis may undermine a non-democratic regime. Also in a recent review de Mesquita and Downs (2005) argue that while economic growth results in higher incomes and increases demand for democracy, it may also foster the ability of autocratic regimes to strengthen their power as they are able to shape institutions and political events to their advantage. Acemoglu and Johnson (2005) show that the strong cross-country correlation between income and democracy does not mean there is causality and that this correlation can be explained by historical factors which jointly determine both the economic and political development paths of various societies. In the most ambitious analytical undertaking to date Acemoglu and Robinson (2006) develop a general framework using game theory for understanding how democratic development takes place and consolidates or not. This work shows that there are problems of simultaneity between democratic development and economic development which will be discussed when relevant. However, these issues go well beyond the scope of this chapter.

We consider the possible effects of a 'given' democratic process without dwelling much on how it may have come about. Its scope is the relationship between 'democratic development' and 'economic growth'. From an economic perspective the objective is to determine whether there is a well-defined relationship (or lack thereof) between the two, and, more specifically, whether one should expect democracy to 'help' or 'hinder' stronger economic performance in general and in the context of the MENA region in particular.

In Section 2 we provide the general context for the democracy–growth linkages discussion in the MENA region which is characterized by the existence of a democracy deficit as well as a growth deficit for the past two decades. Section 3 reviews the empirical literature on the links between democracy and growth, focusing on direct links and using mostly reduced form type models. It concludes that the nature and strength of these links are at best ambiguous. More recent work on the relationship between democracy and growth surveyed in Section 4 pursues a more structural approach, looks at the intermediation channels and indirect links between democracy and growth as well as the role of the nature of democratic regimes. One main conclusion is that the effect of democracy on growth, especially in MENA, depends to a large extent on whether a democratic transition leads to better governance and, therefore, a better business climate and higher private physical capital accumulation. Then Section 5 explores the extent to which achieving better governance is more likely under democratic regimes or non-democratic ones. Section 6 provides a brief discussion of a different approach to looking at the links between democracy and growth by postulating that while such a link may not be established systematically for any country at any time it may be important for most MENA countries today. In this case democratic reform may be needed to unlock the prevailing *status quo* of low public accountability and the maintenance of prevailing economic policies and networks of privilege and generate a great political and economic transformation which could jointly produce better democracy and greater economic growth in the region. The last section concludes that democratic development could be a strong lever for economic growth in the MENA region and that these countries should strive for democratic regimes which are sustainable in the sense of having characteristics which make them more likely to produce good governance. 'Quality democracy' which produces quality governance, improves the investment climate and encourages the emergence of a dynamic private sector, and can help to meet the development challenges of the MENA region, which needs to achieve average growth rates of 6–7 per cent a year in order to absorb the fast growing, increasingly educated and feminized labour force. The main focus should be on the design of the appropriate democratic institutions which:

(i) minimize imperfections in the political market, with more freedom of information and a free press, adequate mechanisms to contain clientelism and increased credibility of political promises,
(ii) introduce safeguards and effective checks and balances,
(iii) increase the legitimacy of the democratic transformation, and
(iv) in cases where there is significant ethnic and or religious fragmentation minimize the risks of social conflict.

2 The democracy and growth deficits in the MENA region

At this point, it is perhaps useful to discuss the links between democracy and economic growth in the MENA region. This context can be summarized by the existence of both a 'democracy deficit' and a 'growth deficit'. Their simultaneous presence in practically all countries of the region (even though at different degrees) leads one to wonder whether any links exist between the two.

Before presenting the evidence on the democratic deficit we consider the definition of democracy.[3] At its most abstract level, democracy is a system of government (or of exercise of authority) in which effective political power is vested in the people and where major decisions of government and the direction of policy behind these decisions rests directly or indirectly on the freely given consent of the majority of the adults governed. At a more practical level, democracy tends to be defined in procedural terms as the body of rules and procedures that regulate the transfer of political power and the free expression of disagreement at all levels of political life. More concretely, it is defined as a political system where access to political power is regularly achieved through competitive, free and fair elections. As stated by Schumpeter (1942), it is '... the institutional arrangement for arriving at political decisions in which individuals acquire the power to decide by means of a competitive struggle for the peoples' vote' (p. 250).

The democracy deficit in the MENA region

Democracy has gained worldwide acceptance in recent decades. Without exception all developed countries maintain democratic systems, and many

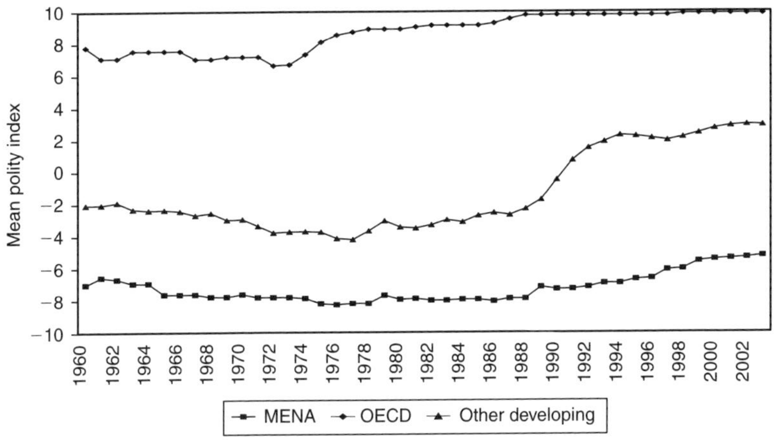

Figure 3.1 Democracy trends in MENA and other regions
Source: University of Maryland Center for International Development and Conflict Management.

developing ones are selecting their leaders through competitive elections, that is, moving towards more democratic political regimes. A recent publication on lessons of the 1990s by the World Bank (2005a) pointed out that '... a striking phenomenon of the 1990s was the rise in the number of countries selecting their leaders through competitive elections. The number rose from 60 countries in 1989 to 100 in 2000. Among poorer countries (those with less than the median country's per capita income) the number nearly tripled, from 11 in 1989 to 32 in 2000; 15 per cent of the poorer countries elected their governments in 1989 and 42 per cent in 2000.' This shows a remarkable move towards democracy, but this trend did not spread as vigorously to MENA. There is now a wide body of evidence about the 'democracy gap or deficit' in the MENA region. It will suffice here to highlight some of this empirical evidence.

First, evidence can be observed when using the well-known composite Polity Index from the Polity IV dataset.[4] The composite Polity Index (which ranges from −10 for the least democratic regimes to +10 for the most democratic regimes) shows that the MENA region has consistently lagged behind the rest of the world, suggesting that there is a persistent democracy deficit in the region (Figure 3.1). The MENA democracy deficit has existed over the last forty years, with the average regime in MENA remaining authoritarian according to this metric (negative values for the Polity Index). While the Organisation for Economic Co-operation and Development (OECD) countries have been consistently democratic other regions in the world were traditionally not very democratic. From around 1977, however, the Polity Index shows a clear tendency towards democratization in developing countries outside MENA. In developing countries (other than MENA) the average

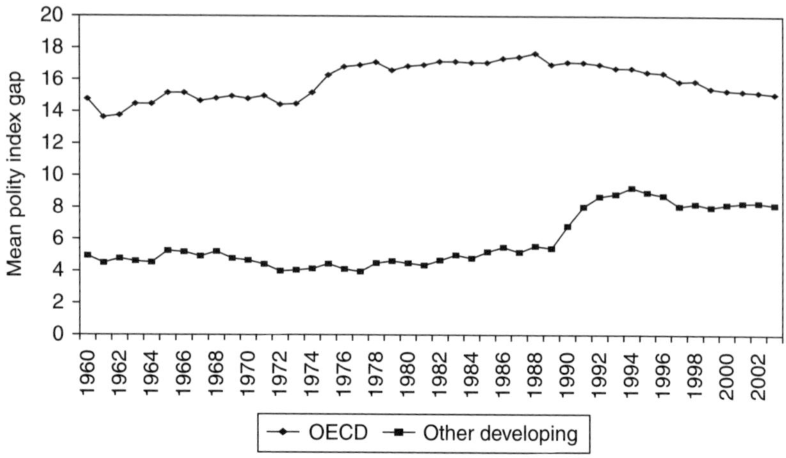

Figure 3.2 Democracy gap between MENA and other regions
Source: University of Maryland Center for International Development and Conflict Management.

Polity Index had turned positive by 1991, with a gain of 7 points (30 per cent of the scale) during the period 1977–2002.

During the 1960s on average the democracy level of countries in MENA and other developing regions was declining. The democracy gap between the two regions remained, however, relatively stable with a small declining trend during the period covering the mid-1960s and the mid-1970s. The democracy gap reached its lowest point around 1977. Since then, the gap has increased steadily, accelerating around 1990 when the Soviet Bloc disintegrated and new democracies emerged, particularly in Central and Eastern Europe. Since 1994 there has been a decline in the democracy gap between MENA and other developing regions, but the gap remains significantly above the level attained in the 1970s. The democracy gap between MENA and the OECD increased steadily until 1988 when the average OECD Polity Index reached its high plateau. At that point, the gap was almost 17.5 points – 88 per cent of the scale. Since then the gap between MENA and the OECD has declined with the gradual progress towards democratization in MENAs. Nonetheless, the gap remains at 15 points or 75 per cent of the scale, above the 1960s level.

Further evidence comes from analysing the trends in the Freedom House Political Rights Index. This alternative measure of democracy has been used by several scholars including Acemoglu and Robinson (2006) and Barro (1999). The original Freedom House index ranges from 1 to 7, with 1 representing the most political freedom and 7 the least. We use the transformed Freedom House index (Acemoglu and Robinson, 2006) which, following Barro (1999), is supplemented with data from Bollen (1990, 2001) for 1960

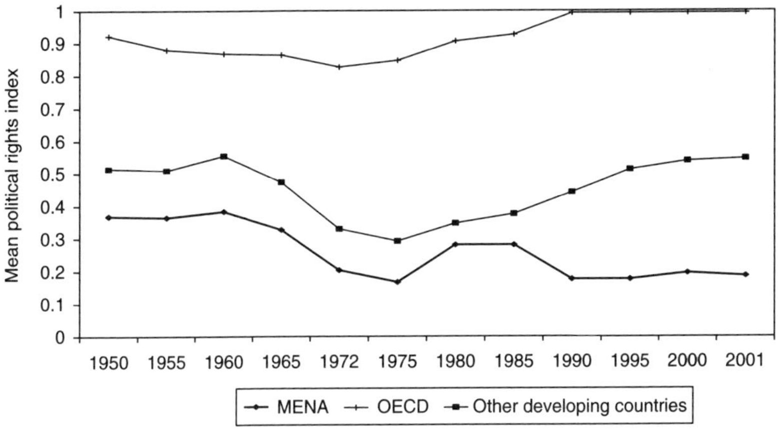

Figure 3.3 Freedom House political rights index in MENA and selected regions
Source: Freedom House.

and 1965, normalized and transformed to lie between 0 and 1, with 0 corresponding to the least democratic set of institutions and 1 to the most.[5] This facilitates the comparison with the other indicators of democracy used in the paper.

Figure 3.3 plots the time series of the normalized Freedom House Political Rights index. The index confirms the low level of democracy in the MENA region, and a growing democracy gap with OECD and other developing regions in the world. As Figure 3.3 shows, the MENA region has a declining trend in the political rights index, losing considerable ground between 1960 and 1975, and between 1985 and 1990. The index reveals a small improvement in political rights in the period 1975–80, at the height of the oil boom. The index also indicates little, if any, gains in political rights during the 1990–2001 period, contrary to the trends of the Polity index. This may indicate that while some elements of democratization were implemented, those related with political rights lagged.

Analysis of the democracy gap using the Freedom House index shows an increasing gap *vis-à-vis* OECD countries until the early 1990s. With respect to countries in other developing parts of the world, the democracy gap declined marginally during the 1960–80 period. Since 1985, however, it has increased sharply as other regions of the world have moved more rapidly towards increasing political rights and advancing democratic reforms.

Additional evidence on the gap can be found from the work of Papaioannou and Siouroumis (2004) who constructed a complete dataset on democratization in the world since the 1970s. The data used are wide ranging and go beyond the various quantitative indicators and use the historical review of episodes. The authors find that 38 episodes of 'full democratization' and 24 episodes of 'partial democratization' occurred in the world over the last 30 to 40 years. None of these episodes took place in the MENA region.

Finally, a fourth piece of evidence on the 'democracy deficit' is the absence of any positive correlation between democracy and *level of incomes* in the MENA region, unlike what is typically found for the rest of the world. Przeworski *et al.* (2000) found that democracies were more frequently found in developed (wealthier) countries while dictatorships were more frequent in poor countries. In typical charts showing the correlation between level of income and democratic development, MENA counties tend to cluster way below the line. In particular, the many oil-producing countries tend to be less democratic than other less wealthy countries. The Gulf Cooperation Council (GCC) countries have among the lowest scores in the region using the Polity IV index.

Driving the gap between MENA countries and the rest of the world are striking weaknesses in external accountability and in access to basic political and civic rights. Word Bank (2003e) constructed an index of public accountability (IPA). The IPA assesses the process for selecting and replacing those in authority. It measures the quality of governance according to the inclusiveness of access to basic political and civic rights and the relative strength of external accountability mechanisms. It aggregates 12 indicators that measure the level of openness of political institutions in a country and the extent to which political participation is free, fair, and competitive; civil liberties are assumed and respected; and the press and speech are free from control, violation, harassment, and censorship. It also captures the transparency and responsiveness of the government to its people and the degree of political accountability in the public sphere.

All countries in the MENA region, whatever their income, score far below the world trend in the IPA (Figure 3.4). Some richer MENA countries score especially low on the IPA – with scores equal to those in some of the poorest countries of the world. Oil seems to matter as oil-exporting countries have the worst IPA scores.

Economic growth deficit in the MENA region

MENA's historic model of economic development was based on state-led development and central planning, with economic and social policies designed for redistribution and equity, and a strong social contract between governments and the people they represented. During 1965 to 1985 economic growth per capita averaged 2.9 per cent per year, second only to the East Asia and Pacific region (Figure 3.5). Many factors contributed to this performance, including rapid progress in early-stage industrialization; high levels of public employment and spending, especially on infrastructure; trade protection for domestic producers; and rising oil prices that yielded large capital inflows, created jobs and promoted remittance flows into

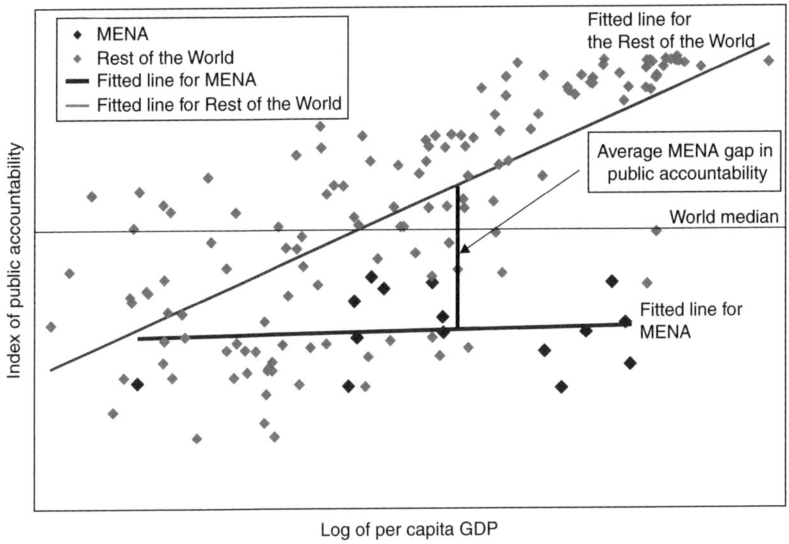

Figure 3.4 Public accountability and per capita incomes in MENA
Source: World Bank (2003e).

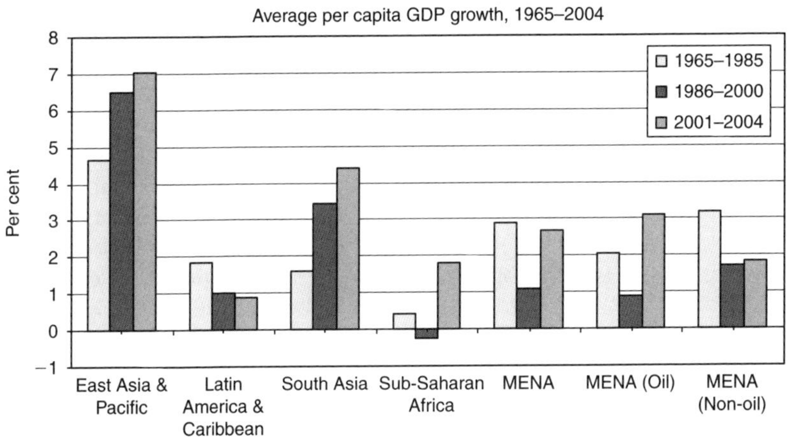

Figure 3.5 Average per capita GDP growth, 1965–2004
Note: MENA (oil producers) include Algeria, Bahrain (1986–2004). Iran (1986–2004). Kuwait, Oman, Saudi Arabian and UAE (1986–2004). MENA (non-oil producers) includes Egypt, Jordan, Lebanon (1986–2004), Morocco, Syria, Tunisia, and Yeman (1986–2004).
Source: World Development Indicators 2005.

non-oil-producing MENA states. While this development model paid large dividends in the beginning, there were also significant costs. Centralized and hierarchical governments emerged in MENA, with limited transparency and contestability of representatives or policies. The MENA development model also created economies that had great difficulty in adapting to shocks and economic change.

As early as the late 1970s the economic systems that had developed in MENA – and that carried the people in the region through an unprecedented era of achievements – showed signs of cracking under stress. The high growth rates were becoming increasingly costly to achieve. Though investment was at record levels, with the rate of growth of physical capital per worker increasing by more than 80 per cent in the 1970s compared to the 1960s, this investment was inefficient, having increasingly smaller growth pay-offs. As a result of large inefficiencies total factor productivity growth was lower than in any other region of the world and turned negative during the 1970s.

The MENA region entered the 1980s with mounting evidence of strains and difficulties to sustain the promise of continued prosperity. Facing declining public revenues following the oil shock in the mid-1980s, governments struggled to maintain their growth performance and redistributive commitments. With a public-sector wage bill accounting for as much as 20 per cent of gross domestic product (GDP), deficits mounted and debt grew at an alarming rate. The fiscal strains contributed to large macroeconomic imbalances. Productivity growth, already declining by the 1970s, plummeted to −1.5 per cent a year on average over the 1980s. Real output growth collapsed under the multiple blows of declining public spending, in part a result of the negative oil shocks, an unattractive private investment climate, and continuing losses in efficiency. GDP per capita stagnated during the 1980s, averaging an imperceptible 0.3 per cent a year during the decade.

In the 1990s several macroeconomic stabilization reforms were implemented which paid important dividends. By and large, MENA countries recovered from the instability of the 1980s. Inflation was brought under control, debt levels declined, and macroeconomic performance mostly turned positive. These were fundamental pre-conditions for higher private investment and growth, but strong growth rates required to cope with the demographic transition of the region failed to materialize. Despite the reforms mentioned the effort failed to translate into the strong economic recovery anticipated. Though GDP growth improved compared to the crisis-ridden 1980s, per capita growth remained weak, averaging 1.5 per cent a year in the 1990s. While the decline in productivity growth was arrested, productivity growth was close to 2 percentage points lower than the world average and 3.5 percentage points lower than East Asia with about the same level of investment.

With the coming of the new millennium, the region has experienced a new set of favourable conditions. As a result, the region has achieved exceptional growth during recent years. Accelerating in the early 2000s, economic growth in the MENA region (excluding Iraq) averaged 5.1 per cent a year between 2002 and 2004, the strongest growth rate in a decade, and significantly higher than the average yearly growth during the 1990s. On a per capita basis, the

MENA region's 3.2 per cent average growth over 2002–04 was its strongest growth performance since the mid-1970s.

Despite the oil-driven growth boom, on a per capita basis, the region's growth rate over the last few years continues to lag behind that of most other regions, a reflection of both the firming of GDP growth rates across developing regions and MENA region's high population growth rate which continues to be a key development challenge. At the regional level, per capita income growth in East Asia and the Pacific, South Asia, Central Asia and Europe all outpaced MENA's per capita GDP performance in both 2003 and 2004.

To summarize, over the past two decades the MENA region has experienced a growth deficit with low per capita income growth. This growth performance has been weaker than that achieved by most other regions of the world, except for Sub-Saharan Africa.

3 Empirical correlation and direct links between democracy and economic growth

The previous discussion tempts one to hypothesize that there is a strong link between the low growth and the democracy deficit in the MENA region. In this section we review more thoroughly the international experience on the empirical relationship between democracy and growth and investigate how it applies the MENA region.

International experience suggests that the economic success of many authoritarian regimes such as Singapore, South Korea, and Indonesia during the 1970s and 1980s, Chile in the 1980s, and China over the last 20 years has always cast some doubt on the existence of any robust (positive) linear relationship between economic growth and democracy. Empirical studies using standard growth regressions models and cross-country data have found mixed evidence for such direct links. Reviews of a large number of these studies (see Borner, Brunetti and Weder, 1995) found that only a few showed any strong positive relationship, with most showing either insignificant results or even a negative link. Using the Freedom House indicator for democracy (electoral rights), Barro and Sala-i-Martin (2003) showed that a non-linear relationship might exist, similar to a Laffer Curve, in which democratization appears to enhance growth for countries that are not very democratic but to retard growth for countries that have already achieved a high degree of democracy. Przeworski *et al.* (2000) analysed data over a long period of time and concluded that when countries were observed across the entire spectrum of conditions total income grew at about the same rate for democratic and non-democratic regimes. However, they found that patterns of growth varied between democracies and non-democracies, particularly in wealthy countries.

The history of the MENA region over the last 50 years shows limited experience with democracy and political openness. But while no country in the

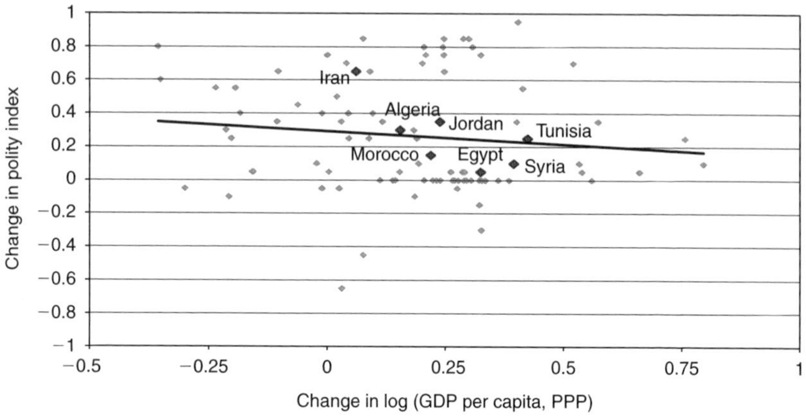

Figure 3.6 Democracy growth and income growth, 1970–2003

region achieved full transition to democracy, the degree of political openness and use of the electoral process to choose the government in power has varied significantly over time and across countries. The high income growth rates achieved in the 1970s and early 1980s were not accompanied by any significant degree of political openness, while the growth collapse in the later 1980s saw some degree of political liberalization in several MENA countries. During the 1990s the experience of low economic growth countries, such as Morocco, was associated with gains in democratization, while higher growth countries like Tunisia were increasingly autocratic. At the same time Jordan experienced higher growth and political openness while low growth and limited democratization was the norm in most Gulf countries Overall, there is little correlation between changes in democracy and changes in income per capita during 1970 to 2003 in MENA and the rest of the world (Figure 3.6). Countries that grew faster than others have not become more democratic.

The lack of any strong empirical evidence of *direct positive links* between democracy and economic growth, the MENA region including has led research to explore new directions for the study of the linkages between democratic and economic development. We look at some of these in the next section.

4 Structural analysis of the links between democracy and economic growth

Indirect links between democracy and economic growth

Recent research has moved in three directions to explore the *indirect* linkages between democratization and economic growth.[6] The *first direction* explores in greater depth the theoretical and empirical links between democracy and economic growth, going beyond simple correlations and cross-country regressions considered with the direct links. These studies look at the indirect effects of democracy on economic growth through a number of intermediation channels. They use structural models which involve income growth, democracy and variables which represent such intermediation or transmission channels. Some of these channels show a negative impact of democracy and economic growth, while others show a positive link. A focus on the inefficiencies of representative government, using the 'median voter model' or the public choice approach, would imply that democratic regimes result in greater demand for redistribution and the prevalence of special interest politics. This may result in higher government consumption, higher taxation, more redistribution and lower private investment. All these channels would imply lower growth rates.

But many other channels would lead one to expect a positive impact on democracy leading to economic growth. First, redistribution and higher taxation may result in higher human capital accumulation through larger subsidies and the handling of capital market failures. Second, democracy deals better with economic instability through commitment achieved through the political process. Political instability is part of everyday life in democracies but does not affect economic growth as much as in the case of authoritarian regimes. In non-democracies any change or expectation of leadership change negatively affect investment and growth: whenever dictators are expected to be removed growth declines sharply (Przeworwski *et al.* 2000). These non-democratic regimes are only successful if they are stable. Shocks, therefore, have a major negative impact on economic growth. In addition, democratic regimes are better suited to both the mediation of conflicts among interest groups, and responding to exogenous negative shocks (Rodrik 1997, 2000). Countries with a higher degree of social and ethnic fragmentation and weak democratic institutions are suffer the sharpest drops in GDP after shocks.

Tavares and Wacziarg (2001) used a full system of simultaneous equations and panel data for the period 1970–89. They found that democracy fosters growth because it improves human capital accumulation and, in a weaker way, because it reduces income inequality. At the same time, they found that democracy hinders growth by reducing physical capital accumulation and in a less robust way by increasing the government consumption to GDP ratio. However, no significant impact was found through the channels of political instability and policy distortions. The overall effect of democracy on growth was slightly *negative* mainly attributable to the large impact on the reduction in the rate of physical capital accumulation. In a similar vein Feng (2003) conducted a wide-ranging empirical study of the impact of political institutions on economic growth. He found that democracy had an insignificant direct effect on economic growth, but that the indirect effects were strong and significant. These indirect channels include political instability, policy uncertainty, investment, education, property rights and birth rates.

The *second direction* ranged beyond cross-country analysis and used event analysis intensively and differences in performance for *before and after* democratization episodes. Empirical findings from this analysis suggested a positive impact for democratization in a given country's economic growth. From a theoretical standpoint the evidence presented in this new branch of the democracy–growth nexus literature offers direct support for so-called development theories of democracy and growth which highlight the growth enhancement aspects of the democratic process. From a policy perspective the results suggest that democratic institutions, *if properly introduced and adapted*, can bring substantial growth benefits. They also suggest an important role for the international community, to help mitigate the transition costs, which may be high and impede the consolidation of democratic rule.

To assess whether successful democratic transition is associated with faster growth, Papaioannou and Siourounis (2004) first identified the countries and the exact timing of the establishment of their *permanent democratization* in the period 1960–2000. They employed an event study approach and analysed the evolution of GDP growth before and after incidents of political modernization. Using a dynamic panel with annual observations, and econometric techniques that address concerns on the shortcomings of previous research, the study reveals that conditioning on various growth determinants, global shocks and business cycle effects, a permanent democratization is associated with approximately one per cent increment in real per capita growth. The analysis also reveals a *J-shaped growth* pattern. This implies that output growth drops during the democratic transition, but then fluctuates at a higher rate suggesting 'short-run pain', due perhaps to high transition costs and learning, followed by 'long-run gain' due to higher growth after the consolidation of democracy. The effect is robust according to various model specifications, panel data methodologies, alternative democratization dates, and to the potential endogeneity of democratization. Their methodology enables them to quantify both the short- and the long-run correlations of political modernization and growth. Their results support the Aristotelian notion, recently put in another way by Friedrich Hayek, that the merits of democracy will be achieved in the long run.[7] That is, stable democracies foster growth.

The work of Papaioannou and Siourounis is related to a new wave of research into the effect of institutions on economic performance.[8] Their results suggest that besides legal norms or property rights protection, the type and quality of political institutions correlates strongly with economic growth. The overall effect of democracy on growth is then *positive* in these studies.

The *third direction* of the literature goes beyond the general dualistic specification of political regimes into democratic and non-democratic and explores a number of dimensions. A significant amount of work, mostly on advanced countries, looks at how the nature and rules of democratic regimes affect outcomes. Whether these regimes are presidential or parliamentarian or whether they use majoritarian or proportional representation influences the way democracy affects economic outcomes.

In recent parallel studies, Persson (2004) shows that income gains following democratization are highest when the transition leads to a proportional representation (versus a majoritarian) or when it leads to a parliamentary (versus presidential) system. Giavazzi and Tabellini (2004) document significant interactions between economic and political liberalization and show that countries experience substantial growth gains when they liberalize first the economy and then the polity. The focus in developing countries has been on how imperfections in electoral markets tend to make democracy less effective in achieving good government compared to advanced countries (World Bank 2005a). Imperfections in electoral markets – lack of voter information, the inability of political competitors to make credible promises, and social polarization – are important to understanding policy formulation and explaining differences in economic performance between rich and poor democracies. Voters in developing countries tend to be less informed, the role of the media weaker and campaign financing more prone to capture resulting in worse governance outcomes. At the same time, politicians tend to be less credible, and clientelism more pervasive, especially as the length of exposure to elections tends to be shorter. In addition, social polarization and ethnic fragmentation distort the electoral process.

The empirical findings from this strand of the literature tend to *condition* the possible impact of democratization on growth depending on the severity of political market imperfections. Differences in economic performance across democracies can be explained by these electoral imperfections. Numerous imperfections in electoral markets make it difficult for citizens to hold politicians accountable for policies. Elected governments are most likely to enact policies which favour narrow segments of the population at the expense of the majority when citizens lack good information mechanisms, cannot trust promises made prior to elections, or live in societies that are deeply polarized. These are three of the most important political market imperfections affecting policy outcomes. In contrast, elected governments are most credible and most likely to respect private property rights when they confront checks and balances on their decision-making. Thus, accountability becomes an essential component.

Informed voters are essential to good political outcomes. Without information about what politicians are doing, how their policies affect citizens' welfare, or about the attributes of their political competitors, citizens cannot easily identify and reward high-performing politicians. As a result, bad performance is encouraged and bad political outcomes are likely to occur. In political markets, information on the characteristics of political competitors and government performance is key. Proxies such as newspaper circulation are commonly used in empirical analysis for voter information, and reveal, controlling for income and other factors, that higher newspaper circulation is associated with lower corruption, greater rule of law, better bureaucratic quality, and greater secondary school enrolment (Keefer and Khemani, 2005).

Credible commitments by politicians are also important for good governance. When challengers do not make credible policy commitments, citizens have no reason to prefer them over incumbents. Even if incumbents do badly, citizens have no reason to believe that challengers will do any better. This insulates incumbents from competition and diminishes pressure to perform well. Politicians may only make credible promises to some voters; this not only generates clientelism; it also creates incentives for politicians to under-provide public goods and extract large rents.

In the same way social polarization hinders the capacity for political systems to generate good outcomes. Social polarization undermines the accountability of a government to its citizens. In extreme cases, deep divisions among social groups hinder the capacity of one group to elect a representative from the other, irrespective of his/her characteristics, political platform or qualities as a representative. Elected representatives from one group then have no incentive to address the concerns and solve the problems of the other, generating distortions in the provision of public goods. Empirical studies show that ethnic tension is higher in poorer democracies than in richer ones. The consequences of social polarization will be exacerbated by all the factors that undermine voters' ability to hold politicians accountable.

Implications for MENA countries?

What can be concluded from our survey of MENA countries? Does it mean that democratic reform is unimportant for economic growth? Since the survey shows a lot of uncertainty about the causal links from democracy to economic growth, MENA countries should not expect the pursuit of democratization in itself to bring quick benefits in terms of economic growth. One is tempted to conclude that the search for higher economic growth should focus more on traditional policy and institutional reforms within the existing political regime. In that case the path towards adopt democratic development would be different track separate from that of economic growth.

But such a conclusion would be premature. In fact, the previous discussion suggests that there are some robust positive effects of democracy on growth through higher human capital accumulation. But is such a link relevant or significant to MENA countries? There is empirical evidence that MENA countries achieved strong gains in terms of human development during the last 4–5 decades under non-democratic regimes (World Bank, 2006). Impressive improvements in human development indicators took place in the MENA region between 1960 and 2000, surpassing the performance of countries in other regions with similar Purchasing Power Parity (PPP) income levels. For instance, average years of education in MENA increased by over 500 per cent and in the case of women by over 800 per cent during the 1960–2000 period. Child mortality decreased from an average of 262 deaths per 1,000 births to an

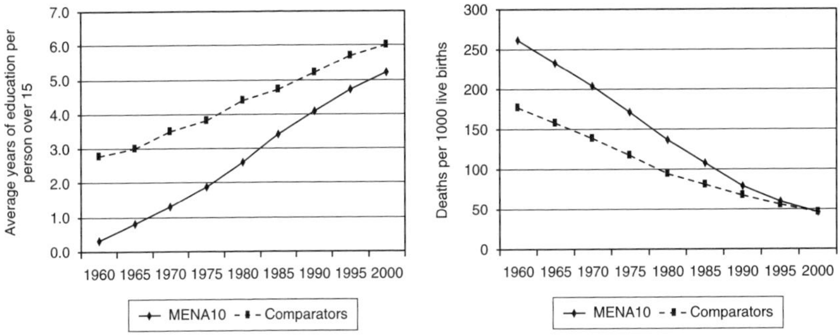

Figure 3.7 Human development indicators in MENA
Note: MENA10 refers to Algeria, Egypt, Iran, Jordan, Lebanon, Libya, Morocco, Syria, Tunisia and Yemen. Comparators include 32 countries with similar income levels of MENA countries in PPP terms in 1980.
Source: World Bank (2006).

average of 47 deaths per 1,000 births during the same period. Life expectancy at birth improved from 47 to 68 years, a 45 per cent increase.

Actually one could argue that regimes in MENA attempted to buy the loyalty of their citizens through strong redistributive programmes, such as free access to education and health, public sector jobs and subsidized prices for basic commodities. It is unlikely that increased investment in education would be important for increasing income growth in MENA countries over the coming period. On the other hand, there is a general recognition of the need for educational reform to improve the quality and adequacy of education to meet changing economic conditions, and governance mechanisms may turn out to be critical to the success of these reforms.

The previous analysis shows that there are some robust positive effects of democracy on growth through better commitments to policies with a more credible and predictable political process and through better intermediation of conflicts. Such effects are likely to be relevant in many MENA countries and situations. Another conclusion from this review is that for a number of other links from democracy to economic growth the effects are largely contingent on whether a move towards more democratic government would lead to better governance. In particular, there is uncertainty about the impact of democracy on capital accumulation and policy distortions. This uncertainty is probably related to the extent to which democracy leads to more or less respect for property rights, policies which favour broader or narrow interests, and adequate or under-provision public goods; which in turn depends on the strength of politicians' credibility and pervasiveness of clientelism.

The main general conclusion is that the net impact of democracy on growth depends on the severity of political market imperfections or, in other words, whether democracy produces good governance and thereby enhances physical capital accumulation. This conclusion is strengthened by two complementary findings from the literature on governance (without reference to democracy): First, direct strong positive links between good governance and economic growth; and second, between better governance and higher private investment. The latter linkage is particularly important for the MENA region.

Governance and growth

The work of Buchanan, Tollison and Tullock (1980), Evans (1989, 1995), North (1981, 1990), and de Soto (1989) systematically linked country characteristics, such as the security of property rights, directly to the wealth of nations, improving the understanding of the effects of the non-policy characteristics of government performance on economic development and growth. Research stemming from this strand of the literature highlighted the contribution of previously under-examined issues such as the security of property rights, the rule of law, expropriation, bureaucratic quality, red tape and the quality of regulation.

Both theory and empirical evidence support the influence of *individual* components of governance rather than *aggregated* concepts of governance on development and growth. Studies have found that some governance components have stronger links than others (Keefer 2004b). The security of property rights, the credibility of governments (see Knack and Keefer 1995; Acemoglu and Johnson 2005; Acemoglu, Johnson and Robinson 2001; Rodrik, Subramanian and Trebbi 2004; Hall and Jones 1999) and an honest and efficient bureaucracy emerge as the components with the best documented and strongest links to economic development and growth. On the other hand, causality problems cloud estimates of the influence of bureaucratic capacity and corruption on development. In addition, analyses of freedom of expression and accountability, while the subject of substantial attention among researchers, have suffered from a lack of theoretical and empirical precision that clouds interpretation.

The theoretical case for secure property rights is inimical and they fear confiscation of their assets by government. Still, there are objections to the theoretical case linking the security of property rights to growth.[9] One relates to the fact that often two important notions of property rights are confused, the *allocation* of property rights and the *security* of property rights. Democracy may render property rights less secure because the introduction of democracy creates opportunities for the poor to redistribute incomes away from the rich. However, it is not democracy, *per se*, that creates insecurity, but the transition to democracy. Once democracy is established, there is no reason to expect the distribution of property rights to change further. Some contributions to the governance literature refer not only to the security of property rights but also to the closely related but somewhat broader concept of 'government credibility'. This is the case with Knack and

Keefer (1995), for example. Only credible governments can assure investors that their assets are safe from expropriation.

In the context of MENA, some empirical evidence shows that better governance might have a significant positive effect on economic growth. Weaker governance in MENA costs 1.0 to 1.5 percentage points in forgone annual GDP growth (World Bank, 2003e). On average, improving the quality of institutions by one standard deviation – approximately equal to raising the average institutional quality in MENA to the average institutional quality of comparable East Asian countries (Indonesia, Malaysia, the Philippines, Singapore, Thailand, and Vietnam) – would have resulted in an increase of almost 1 percentage point in average annual GDP growth for the region as a whole. This figure would imply an income level that is 50 per cent higher in a period of 40 years due to compounding. The gain in growth rate from better governance will rise to a 1.5 percentage point difference for the group of MENA countries with substantial oil and gas revenues, implying an income level 81 per cent higher in the same comparable period. Similar results have been found by Elbadawi (2002).

Governance and private investment

The influence of the quality of governance on growth works primarily through its effect on private business and the capacity to invest. Numerous studies (see World Bank, 2003e) have documented the relationship between governance and private sector activity. Businesses react to the incentives, costs and constraints that control their business environment which, in turn, are influenced by the shaping and implementation of public policies. Improved governance produces a better business climate that fosters investment, productivity and growth. It reduces the scope for arbitrary government policy-making, providing mechanisms that help countries to minimize the persistence of policy distortions. By ensuring the public accountability of politicians and bureaucrats, better governance also contributes to the effective implementation of economic policies conducive to growth.

Better governance also improves bureaucratic performance and predictability, reducing uncertainty and the costs of doing business. This enhances the business environment. Better governance makes it easier to start new businesses and to run and expand existing ones. It lowers transaction costs at all levels (entry, operation, and exit), reduces information asymmetries between business and governments, and lowers uncertainties and unpredictability. It does so by protecting and enforcing property rights, curbing burdensome administrative and judicial rulings, reducing red tape, ensuring good regulatory quality, and improving access to affordable and reliable recourse to dispute resolution. By helping ensure more orderly public accountability processes, better governance also reduces political risk.

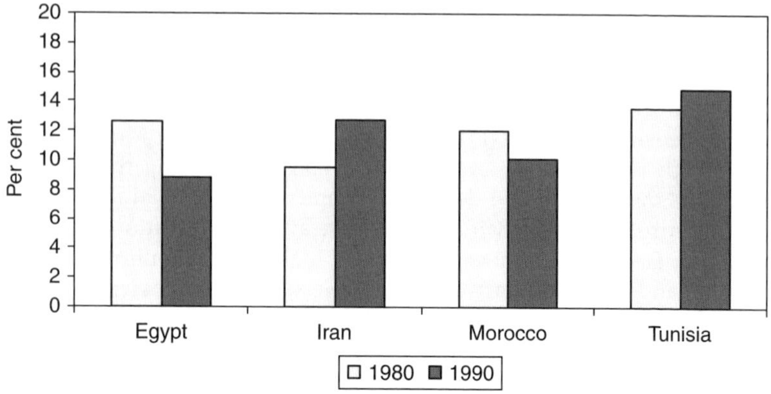

Figure 3.8 Private investment in the MENA region
Source: Aysan, Nabli and Véganzonès-Varoudakis (2006).

Better governance contributes to the effective delivery of the public goods necessary for productive business. Firms operate in a commercial environment that depends on many key public goods. And better governance helps to ensure that these goods are available in a timely, equitable, and cost-efficient manner. Public goods that are essential for a good business environment include appropriately regulated public utilities and natural monopolies, a stable and prudently regulated financial system, public safety and low crime, and good quality health and education. Effective delivery of these and other public goods boosts the productivity of private investment and leads to faster growth and development.

A recent empirical study by Aysan, Nabli and Véganzonès-Varoudakis (2007) quantified the possible impact of better governance on private investment for a few MENA countries (Egypt, Iran, Morocco, Tunisia). They used panel data and a simultaneous equation model for private investment and governance indicators to estimate this impact. They found that improved governance indicators, in terms of quality of public administration and public accountability, equivalent to one standard deviation of observed variability would yield about 3.5 percentage points on increase in private investment to GDP ratios. For MENA countries this would have increased the ratio of private investment to GDP on average from 12 per cent to 15.5 per cent which is a significant impact.

5 Better governance is critical but how?

Governance is among the more elastic concepts in the social science and development lexicons (Keefer, 2004a). Definitions tend to include the extent to which governments are responsive to citizens and provide them with certain core services, such as secure property rights and rule of law, and the extent to which public sector institutions and processes give government decision-makers an incentive to be responsive to citizens.

Good governance requires inclusiveness, transparency and accountability in the management of public affairs. The governance challenge in the MENA region is to strengthen these incentives, mechanisms, and the capacity for greater accountability and inclusive public institutions and to expand allegiance to equality and participation throughout society. Those good governance mechanisms which are the first steps towards better economic policies are themselves the instruments for improving economic growth.

The previous discussion makes a strong argument that democracy can have a positive impact on economic growth if it leads to better governance. But is democracy likely to generate good governance and are there alternatives to achieving good governance?

From democracy to better governance?

Researchers have developed various arguments that link democracy to the quality of governance. The introduction of democratic institutions in the form of more political and civil rights, and freedom of the press, among others, may or may not be associated with improved governance. On the one hand, democracies allow populations to peacefully and regularly oust inept, inefficient and corrupt public administrations and to keep more efficient, successful regimes, thus tending to make the quality of governance on average higher in the long run. On the other hand, a number of studies have noted that the proliferation of interest groups lobbying for power or for rents under democratic institutions may lead to policy gridlock, pervasiveness of clientelism and lack of accountability. This could hinder growth prospects.

The empirical literature appears to confirm that stronger democratic institutions are positively associated with a higher quality of governance, as well as with its positive impact on growth (Rivera-Batiz 2002; Keefer 2004a). Stronger democratic institutions influence governance by constraining the actions of corrupt and inept officials. They also facilitate the activities of the press, which can monitor corruption and disseminate information on government officials to the public so that they can be held accountable.

But research and experience have uncovered many situations where democracy is unlikely to produce better governance. For instance, it has been often observed that younger democracies are more corrupt, exhibit less rule of law, and lower levels of bureaucratic quality. These young democracies spend more on public investment and government workers. The politicians are less credible (Keefer, 2005), and the inability of political competitors to make credible promises to citizens leads them to under-provide public goods, over-provide transfers to narrow groups of voters, and engage in excessive rent-seeking. Young democracies seem to require time to mature to generate the desirable results.

Democracy may also fail to induce better governance and higher growth in MENA because of social cleavage and fragmentation, as discussed above in the context of the importance of political market imperfections. The literature on these issues has shown that getting democracy right is also affected by the extent of social cleavage. Elbadawi (2004) tests for the impact of social cleavage on growth. In his model, social cleavage is measured by indexes of (ethnic, cultural or religious) fractionalization and polarization. He finds that several MENA countries have highly ethnically and/or religiously fractionalized societies; including Djibouti, Jordan, Lebanon, Iraq, and Syria. Like other authors (Alesina *et al.* 2003; Easterly and Levines 1997, and Rodrik, 1998), Elbadawi finds that the conflict variable that measures the social cleavages in his model has a negative effect on growth. The conflict variable was highly significant in the case of ethnic fractionalization and moderately significant for language, religious and dominant polarizations. In all cases, it was negatively associated with long-term stability of growth. The results are much less robust for the case of the polarization-based conflict. However, ethnic and, especially, language polarization were negatively and significantly associated with long-term growth stability.

This analysis indicates that relatively socially homogenous societies in MENA (Egypt and Tunisia) may be better suited to achieve good governance through democracy while less homogenous societies in MENA (Iraq, Lebanon, Syria) may find it more difficult to achieve the needed socio-political consensus for good governance and good economic policy.

Should the goal be just 'better governance'?

If there are risks that democracy does not lead to better governance, that is, more transparency, greater freedom of expression and accountability, more secure property rights, less corruption, a more efficient civil service and more effective public service delivery, what are the implications for the MENA region?

One possible implication may be that MENA countries should strive to achieve 'better governance' and not bother with seeking democracy. Countries should try to develop features of good governance such as secure property rights, rule of law, efficient and less corrupt government and public administration, predictable rules and laws and so on. The economic success of authoritarian regimes particularly in Asia, such as China, Taiwan, Singapore and South Korea, and even in some MENA countries such as Tunisia and Egypt who achieved relatively high rates of growth over the long run suggests that this is possible, and that an adequate quality of governance can be secured under such regimes. One might question whether the very authoritarian discretion of such regimes actually helped growth by enabling the leading parties to push through economic reforms which in a democratic setting might have been either slow or impossible to achieve because of the need for consensus. This argument would be even more compelling in situations where there is a high likelihood that democracy would not generate better governance because of significant social cleavages.

Many argue that this is not the case and that democracy need not be sacrificed on the altar of development. While East Asian countries prospered under authoritarianism, many more countries have seen their economies deteriorate due to the lack of democracy and accountability – for example, Zaire, Uganda, or Haiti. Such cases abound in MENA with the examples of Iraq, Libya or Syria. In addition, some of the most successful economic reforms of the 1980s and early 1990s were implemented under newly-elected democratic governments in many regions – for instance Latin America Countries (LAC) (Bolivia, Argentina, and Brazil) and Europe and Central Asia (ECA) [transition economies like Hungary, the Czech Republic, Poland, Slovenia and Slovakia among others].

The critical question is whether 'better governance' is more likely to emerge under democratic or non-democratic regimes. Some of the previous discussion indicates that democracy leads to better governance, despite the risks faced by developing young democracies and countries with significant social cleavages. How about non-democratic regimes? Are they able to produce governance systems which can enhance the quality of the business environment, leading to higher investment and sustained economic growth? Rodrik (1999) and Rodrik and Wacziarg (2005) have even argued that the performance record for democracies is even better than usually acknowledged. Claims that democratization leads to disappointing economic results are often used to justify calls to delay political reforms in poor, ethnically divided countries until they become 'mature enough' for democracy. However, the hypothesis that democratization is followed by bad economic performance, particularly in poor, fractionalized countries, is not supported by their analysis. In any event, the cases of 'enlightened dictatorship' appear to be the exception rather than the rule in the recent past. Authoritarian regimes may only randomly provide high-quality governance and for each case of a non-democratic regime which seems to produce better governance and growth outcomes one can find many more cases of bad governance and dismal economic outcomes. Democracies appear to be more likely to generate better governance than non-democratic regimes.

The case of oil-producing countries

Oil rents have shielded many MENA countries from economic crises, but they also seem to have helped to reduce the likelihood of the region becoming more democratic (Ross, 2001). At the same time, the economic record of mineral-exporting countries over the past few decades, especially oil exporters, has been disappointing. Studies such as Eifert, Gelb and Tallroth (2003) argue that this performance may be the result of poor public sector governance leading to poor oil-revenue management. This phenomenon has sometimes been described as 'political Dutch disease' and was noted by political scientists in the context of the MENA region. Several authors (Wantchekon 2002; Ross 2001; and Lam and Wantchekon 2002) identified a positive correlation between resource dependence and authoritarian governments controlling for characteristics such as GDP, human capital, income inequality and other possible determinants.

But can such regimes generate better governance in the absence of democracy? In fact, a recent study by Collier and Hoeffler (2005) founds major differences in the economic performance of autocracies and democracies when controlling for natural resource endowments. Richly endowed countries, such as oil-producing countries, seem to perform better economically if they are not restrained by democratic institutions. The underperformance of oil-rich democracies is explained by economic policy choice, namely the size and quality of investment. In view of the finding by Tavares and Wacziarg (2001) that democracies in general tend to under-invest in physical capital as they focus more on policies related to human capital development and a more equitable society, Collier and Hoeffler conclude that oil-rich democracies not only underinvest but invest badly since they face fewer financial, and consequently, political restraints. Resource-rich countries do not need to tax so much which results in less scrutiny on their delivery of public services by their citizens. Therefore, the key argument is that resource-rich democracies need a distinctively different design which places more importance on checks and balances, that is, on instruments which rebalance how power is used rather than on mechanisms that determine how power is achieved.

However, the empirical evidence demonstrates that major oil-producing countries tend to have lower governance indicators. While they may need to have more checks and balances, oil-reliant countries have the worst index of public accountability scores. Having the substantial oil and gas revenues accrue directly to government budgets means that governments can maintain a deficient governance environment as long as they do some redistribution and provide public goods to the population. In a situation of 'no taxation, no representation' governments face little pressure to improve governance so as to increase economic development. The substantial revenue from natural resources relieves a government from the need to tax, thus reducing its obligation to be accountable. In addition, they are able to redistribute a significant share of oil revenue through public employment and broad access to cheap public services. These two factors – no taxation and some redistribution – mute demands for accountability (World Bank, 2003e). While the presence of mineral wealth in a country may not be the cause for a governance deficit, it could make it more difficult for good governance institutions to emerge.

Eifert, Gelb and Tallroth (2003) reinforce this conclusion and the importance of democracy for these countries. They analyse oil-rich regimes in the world according to their characteristics, and divide political systems into

(i) mature democracies; (ii) fractional democracies; (iii) paternalistic autocracies; (iv) reformist autocracies; and (v) predatory autocracies. The study concludes that mature democracies have clear advantages in managing oil revenues for the long term because of their ability to reach consensus, their educated and informed electorates, and the level of transparency that facilitates clear decisions on how to use the oil revenues over a long-term horizon. Reformist and paternalistic autocracies lack transparency and face the risk of oil-led spending being the legitimizing force behind the state, which tends to foster corruption as well as creating problems with political transitions. These countries tend to be locked in high-spending patterns that are unsustainable in the very long term. Fractional democracies lack an effective political system to create consensus among competing interests. Finally, predatory autocracies have short-term horizons and the characteristics of kleptocratic regimes that syphon money from state coffers, eventually drying up the oil wealth.

6 The 'binding constraint' to growth approach

The previous review of the links between democracy and economic growth has relied mostly on work which tries to find systematic relationships from cross-country comparisons. While such research finds complex relationships and sometimes uncertain results it tends to show the existence of a strong positive relationship between democracy and growth, especially if democratic institutions are designed in such a way as to lead to better governance and minimize the possible negative impact of political market failures and avoid the risks from social cleavages.

But even with this analytical framework to try to find systematic relationships between democracy and growth Barro and Sala-i-Martin (2003) demonstrate that a non-linear relationship may exist. Democratization appears to enhance growth for countries that are not very democratic, but to retard growth for countries that have already achieved a high degree of democracy. This finding applied to MENA countries would mean that democracy is important for growth given their present low scores in terms of democratic development.

A completely different approach for looking at the relationship between democracy and growth is to recognize that expectations of an overall systematic relationship between democracy and growth are ill-placed. The impact of democratization on growth should be country- and time-specific and the static search for a stable relationship may be counter-productive. Such an alternative way to link democracy and economic growth is to use the recently-developed approach of 'binding constraint' by Hausmann, Rodrik and Velasco (forthcoming). This approach holds that constraints to growth are time- and country-specific. It rejects cross-country findings and 'one-size-fits-all' solutions as useless tools for studying relationships between reforms and economic growth. In that framework, the question is whether at a given time and in a given country the 'democracy deficit' as compared to other factors may be the binding constraint on growth. For MENA countries this could imply that democracy did not matter in the past but that it may be critical now. It may also imply that there is no general answer to this question for the 'region' as a whole, but that one has to be country specific.

The argument for the binding-constraint approach for most countries in the region is as follows: low economic growth in the MENA countries is due to low private investment, which is itself due to a weak investment climate and poor public-sector governance. Major and credible reforms are needed, especially in terms of public sector governance and investment climate, in almost all countries of the region in order to unlock the growth potential (see World Bank 2003a).[10] On the other hand, experience shows that after 20 years of attempts at reform the depth and scope of such reforms, while they vary from country to country, remain limited. Political economy analysis suggests that existing political regimes have been unable to generate the required reforms (Nabli, 2005). The existing political economy equilibrium favours the *status quo* of low public accountability and the maintenance of prevailing economic policies and networks of privilege. In such a situation democratic reform may be able to unlock this state of affairs and generate a great political and economic transformation which could produce both greater democracy and economic growth in the region.

7 Conclusion: striving for democracy in the MENA region?

Democratization yields benefits in terms of individual freedom and empowerment that are valued independently of their consequences for growth and material wealth. But democratization is also beneficial because democracies can: (a) yield long-run growth rates that are more predictable; (b) produce greater short-term stability; (c) handle adverse shocks better; and (d) deliver better distributional outcomes.

Our review of the literature about the links between democracy and economic growth and its application to the conditions of the MENA region leads to the conclusion that MENA countries should strive for democratic regimes which are sustainable in the sense of having characteristics which make them more likely to produce good governance. This means that democratic development requires going beyond an electoral process which guarantees free, open and competitive elections. These formal democratic processes have to be complemented with a number of reforms aimed at:

(i) minimizing imperfections in the political market, with more freedom of information and a free press, adequate mechanisms to contain clientelism and increased credibility of political promises;
(ii) introducing safeguards and effective checks and balances; and

(iii) increasing the legitimacy of the democratic transformation.

In cases where there is significant ethnic and or religious fragmentation it is vital that the democratic institutions be designed so as to minimize the risks of conflict and the emergence of unaccountable government. These reforms should ensure or maximize the likelihood that democracy leads to better governance and therefore higher economic growth. In such a situation one would not have to face short-term trade-offs between democracy and economic growth.

This conclusion is reinforced by the 'binding constraint to growth' approach. Democracy may not be a 'binding constraint' to growth in the strict sense that if it were achieved today it would result in higher economic growth in MENA countries. However, one can argue that progress in democracy is probably critical at this stage of the MENA world's history for achieving the required transformation which would ensure better governance, more accountability, a better investment climate and credible policies for increased private sector investment, employment and growth.

Finally, one might argue that while democracy can lead to better governance and, therefore, better economic policies and credible reforms, the design of such economic reforms may in itself enhance democratic development. This should produce a virtuous circle where democratic development enhances governance, and economic growth will itself support the consolidation of democratic development. For instance, following Acemoglu and Robinson (2006), increased economic transparency which improves the relative incomes of the owners of human and physical capital and greater economic equality would enhance the development of democracy.

Notes

1. The MENA region in the World Bank definition includes all Arab countries except Sudan, Somalia, Mauritania and Comoros, plus Iran.
2. A recent paper by Gause (2005) reviews the question and challenges the view that promotion of democracy in the Middle East would stop generating anti-American terrorism.
3. The political regime universe has on one side democracy and on the opposite side dictatorship (or authoritarian regimes). Dictatorships are defined here as regimes in which political rulers accede to power and maintain themselves in power by force. They use force to prevent societies from expressing their opposition to rulers' decisions. Because they rule by force, they are vulnerable to visible signs of dissent. These opposing political regimes represent different ways of selecting rulers, processing and resolving conflicts, and making and implementing public policy. In a sense, they are different ways of organizing political lives. As such, they are likely to impact people's lives and welfare in different ways.
4. The Polity IV index is produced by the Integrated Network for Societal Conflict Research Program of the University of Maryland's Center for International Development and Conflict Management (CIDCM)). Polity IV contains coded annual

information on regime and authority characteristics for all independent states (with greater than 500,000 total population) in the global state system and covers the years 1800–2003.

5. We thank Daron Acemoglu for providing the transformed Freedom House data.
6. Friedman (2005) provides a useful review and summary of the findings on this issue (Chapter 13).
7. Friedrich Hayek (1960) summarized this point by stating that '...it is in its dynamic, rather than in its static, aspects that the value of democracy proves itself. As is true of liberty, the benefits of democracy will show themselves only in the long run, while its more immediate achievements may well be inferior to those of other forms of government.'
8. See Acemoglu et al. (2005).
9. In a recent study by Harber, Razo and Mauer (2003) on the politics of property rights the authors challenge the idea that political stability and broader property rights are necessary for economic growth, based on Mexican historical evidence. They claim that economic growth does not always requires a government that is constrained from preying upon property rights, it only needs a government that make selective credible commitments to a subset of asset holders.
10. The Middle East and North Africa Region of the World Bank produced four major regional reports on the occasion of the World Bank–International Monetary Fund Annual Meetings in Dubai in September 2003. These reports – on trade and investment, governance, gender, and employment–are intended to enrich the debate on the major development challenges of the region at the beginning of the twenty-first century.

References

Aysan, A. F., Nabli, M. K. and Véganzonès-Varoudakis M.-A. (2007) 'Governance, Institutions and Private Investments. An Application to the Middle East and North Africa', *The Developing Economics*, vol. 45, no. 3.

Acemoglu, D. and Johnson, S. (2005) 'Unbundling Institutions', *Journal of Political Economy*, vol. 113, no. 5, pp. 949–95.

Acemoglu, D. and Robinson, J. (2006) *Economic Origins of Dictatorship and Democracy* (Cambridge: Cambridge University Press).

Acemoglu, D., Johnson, S. and Robinson, J. (2001) 'The Colonial Origins of Comparative Development: An Empirical Investigation', *American Economic Review,* vol. 91, pp. 1369–401.

Acemoglu, D., Johnson S. and Robinson, J. (2005) 'Institutions as the Fundamental Cause of Long-Run Growth?' In P. Aghion and S. Durlauf (eds), *Handbook of Economic Growth* (Amsterdam: Elsevier), pp. 386–472.

Acemoglu, D., Johnson, S., Robinson, J. and Yared, P. (forthcoming) 'Income and Democracy', *American Economic Review*.

Alesina, A., Devleeschauwer, A., Kurlat, S., Wucziarg, R. and Easterly, W. (2003) 'Fractionalization', *Journal of Economic Growth*, vol. 8, pp. 155–94.

Barro, R. J. (1994) 'Democracy and Growth', working paper no. 4909, National Bureau of Economic Research.

Barro, R. J. (1999) 'The Determinants of Democracy', *Journal of Political Economy,* vol. 107, pp. S158–S183.

Barro, R. J. and Sala-i-Martin, X. (2003) *Economic Growth* (Cambridge, Massachusetts: MIT Press, 2nd edition).

Bollen, K. A. (1990) 'Political Democracy: Conceptual and Measurement Traps', *Studies in Comparative International Development*, vol. 25, pp. 7–24.

Bollen, K. A. (2001) 'Cross-National Indicators of Liberal Democracy, 1950–1990' [Computer file]. 2nd ICPSR version (Chapel Hill, NC: University of North Carolina [producer], 1998) Distributed by the Inter-university Consortium for Political and Social Research.

Borner, S., Brunetti, A. and Weder, B. (1995) *Political Credibility and Economic Development* (London: Palgrave Macmillian).

Bourguignon, F. and Verdier, T. (2000) 'Oligarchy, Democracy, Inequality and Growth', *Journal of Development Economics*, August. vol. 62, no 2, pp. 285–313.

Buchanan, J. M., Tollison R. D., and Tullock, G., (eds). (1980) *Toward a Theory of the Rent-Seeking Society* (College Station Texas: A & M University Press).

Collier, P. and Hoeffler, A. (2005) 'Oil Democracies', University of Oxford, Department of Economics (mimeo).

de Mesquita, Bueno B. and Downs G. W. (2005) 'Democracy and Development', *Foreign Affairs*, September/October, vol. 84, no. 5.

de Soto, H. (1989) *The Other Path* (New York: Harper and Row).

Easterly, W. and Levine, R. (1997) 'Africa's Growth Tragedy: Policies and Ethnic Divisions,' *Quarterly Journal of Economics,* vol. 111, no.4, pp. 1203–50

Eifert, B., Gelb, A. and Tallroth, N. B. (2003) 'Managing Oil Wealth' *Finance and Development'*, vol. 40, no.1, Washington DC.

Elbadawi, I. A. (2002) 'Reviving Growth in the Arab World', Working Paper Series no. 0206, Arab Planning Institute. Safat, Kuwait.

Elbadawi, I. A. (2004) 'The Politics of Sustaining Growth in the Arab World: Getting Democracy Right', Lecture and Working Paper Series, no. 2, American University of Beirut, Faculty of Financial Economics.

Elbadawi, I. A. and Makdisi, S. (2007) 'Explaining the Democracy Deficit in the Arab World', *The Quarterly Review of Economics and Finance*, vol. 46, no. 5, pp. 813–31.

Evans, P. (1989) 'Predatory, Developmental, and Other Apparatuses: A Comparative Political Economy Perspective', *Sociological Forum,* vol. 4, no 4, pp. 561–87.

Evans, P. (1995) *Embedded Autonomy: States and Industrial Transformation* (Princeton: Princeton University Press).

Feng, Y. (2003) *Democracy, Governance and Economic Performance: Theory and Evidence* (London: MIT Press).

Friedman, B. M. (2005) *The Moral Consequences of Economic Growth* (New York: Knopf).

Gause, F. G. III (2005) 'Can Democracy Stop Terrorism?', *Foreign Affairs*, September/ October, vol. 84, no. 5.

Giavazzi, F. and Tabellini, G. (2004) 'Economic and Political Liberalizations'. *National Bureau of Economic Research* (Cambridge, MA), Working Paper, no. 10657

Haber, S., Razo, A. and Mauer, N. (2003) *The Politics of Property Rights: Political Instability, Credible Commitments, and Economic Growth in Mexico, 1876–1929* (Cambridge: Cambridge University Press).

Hall, R. E. and Jones, C. I. (1999) 'Why Do Some Countries Produce So Much More Output per Worker than Others?' *Quarterly Journal of Economics,* vol. 114, no 1, pp. 83–116.

Hausmann, R., Rodrik, D. and Velasco, A. (forthcoming) 'Growth Diagnostics', in J. Stiglitz and N. Serra (eds), *The Washington Consensus Reconsidered: Towards a New Global Governance* (Oxford: Oxford University Press).

Hayek, F. A. (1960) *The Constitution of Liberty* (Chicago: The University of Chicago Press).

Keefer, P. (2004a) 'Does Democracy Help?' The World Bank, Development Research Group (mimeo).
Keefer, P. (2004b) 'A Review of the Political Economy of Governance: From Property Rights to Voice' The World Bank, Development Research Group (mimeo).
Keefer, P. (2005) 'Democratization and Clientelism: Why are Young Democracies Badly Governed?' The World Bank, Development Research Group (mimeo).
Keefer, P. and Khemani, S. (2005) 'Democracy, Public Expenditures, and the Poor: Understanding Political Incentives for Providing Public Services', *The World Bank Research Observer*. vol. 20, no. 1
Knack, S. and Keefer, P. (1995) 'Institutions and Economic Performance: Cross-Country Tests Using Alternative Institutional Measures', *Economics and Politics,* vol. 7, no. 3, pp. 207–28
Lam, R. and Wantchekon, L. (2002) 'Political Dutch Disease' (mimeo).
Lipset, S. M. (1959) 'Some Social Requisites of Democracy: Economic Development and Political Legitimacy', *American Political Science Review,* vol. 53, pp. 69–105
Madison, J., Hamilton, A., A., and Jay, J. (1987) *The Federalist Papers* (London: Penguin Classics).
Nabli, M. K. (2005) 'Restarting the Arab Economic Reform Agenda', *The Arab World Competitiveness Report 2005*, World Economic Forum (Basingstoke: Palgrave Macmillan).
North, D. (1981) *Structure and Change in Economic History* (New York: W.W. Norton).
North, D. (1990) *Institutions, Institutional Change and Economic Performance* (Cambridge: Cambridge University Press).
Papaioannou, E. and Siourounis, G. (2004) 'Democratization and Growth', *London Business School Economics Working Paper.*
Persson, T. (2004) 'Forms of Democracy, Policy and Economic Development', *Institute of International Economics* (Stockholm, Sweden), working paper.
Przeworski, A., Alvarez, M. E., Cheibub, J. A., and Limongi, F. (2000) *Democracy and Development: Political Institutions and Well-Being in the World, 1950–1990* (Cambridge: Cambridge University Press).
Rivera-Batiz, F. L. (2002) 'Democracy, Governance, and Economic Growth: Theory and Evidence', *Review of Development Economics*, vol. 6, no. 2, pp. 225–47.
Rodrik, D. (1997) 'Democracy and Economic Performance', Harvard University, John F. Kennedy School of Government (mimeo).
Rodrik, D. (1999) 'Where Did All the Growth Go? External Shocks, Social Conflict, and Growth Collapses', *Journal of Economic Growth* December.
Rodrik, D. (2000) 'Institutions for High-Quality Growth: What They Are and How to Acquire Them', *Studies in Comparative International Development*, vol. 35, no. 3.
Rodrik, D. (2005) 'Growth Strategies', in P. Aghion and S. Durlauf (eds), *Handbook of Economic Growth* (Amsterdam: North-Holland).
Harvard University, John F. Kennedy School of Government, forthcoming
Rodrik, D., Subramanian, A., and Trebbi, F. (2004) 'Institutions Rule: The Primacy of Institutions over Geography and Integration in Economic Development', *Journal of Economic Growth*, vol. 9, no. 2.
Rodrik, D. and Wacziarg, R. (2005) 'Do Democratic Transitions Produce Bad Economic Outcomes?', *American Economic Review, Papers and Proceedings*, vol. 95, no. 2, pp. 50–5.
Ross, M. (2001) 'Does Oil Hinder Democracy?', *World Politics,* vol. 53, pp. 325–61.
Sen, A. (1999) *Development as Freedom* (New York: Alfred Knopf).

Schumpeter, J. A. (1942) *Capitalism, Socialism and Democracy* (New York: Harper and Brothers).

Tavares, J. and Wacziarg, R. (2001) 'How Democracy Affects Growth', *European Economic Review,* vol. 45, pp. 1341–78

Wantchekon, L. (2002) 'Why Do Resource Abundant Countries Have Authoritarian Governments?', *Journal of African Finance and Economic Development,* vol. 5, no. 2, pp. 57–77.

World Bank (2003a) *Jobs, Growth, and Governance in the Middle East and North Africa: Unlocking the Potential for Prosperity* (Washington, DC: The World Bank).

World Bank (2003b) *Trade, Investment, and Development in the Middle East and North Africa: Engaging the World* (Washington, DC: The World Bank).

World Bank (2003c) *Unlocking the Employment Potential in the Middle East and North Africa: Toward a New Social Contract* (Washington, DC: The World Bank).

World Bank (2003d) *Gender and Development in the Middle East and North Africa: Women in the Public Sphere* (Washington, DC: The World Bank).

World Bank (2003e) *Better Governance for Development in the Middle East and North Africa: Enhancing Inclusiveness and Accountability* (Washington, DC: The World Bank).

World Bank (2005a) *Economic Growth in the 1990s: Learning from a Decade of Reform* (Washington, DC: The World Bank).

World Bank (2005b) *Middle East and North Africa: Economic Development and Prospects. Oil Booms and Revenue Management* (Washington, DC: The World Bank).

World Bank (2006) *Sustaining Gains in Poverty Reduction and Human Development in the Middle East and North Africa: Orientations in Development* (Washington, DC: The World Bank).

Part 2
Supply of Productive Factors

4

Distance to the Efficiency Frontier and Foreign Direct Investment and Spillovers*

Klara Sabirianova Peter, Jan Svejnar and Katherine Terrell

1 Introduction

Are firms in the former communist economies converging to the world standard? This is the key question in the most challenging economic transformation at the start of this century. While expert opinions differ on what constitutes a successful and complete transition, it is generally acknowledged that transition economies need to raise their productivity substantially in order to catch up with the advanced countries.[1] In this chapter, we show how much progress has been made in reducing the distance between the efficiency of domestic firms and the world technology frontier in two transition economies – the Czech Republic and Russia – and we assess whether the presence of foreign firms in these countries contributes to the reduction of the productivity gap (either through knowledge spillovers or competition).

Russia and the Czech Republic are desirable model economies because they share useful similarities in their initial conditions, yet they represent polar cases of the strategy and implementation of the transition. Unlike, for instance, Hungary and Poland, Russia and the Czech Republic maintained a relatively unreformed centrally planned system until the very end of the communist period, thus providing us with 'authentic' initial conditions. During the transition, both countries privatized most of the state assets in a way that was both rapid and controversial. Otherwise these economies pursued different paths, becoming prototypes of two distinct patterns of the transition process. The Czech Republic exemplifies the Central European model. It opened up to trade and capital flows, developed a relatively functioning market economy and gradually established institutions, rules and regulations

* The authors would like to thank Barry Ickes, Josef Brada, Chris Woodruff and participants at the 2004 EEA meeting in Madrid; the 2004 WDI/CEPR conference in Hanoi; the 2004 and 2004 AEA meetings in Atlanta and San Diego for their useful comments. We are grateful to Yuriy Gorodnichenko for his stellar research assistance and to the NSF (Research Grant SES 0111783) for its generous support.

that made it eligible, together with other Central European countries, for accession to the European Union. Like the other Commonwealth of Independent State (CIS) countries, Russia has remained more closed to the world. It has changed its laws, regulations and institutions more slowly and without attempting to harmonize them with those of the European Union. Hence, to the extent that private corporate governance and competition are effective in strengthening performance, we should expect firms in the Czech Republic to be closing the productivity gap and converging to the frontier more rapidly than firms in Russia.

2 Evolution of the productivity gap and distance to the frontier

We start by estimating and comparing changes in the levels of productive efficiency of domestic and foreign-owned firms in each of these two countries over the 1992–2000 period.[2] Specifically, we estimate the following augmented translog production function with panel data on medium-sized and large firms in the industrial sector (manufacturing, mining, and utilities) in the Czech Republic and in Russia for three consecutive periods: 1992–4 (early transition), 1995–7 (middle transition) and 1998–2000 (mature transition):[3]

$$\ln y_{it} = X_{it}\beta + Z_{it}\rho + v_i + \varepsilon_{it} \tag{4.1}$$

where y_{it} represents the output (revenue) of firm i in year t, X_{it} is a vector of inputs (in translog specification) and dummy variables for (two-digit level ISIC) industries and years, Z_{it} is a dummy for domestic ownership (with foreign ownership serving as the base), v_i are unobserved time-invariant firm-specific effects, and ε_{it} is an independently distributed error term, with $\mathrm{E}(v_i) = \mathrm{E}(\varepsilon_{it}) = \mathrm{E}(v_i\varepsilon_{it}) = \mathrm{E}(\varepsilon_{it}\varepsilon_{is}) = 0$ for $\forall t > s$. We treat domestic firms with private, mixed and state ownership as one category since we find in a companion paper that their efficiency is similar (Sabirianova, Svejnar and Terrell, 2004, henceforth SST, 2004).

Next, for each firm i we calculate firm-specific productive efficiency in log points as $\varphi_i = \rho + v_i$, with $\mathrm{E}(\varphi_i) = \rho$ and $\mathrm{E}(v_i) = 0$, and we measure how far the productive efficiency of domestic firms is from that of the frontier firms.[4] An important methodological question is how to define the world technology frontier. Since in SST (2004) we find that the efficiency of foreign firms is above the efficiency of domestic firms at all respective points of the two efficiency distributions, in this chapter we use the average level of the estimated efficiency of the top third of foreign firms in a given two-digit industry as the benchmark for the frontier.[5] We believe this is superior to the alternative of using firms operating in advanced market economies as the benchmark since the latter approach is plagued by comparison problems associated with wide exchange-rate fluctuations and different shocks and institutions across countries.

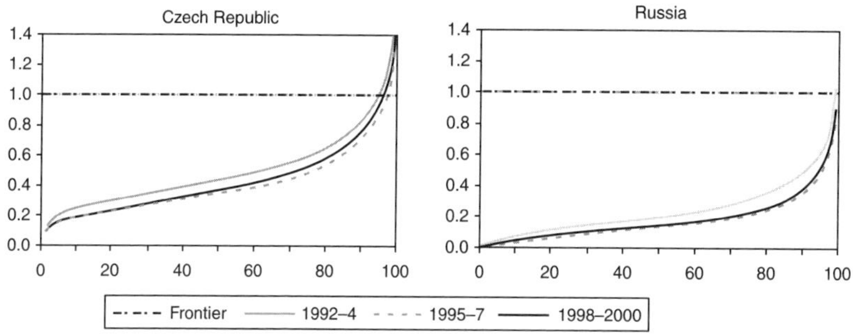

Figure 4.1 Distance of domestic firms to the frontier by period

Notes: The frontier is defined as the mean productive efficiency of the top third of foreign owned firms in a 2-digit ISIC industry. The efficiency estimates are obtained from the translog production function (specified in equation 1) estimated with a random effect estimator for each period separately. The (inverse) measure of the firm's distance to the frontier is calculated as the ratio of the firm's efficiency to the frontier in its industry. Percentiles are constructed from the distribution of the firm-specific distance to the frontier for each ownership type.

We therefore estimate the (inverse) distance from the frontier as the ratio of each firm's efficiency to the mean productive efficiency of the frontier foreign firms within a two-digit industry in each period. The ratio indicates how far a firm is from the efficiency frontier. When the ratio is large (closer to 1), the firm is approaching the frontier. Since our measure of productive efficiency is in log form, we apply the following exponential transformation:

$$\alpha_i = \exp(\varphi_i - \overline{\varphi}_{k,FOR}|_{\theta>.66}) \tag{4.2}$$

where α_i is the firm-specific (inverse) measure of the distance to the frontier and $\overline{\varphi}_{k,FOR}|_{\theta>.66}$ is the mean productive efficiency of the top third of foreign firms (above the 66th percentile in θ) in industry k. We use random effect (RE) estimates to obtain our measure of productive efficiency.[6]

In Figure 4.1 and Table 4.1 we show for each time period the distribution of the domestic firms' distance to the frontier (α_i). Two important findings emerge: (a) in every period domestic firms in Russia are further away from the frontier than domestic firms in the Czech Republic; (b) the distance from the frontier has grown from 1992–4 to 1995–7 and it did not change much from 1995–7 to 1998–2000. During the period 1998–2000 the efficiency of the median domestic firm in the Czech Republic was 37.4 per cent of the frontier, whereas it was only 14.6 per cent in Russia. While the top 5 per cent of the Czech domestic firms operated at the level of the frontier, the best Russian firms were not even close to this level. Even more dramatic is the fact that the Russian firm at the 90th percentile was the same distance from the frontier as the median Czech firm.

In Table 4.1 we also show the distribution of the distance of foreign-owned firms from the frontier. In both countries, the distribution of foreign firms lies

Table 4.1 Distance to the frontier by ownership and period

Czech Republic						
	Foreign			*Domestic*		
Percentile	*1992–4*	*1995–7*	*1998–2000*	*1992–4*	*1995–7*	*1998–2000*
10	0.286	0.218	0.205	0.250	0.186	0.189
25	0.414	0.350	0.346	0.329	0.249	0.263
50	0.612	0.574	0.556	0.445	0.345	0.374
75	0.912	0.856	0.835	0.609	0.493	0.531
90	1.125	1.118	1.109	0.829	0.732	0.766
Russia						
	Foreign			*Domestic*		
Percentile	*1992–4*	*1995–7*	*1998–2000*	*1992–4*	*1995–7*	*1998–2000*
10	0.079	0.077	0.092	0.072	0.048	0.043
25	0.158	0.156	0.167	0.122	0.085	0.083
50	0.278	0.322	0.338	0.195	0.144	0.146
75	0.717	0.673	0.699	0.317	0.230	0.240
90	1.349	1.350	1.324	0.482	0.353	0.371

Note: See notes in Figure 4.1 for definitions.

closer to the frontier than the distribution of the domestic firms. Moreover, the distribution of the distance of foreign firms is fairly constant over the three periods, although in the Czech Republic there is a slight increase in the distance from the first to the second period. However, this increase is not as great as that of the domestic firms.

Overall, in both countries domestic firms diverged from the frontier set by foreign firms during the first half of the transition and they stabilized this enlarged gap but did not succeed in diminishing it during the second half.

3 Effect of foreign presence on the productivity gap

If domestic firms are not catching up to the world efficiency standard in general, is it the case that they are converging to this standard in industries with a greater foreign presence and falling behind in industries with a smaller foreign presence, or vice versa? In this section we explore these propositions. Moreover, since foreign-owned firms are more technologically advanced and globally accustomed to absorbing knowledge, we test if greater foreign presence has a positive effect on these firms and a less positive or negative effect on the domestic firms.

Part of the FDI literature argues that foreign firms have beneficial 'spillover' effects on the productivity of domestic firms by allowing the latter to observe and learn from the introduction of new products and processes to the domestic market (horizontal spillovers).[7] Foreign firms may also act as a new and large source of demand for inputs, thus stimulating new production in upstream activities (vertical spillovers). On the other hand, foreign firms can have a negative effect on domestic firms' output and productivity, especially in the short run, if they compete with domestic firms and 'steal their market'. This may force domestic firms to cut back production and experience a higher average cost as fixed costs are spread over a smaller scale of production (Aitken and Harrison, 1999). The question is which effects dominate.

Studies of the effect of foreign presence on the productivity of domestic firms use data on domestic firms and include as an explanatory variable some measure of foreign presence, usually the share of foreign firms in a given industry's output or employment. The evidence from this research is mixed. Studies of the same industry (horizontal spillovers) suggest that the effect is negative in developing countries such as Morocco (Haddad and Harrison, 1993) and Venezuela (Aitken and Harrison, 1999) as well as in transition economies such as Bulgaria and Romania (Konings, 2000), the Czech Republic (Djankov and Hoekman, 1998; Kosova, 2004) and Russia (Yudaeva *et al.*, 2003). However, Damijan *et al.* (2003) detect positive horizontal spillovers in five of the ten transition countries they examine. The negative effect is usually attributed to a low 'absorptive capacity' of domestic firms in the less developed countries. It is argued that the larger the technology gap between the domestic and foreign firms, the less likely the domestic firms will be able to gain from foreign firms; by implication positive spillovers should be found in more technologically advanced sectors or in the more industrialized countries.[8] This latter hypothesis receives some support as Kinoshita (2000) finds positive horizontal spillovers in the R&D sector in the Czech Republic, while Haskel, Pereira and Slaughter (2007) find evidence of positive spillovers on the productivity of domestic plants in the UK.

Unlike the existing studies in this area, we combine data on domestic and foreign-owned firms and test whether foreign presence in a given industry affects productive efficiency of domestic and foreign firms differently. In particular, we hypothesize that foreign presence in emerging market economies affects positively the efficiency of foreign firms, which are more advanced and have a globally developed absorptive (learning) capacity, while having a smaller positive or a negative effect on the efficiency of domestic firms, which are less efficient and may not yet have developed their absorptive capacity. In order to implement this test, we augment the production function specified in equation (4.1) by including as explanatory variables the interaction of foreign presence with the dummy variables for domestic ownership and foreign ownership. We measure foreign presence as the lagged share of foreign firms in total output in a given two-digit ISIC industry ($FS_{(-i)t-1}$).[9] This measure is

Table 4.2 Descriptive statistics of foreign presence for selected years

	Czech Republic			*Russia*		
Foreign Firms' Average	*1992*	*1996*	*2000*	*1992*	*1996*	*2000*
Share of industrial firms	0.035	0.126	0.307	0.001	0.034	0.056
	(0.184)	(0.332)	(0.461)	(0.026)	(0.182)	(0.229)
Share of total output	0.077	0.214	0.511	0.001	0.030	0.196
	(0.266)	(0.410)	(0.500)	(0.031)	(0.171)	(0.397)
Share of total employment	0.026	0.121	0.336	0.001	0.019	0.115
	(0.159)	(0.326)	(0.473)	(0.036)	(0.137)	(0.319)
No. of firms	1537	2283	2084	16633	17138	15035

Note: Standard deviations are in parentheses.

firm-specific because for each firm we exclude its own output in calculating $FS_{(-i)t-1}$. Such a specification helps capture what each firm learns from others rather than from itself and it also avoids the bias induced by having the firm's own output on both sides of the equation. In addition to estimating the average effects over the 1993–2000 period, we also examine how these effects change over time by introducing the interaction of the above variables with time trend.[10]

In Table 4.2 we present the summary statistics related to foreign presence in the two economies. As may be seen from the table, the three measures of foreign presence that we report – share of the number of industrial firms, share of output, and share of employment – are highly correlated and they all indicate that foreign firms started from a very low share of total economic activity and increased their share over time. Moreover, the three variables show that throughout the period of our analysis the share of foreign firms is much smaller in Russia than in the Czech Republic. For example, the Russian share of industrial firms in 2000 is approximately one-fifth of the corresponding share in the Czech Republic.

The estimated average (time-invariant) and dynamic (time-varying) effects of foreign presence on productive efficiency of domestic and foreign firms in a given industry are reported in Panels A and B of Table 4.3, respectively.[11] In order to assess the sensitivity of the estimates to the estimation method, we report coefficients from pooled OLS, random effects (RE), fixed effects (FE), and the two-stage least squares random effect estimator (2SLS-RE).

The last estimator exploits information on supervisory ministries under central planning in treating the potential endogeneity of ownership, that is, that unobserved firm-specific productivity could determine the type of ownership by influencing the governments' decisions to privatize or investors' decisions to acquire the firm. Since the ministries had significant

Table 4.3 The effect of foreign presence on the efficiency gap, 1993–2000

Panel A: Time-invariant effects

	Czech Republic				*Russia*			
	OLS	*RE*	*FE*	*2SLS-RE*	*OLS*	*RE*	*FE*	*2SLS-RE*
Domestic	−0.275**	−0.090**	−0.017	−0.131**	−0.820**	−0.326**	−0.124**	−0.635**
	(0.023)	(0.018)	(0.020)	(0.029)	(0.028)	(0.021)	(0.024)	(0.029)
Domestic* FS_{t-1}	−0.090	−0.147**	−0.137**	−0.112**	−0.637**	−0.674**	−0.686**	−0.695**
	(0.046)	(0.038)	(0.039)	(0.041)	(0.048)	(0.035)	(0.035)	(0.035)
Foreign* FS_{t-1}	0.119	0.266**	0.354**	0.335**	0.199	0.432**	0.481**	0.367**
	(0.071)	(0.047)	(0.050)	(0.055)	(0.219)	(0.102)	(0.104)	(0.115)
No. of obs.	18434	18434	18434	15133	136769	136769	136769	125795
R^2	0.759	0.740	0.656	0.752	0.681	0.672	0.599	0.690
No. of firms	4313	4313	4313	3777	25594	25594	25594	23899

Panel B: Time-varying effects

	Czech Republic				*Russia*			
	OLS	*RE*	*FE*	*2SLS-RE*	*OLS*	*RE*	*FE*	*2SLS-RE*
Domestic	−0.271**	−0.110**	−0.039	−0.130**	−0.806**	−0.286**	−0.066**	−0.584**
	(0.024)	(0.020)	(0.021)	(0.031)	(0.028)	(0.021)	(0.024)	(0.029)
Domestic* FS_{t-1}	−0.068	−0.371**	−0.383**	−0.342**	−0.317**	−0.209**	−0.195**	−0.210**
	(0.088)	(0.069)	(0.070)	(0.076)	(0.066)	(0.054)	(0.054)	(0.054)
Domestic* $FS_{t-1}*t$	−0.005	0.041**	0.045**	0.040**	−0.109**	−0.165**	−0.176**	−0.177**
	(0.016)	(0.010)	(0.010)	(0.011)	(0.024)	(0.015)	(0.015)	(0.015)
Foreign* FS_{t-1}	0.215	−0.205	−0.150	0.267	−0.629	−0.794**	−1.115**	−0.998**
	(0.207)	(0.131)	(0.134)	(0.182)	(0.393)	(0.207)	(0.215)	(0.245)
Foreign* $FS_{t-1}*t$	−0.016	0.070**	0.074**	0.011	0.156*	0.211**	0.278**	0.234**
	(0.032)	(0.018)	(0.018)	(0.023)	(0.069)	(0.035)	(0.037)	(0.041)
No. of obs.	18434	18434	18434	15133	136769	136769	136769	125795
R^2	0.759	0.740	0.657	0.752	0.681	0.672	0.598	0.689
No. of firms	4313	4313	4313	3777	25594	25594	25594	23899

Notes: FS_{t-1} = the lagged share of foreign firms in total output by 2 – digit industry and year. Standard errors are in parentheses (robust in OLS); * significant at 5%; ** significant at 1%. The estimates are obtained from the translog production function specified in equation (1) and which includes industry dummies, year dummies. t is time trend, with $t = 0$ in 1993. RE – random effects estimator, FE – fixed effects estimator, and 2SLS-RE – two stage least squares random effect estimator, with ministries under central planning as instruments for all ownership variables.

control over the extent and process of privatization, the ministry dummy variables are correlated with (and hence are good predictors of) the ownership variables. We use ministry categories and the one-year lagged X's and Z's to estimate the binary (probit) ownership model for each ownership type:

$$P(Z_t^j = 1 | X_{t-1}, Z_{t-1}, M) = G_j(X_{t-1}, Z_{t-1}, M) \tag{4.3}$$

where j indicates the ownership type (domestic and foreign) and M is a vector of ministry categories. We next use the fitted probabilities from the probit, $\hat{G}_{ij}$, as instruments for ownership categories in the two-stage least squares random effects estimator. These predicted probabilities have several useful properties as instruments for binary endogenous variables (see, Wooldridge, 2002, pp. 621–33). The IV estimator is asymptotically efficient, the fitted probabilities stay within [0,1] range, and the first stage equation need not be correctly specified.

As may be seen from panel A of Table 4.3, all four methods yield the same pattern of key results with respect to the average effect of foreign presence over the 1993–2000 period: productive efficiency of domestic firms declines with greater presence of foreign-owned firms in both countries and the negative spillover is much larger in Russia than in the Czech Republic. Over this period, a 10 percentage point increase in the foreign share of output in an industry reduces efficiency of domestic firms between 10.6 per cent and 13.7 per cent in the Czech Republic and between 47.1 per cent and 50.1 per cent in Russia, depending on the estimate.[12] Conversely, foreign-owned firms experience positive spillovers from greater presence of foreign-owned firms in their industry in both the Czech Republic (around 30.5 per cent to 42.5 per cent) and Russia (around 44.3 per cent to 54.0 per cent).

The time-varying effects, reported in panel B, indicate that the underlying dynamics varies across the two countries. Except for some OLS estimates, the effect of greater foreign presence on domestic firms is (a) negative, but becoming less so over time in the Czech Republic, and (b) negative initially and becoming increasingly negative over time in Russia. The time-varying effects on foreign firms suggest that greater foreign presence has (a) an insignificant initial effect that becomes positive over time in the FE and RE estimates but remains insignificant in the OLS and 2SLS-RE estimates in the Czech Republic, and (b) a negative initial effect that becomes positive over time in Russia.

4 Concluding remarks

Neither the Czech (Central European) nor the Russian (CIS) model of transition has enabled domestically owned firms to converge to the technological frontier set by the most efficient foreign-owned firms. In both countries, the distance of domestic firms to the frontier grew from 1992–4 to 1995–7 and remained about the same from 1995–7 to 1998–2000. On the other hand, the average distance was much greater in Russia than in the Czech Republic.

In both of these economies, greater presence of foreign firms in a given industry is estimated to have a negative average effect on the productive efficiency of domestic firms in that industry, but the effect is positive on the efficiency of other foreign-owned firms. This result parallels the finding of SST (2004) that, both in the Czech Republic and Russia, foreign firms that are closer to the technological frontier have a higher probability of improving their performance than foreign firms that lag further behind, but that domestic firms have approximately the same probability of moving closer or farther from the frontier irrespective of their initial position.

Our dynamic estimates of the spillovers indicate that in the Czech Republic the negative spillover effect on domestic firms is alleviated over time, while in Russia the negative spillover effect becomes stronger over time. These findings suggest that in emerging market economies the hypothesized positive spillover (a) applies to foreign-owned firms, which are relatively more efficient and prepared in terms of their absorptive capacity than local firms, (b) is negative but reversible among domestic firms in countries that open up and gradually adopt market-oriented and enforceable institutional and legal framework, and (c) is increasingly more negative on domestic firms in countries that are more technologically backward, have opened up less to trade and foreign competition, and have not carried out fundamental legal and institutional reforms.

The implication of our findings may be extended further if one takes into account the findings of a parallel study of UK manufacturing by Griffith, Redding, and Simpson (2002), whose estimates suggest that there is convergence to the frontier and that increased foreign presence within an industry raises the speed of convergence to the technological frontier. Taken together, these findings for the Czech Republic (CEE), Russia (CIS) and the UK (EU) are consistent with the notion that the spillovers from foreign presence are positive for all firms in relatively advanced economies, but that in the less developed economies they are positive only for foreign-owned firms and may be (increasingly) negative for domestic firms. Overall, our results suggest that future research needs to examine carefully the differential effects that globalization may have on local and foreign owned firms in both the advanced and emerging market economies.

Notes

1. For example, see Brown (1999) for different views on the end of transition from the symposium on this topic.
2. This part of our analysis relates to Aghion *et al.* (2004), who developed a model showing that firm responses to liberalization are likely to be heterogeneous, with technologically more advanced firms more likely to respond by investing in new technologies and production processes. Their empirical analysis of Indian firms revealed that deregulation of entry elicited heterogeneous performance responses in the same three-digit sector but located in different states of India.
3. Our sample is comprised of industrial firms with more than 100 employees at any point in time. We used data on 1,537 to 2,970 firms a year for the Czech Republic and 15,035 to 19,209 firms in a given year for Russia. For a detailed description of the data and our methodology, see Sabrianova, Svejnar and Terrell (2004).
4. The idiosyncratic errors (ε_{it}) are excluded from the definition of firm-specific productive efficiency in order to reduce the effect of transitory productivity shocks

and statistical noise. To allow for the time variation in productive efficiency, the estimates are performed within the three-year sub-panels defined above.

5. The results are similar if one takes other percentage benchmarks (for example, 10 or 20 per cent). Note that smaller percentages, especially at the level of two-digit industries, are likely to contain more measurement error.
6. The results are not very different from those that would be obtained with fixed effect or two-stage least square random-effect estimators (SST, 2004).
7. Domestic firms can learn about the foreign firms' management style, technology and marketing techniques in many ways: from observation, from employees who worked in these firms and so on.
8. The reverse hypothesis, that firms with a larger technology gap gain more from a foreign presence, was put forward by Findlay (1978).
9. We used the lagged value of foreign presence since spillovers may take time to materialise. By using the lagged value we avoid the potential problem of endogeneity, that is, that foreign firms are attracted to industries with highly productive domestic firms. The panel estimates that control for unobserved firm heterogeneity are also likely to reduce a potential endogeneity bias.
10. Since we are using a lagged variable, we excluded the 1992 data from the analysis.
11. Due to space constraints, we present only the coefficients of the variables of interest. The underlying coefficients on inputs of the translog production function display concavity and monotonicity at the geometric means of the variables.
12. We have converted the coefficients in Table 4.3 into percentages with the formula: $\exp(\beta - 1)$.

References

Aghion, P., R. Burgess S. Redding and F. Zilibotti (2007) 'Entry Liberalization and Inequality in Industrial Performance', *Journal of the European Economic Association Papers and Proceedings*.

Aitken, B.J. and A.E. Harrison (1999) 'Do Domestic Firms Benefit from Foreign Direct Investment? Evidence from Venezuela', *American Economic Review*, vol. 89, pp. 605–18.

Brown, A. (ed.) (1999) *When is Transition Over?* (Kalamazoo, MI: W.E. Upjohn Institute for Employment Research).

Damijan, J.P., M. Knell, B. Majcen and M. Rojec (2003) 'Technology Transfer through FDI in Top-10 Transition Countries: How Important Are Direct Effects, Horizontal and Vertical Spillovers?', Institute for Economic Research, University of Ljubljana, Slovenia.

Djankov, S. and B. Hoekman (1998) 'Avenues of Technology Transfer: Foreign Investment and Productivity Change in the Czech Republic'. World Bank (mimeo).

Findlay, R. (1978) 'Relative Backwardness, Direct Foreign Investment and the Transfer of Technology: A Simple Dynamic Model', *Quarterly Journal of Economics*, vol. 92, no. 1, pp. 1–16.

Griffith, R., S. Redding and H. Simpson (2002) 'Productivity Convergence and Foreign Ownership at the Establishment Level'. CEPR discussion paper no. 3765.

Haddad, M. and A. E. Harrison (1993) 'Are there Positive Spillovers from Foreign Direct Investment?', *Journal of Development Economics*, vol. 42, pp. 51–74.

Haskel, J.E., S.C. Pereira and M.J. Slaughter (2007) 'Does Inward Foreign Direct Investment Boost the Productivity of Domestic Firms?', *Review of Economics and Statistics*, vol. 89(3), pp. 482–96.
Kinoshita, Y. (2000) 'R&D and Technology Spillovers through FDI: Innovation and Absorptive Capacity' CEPR working paper no. 2775.
Konings, J. (2000) 'The Effects of Direct Foreign Investment on Domestic firms: Evidence from Firm Level Panel Data in Emerging Economies', William Davidson Institute working paper no. 344.
Kosova, R. (2004) 'Do Foreign Firms Crowd Out Domestic Firms? Evidence from the Czech Republic'. University of Michigan Business School, Ph.D. dissertation.
Sabirianova, K., J. Svejnar and K. Terrell (2004) 'Foreign Investment, Corporate Ownership and Development: Are Firms in Emerging Markets Catching up to the World Standard?', IZA Working Paper series.
Wooldridge, J.M. (2002) *Econometric Analysis of Cross Section and Panel Data* (Cambridge, MA The MIT Press).
Yudaeva, K., K. Kozlov, N. Melentieva and N. Ponomareva (2003) 'Does Foreign Ownership Matter? The Russian Experience', *The Economics of Transition*, vol. 2, pp. 383–410.

5
A Portrait of the Chinese Entrepreneur

*Simeon Djankov, Yingyi Qian, Gérard Roland and Ekaterina Zhuravskaya**

1 Introduction

It has been increasingly recognised that entrepreneurship plays a crucial role in successful economies. The Schumpeterian approach to growth (Aghion and Howitt, 1997) advances the view that entrepreneurial dynamism is the key to innovation and growth. A growing body of research also emphasizes the role of entrepreneurs and the development of a vibrant small and medium-sized enterprise sector in the process of economic development (World Bank, 2003). Understanding the factors that enable or hinder entrepreneurial activity is thus at the heart of our research.

Paradoxically, entrepreneurship is an under-researched topic in the social sciences, especially in economics. It was not always so. Schumpeter (1934) discusses the role of the entrepreneur in the process of economic development at length. He imagines the entrepreneur as a creative, driven individual who finds 'new combinations of [factors] of production' to develop a new product, corner a new market, or design a new technology. Schumpeter speculates about the psyche of the archetypal entrepreneur: he is motivated by a 'dream to find a private kingdom, or dynasty ... [driven by] the impulse to fight, to prove oneself superior to others, to succeed for the sake of ... success itself'.

In mainstream economics, however, entrepreneurship has never played a central role. For decades, the main focus of economics has been on the allocation of resources and how this is achieved by markets or by governments. It is only recently with the revival of interest in the question of economic growth that Schumpeter's views have acquired greater salience. Empirical research on entrepreneurship in economics is surprisingly limited.[1]

In a broad sense, there are three distinct perspectives on entrepreneurship in the social sciences. The first is the institutional perspective emphasized by

* We thank Xiaolu Wang and Irina Levina for their excellent research assistance, and the international Finance Corporation for financial support.

economists and political economists. This focuses on the role of economic, political, and legal institutions in fostering or restricting entrepreneurship in different countries at various times. Particularly relevant institutional constraints are seen in two aspects. One aspect has to do with the credit market in financing entrepreneurial activities. For example, a major body of research in economic development stressed the role of credit constraints making it impossible for the poor to borrow to set up their own businesses (Banerjee and Newman, 1993). Another aspect dealt with security of property rights in providing the right incentives for entrepreneurs. For instance, the literature on transition from socialism to capitalism emphasized the importance of institutions securing property rights (for example, Johnson, McMillan and Woodruff, 2002; Roland, 2000, Che and Qian, 1998) and the nefarious role of predatory behaviour by government bureaucrats (Djankov *et al.*, 2002), and organized crime (Frye and Zhuravskaya, 2000; Roland and Verdier, 2003). Security of property rights is also an increasingly important theme in the development literature (Acemoglu, Robinson and Johnson, 2002; De Soto, 2000; Besley, 1995).

The second perspective focuses on the sociological variables that shape entrepreneurship. Sociologists have long emphasized the role of values (Cochran, 1971) and social networks (Young, 1971) in promoting or discouraging entrepreneurial activities. Social networks work through a variety of channels, such as family, relatives, friends, or social groups in general.

The third perspective on entrepreneurship emphasizes the individual characteristics of entrepreneurs. For example, psychologists have hypothesized about the psychological traits associated with entrepreneurs – such as a personal need for achievement (McClellan, 1961), belief in the effect of personal effort on outcomes (McGhee and Crandall, 1968; Lao, 1970), attitudes towards risk and individual self-confidence (Liles, 1974). Personal characteristics of entrepreneurs are also a major theme of recent work by Lazear (2002), who used the survey data from Stanford University MBA graduates and found that those with more jobs and shorter job tenure before graduate school were most likely to become entrepreneurs afterwards. He concludes that individuals who become entrepreneurs have a special ability to acquire general skills, which they then apply to their own businesses.

The current project studies entrepreneurship from these three perspectives using a new data set to be collected from several developing countries, including some countries in transition from socialism. Our general plan is to conduct surveys in five large developing countries located in all major continents – Brazil, Russia, India, Nigeria, and China, or BRINC for short. There are several reasons why we chose to study entrepreneurship in these countries. First, they are among the largest emerging economies in the world and are located in all major continents. In particular, Brazil, Russia, India and China are currently perceived as the world's major growth engines. Second, entrepreneurship is only emerging in transition economies (and it is very unequally developed in developing countries) so we can observe out of steady-state phenomena and glimpse the development of entrepreneurship. From that perspective, the study of entrepreneurship in those countries might be more revealing than if conducted in advanced industrialized countries where the development of entrepreneurship has generally been more successful, is more in steady state and exhibits less variation. Third, because these are large countries, we are able to exploit substantial regional variations in institutions and culture within those countries. Identical questions asked across these different countries also allow us to make cross-country comparisons and to draw broad conclusions for developing countries as a whole.

Our surveys cover both entrepreneurs and non-entrepreneurs in order to understand how these groups differ in terms of their individual characteristics, skills, education, intellectual and personality traits, family background, social origins, social networks, values and beliefs, and in their perception of the institutional, social and economic environment businesses face.

In this chapter we report some initial observations from a pilot survey conducted in China in 2003–4.

What are the main results from this pilot study? Interestingly, we find suggestive evidence that social network effects play a major role in determining entrepreneurial behaviour: individuals whose relatives and childhood friends are entrepreneurs are more likely to be entrepreneurs themselves – although this result should be interpreted with caution because of the likelihood of well-known omitted variable biases in the estimation of social effects (see Manski, 1993). Finally, individual characteristics such as greed and willingness to take risks are also important determinants of entrepreneurship, echoing the claims of Schumpeter and others. These preliminary findings are similar to those found in our pilot study of Russia (Djankov *et al.*, 2005) where social networks played an important role.

The rest of the chapter is organized as follows: Section 2 describes the survey data collection; and Section 3 presents summary statistics on the differences between entrepreneurs and non-entrepreneurs in China. Section 4 reports probit and logit analysis on variables associated with entrepreneurship. Section 5 concludes.

2 The survey

The pilot study was carried out in Beijing and six other cities in three different regions of China: in Wuhan and Huanghi in Hubei Province; in Guangzhou and Zhongshan in Guangdong Province; and in Xi'an and Baoji in Shaanxi Province.

Three surveys were conducted. We first surveyed a random sample of 414 entrepreneurs – 50 to 53 in each of the six regional cities and 108 from Beijing in autumn 2004. An entrepreneur was defined as the owner or co-owner of a business with five or more employees.

Early in 2005, an additional 454 non-entrepreneurs – from 53 to 59 in each of the smaller size cities, and 116 in Beijing – were interviewed using a similar survey. Respondents were chosen randomly conditional on matching the age, gender and educational attainment of entrepreneurs from the first survey. In other words, the proportion of men, women, people at various ages and with different levels of educational attainment are near-identical in the two surveys. We opted for this approach to ensure that broad demographic differences between entrepreneurs and non-entrepreneurs were not driving the results, but rather other factors. In addition to the non-entrepreneurs 'matched' to the demographic characteristics of the entrepreneurs, 107 additional non-entrepreneurs were also surveyed without regard to their demographic characteristics (from 19 to 13 in each of the six cities and 17 in Beijing).

Finally, a short survey was run among a random sample of 1,275 respondents (with the same breakdown across cities) asking nine questions about their personal characteristics, including whether or not they were an entrepreneur or self-employed. These data allow us to roughly determine the proportion of entrepreneurs across the study sites. Throughout the empirical analysis, the observations were weighted with weights equal to the inverse of the probability for a particular respondent (entrepreneur or non-entrepreneur) to get into our sample. The weights reflect differences in entrepreneurship, age, gender, and education across cities in the population, as well as the city size.

The limited number of cities and regions in the pilot study makes it difficult to generalize about the impact of regional institutional and cultural differences on entrepreneurship.

3 How do entrepreneurs compare to non-entrepreneurs?

Table 5.1 lists means for a number of variables for entrepreneurs and non-entrepreneurs. For the latter, we use conditional means controlling for age, gender, education and city dummies.[2] In terms of individual characteristics, the major difference that stands out is the difference in the willingness to accept a risk-neutral gamble: accept either (1) win $10 with probability ½ and lose $10 with probability ½ or (2) win $20 with probability ½ and lose $20 with probability ½ – 90 per cent of entrepreneurs in China responded yes (compared to 57 per cent of non-entrepreneurs). There is thus more than a 30 per cent difference in response between both groups. We do not find important differences in either cognitive scores or excellence in education. Intriguingly, only 29 per cent of entrepreneurs mentioned taking part in sports, compared to 81 per cent for non-entrepreneurs. Entrepreneurs viewed themselves as richer than average and this was reflected in their consumption

Table 5.1 Entrepreneurs compared to non-entrepreneurs in China

	Entrepreneurs' mean	*Non-entrepreneurs' conditional mean*	*Standard error for difference in means*	*p-value for difference in means*
Individual Characteristics				
Height, cm	169.04	168.22	0.25	0.02**
No. of localities lived in	1.85	1.55	0.18	0.15
No. of distinct professional activities	2.40	2.13	0.21	0.24
No. of industries worked in	1.85	1.58	0.06	0.00***
Plan to move %	0.04	0.11	0.04	0.09*
Religious believer %	0.12	0.08	0.02	0.09*
Married %	0.84	0.80	0.06	0.53
Speak foreign language %	0.35	0.49	0.11	0.22
Accept a risk neutral gamble %	0.90	0.57	0.09	0.01***
Good health, self-described %	0.51	0.37	0.07	0.09*
Go in for sports %	0.29	0.81	0.06	0.00***
Practice risky sports %	0.12	0.10	0.03	0.62
Overweight %	0.20	0.15	0.05	0.38
Cognitive text score	3.92	3.80	0.26	0.64
Top 10% in secondary school (self-reported) %	0.37	0.38	0.05	0.82
Top 10% in high school, college or university (self-reported) %	0.36	0.38	0.01	0.10
Income and Wealth				
Above average income (self assessed) %	0.50	0.11	0.02	0.00***
Spend more than 50% of household income on food %	0.29	0.56	0.07	0.01***

Own a TV %	1.00	1.00	0.00	0.34
Own a satellite dish %	0.11	0.06	0.05	0.31
Own a microwave %	0.86	0.69	0.03	0.00***
Own a washing machine %	0.98	0.92	0.01	0.01***
Own a dishwasher %	0.18	0.03	0.06	0.05*
Own a computer %	0.85	0.63	0.10	0.07*
Own a car %	0.56	0.19	0.12	0.03**
Own an apartment %	0.88	0.79	0.05	0.12
Own a country house %	0.05	0.03	0.01	0.08*
Sociological Characteristics				
Father has secondary special or higher education %	0.29	0.27	0.04	0.57
Mother has secondary special or higher education %	0.14	0.18	0.06	0.46
Father was a boss or director %	0.30	0.13	0.05	0.02**
Mother was a boss or director %	0.06	0.03	0.02	0.10
Father was a worker or employee without special education %	0.56	0.72	0.05	0.01**
Mother was a worker or employee without special education %	0.70	0.71	0.05	0.86
Father was a member of the Communist Party %	0.40	0.31	0.10	0.42
Mother was a member of the Communist Party %	0.10	0.15	0.01	0.01***
Parent wealth was above average when 16 years old %	0.20	0.09	0.05	0.09*
Number of family members, who are entrepreneurs	0.88	0.38	0.08	0.00***
Number of childhood friends, who became entrepreneurs	0.84	0.55	0.14	0.09*
Number of adolescent friends, who became entrepreneurs	1.26	0.44	0.21	0.01***
Did experience of your friends from school influence your career? %	0.41	0.08	0.03	0.00***

(*Continued*)

Table 5.1 (Continued)

	Entrepreneurs' mean	*Non-entrepreneurs' conditional mean*	*Standard error for difference in means*	*p-value for difference in means*
Motivation, greed, happiness				
Retire if won 100 times GDP per capita %	0.05	0.24	0.06	0.02**
Retire if won 500 times GDP per capita %	0.14	0.37	0.03	0.00***
Retire if won 5000 times GDP per capita %	0.31	0.44	0.05	0.05*
Not retire if won a large sum: I like what I do %	0.74	0.75	0.08	0.93
Not retire if won a large sum: I want more money %	0.70	0.43	0.07	0.01***
Not retire if won a large sum: my work serves useful social purpose %	0.18	0.81	0.08	0.00***
Very happy or quite happy in life %	0.92	0.91	0.02	0.76
Very successful or quite successful in life %	0.64	0.43	0.06	0.01***
Own Values				
Friends are very important %	0.60	0.66	0.04	0.16
Relations with parents are very important %	0.86	0.88	0.01	0.10*
Education of children is very important %	0.91	0.91	0.01	0.43
Financial well-being is very important %	0.73	0.62	0.05	0.08*
Leisure time is very important %	0.19	0.20	0.05	0.85
Health is very important %	0.93	0.88	0.04	0.20
Service to others is very important %	0.19	0.19	0.04	0.92
Political freedom is very important %	0.73	0.28	0.03	0.00***
Power is very important %	0.32	0.26	0.02	0.01**
Religion is very important %	0.06	0.00	0.03	0.11
Work is very important %	0.80	0.63	0.02	0.00***
Intellectual achievement is very important %	0.24	0.33	0.03	0.02**
Values on social norms (own and perceptions of others)				
Not paying a fare can be justified to some degree %	0.08	0.05	0.04	0.48
Shirking at work can be justified to some degree %	0.23	0.07	0.03	0.00***

Accepting a bribe can be justified to some degree %	0.19	0.06	0.03	0.00***
Other people think that avoiding to pay a fare can be justified to some degree %	0.15	0.18	0.04	0.47
Other people think that shirking at work can be justified to some degree %	0.24	0.15	0.03	0.02**
Other people think that accepting a bribe can be justified to some degree %	0.21	0.16	0.03	0.21
Trust				
Most people can be trusted %	0.56	0.54	0.10	0.79
Have a lot of trust in family members %	0.96	0.92	0.05	0.48
Have a lot of trust in friends %	0.58	0.58	0.14	0.98
Have a lot of trust in colleagues %	0.38	0.33	0.07	0.46
Have a lot of trust or some trust in businessmen %	0.71	0.46	0.08	0.02**
Have a lot of trust or some trust in subordinates %	0.95	0.83	0.04	0.02**
Have a lot of trust or some trust in other people from town %	0.42	0.50	0.06	0.29
Have a lot of trust or some trust in compatriots %	0.31	0.38	0.07	0.34
Have a lot of trust or some trust in foreigners %	0.29	0.38	0.11	0.39
Have a lot of trust or some trust in local gvmt. officials %	0.69	0.59	0.04	0.07*
Have a lot of trust or some trust in regional gvmt. officials %	0.68	0.64	0.05	0.43
Have a lot of trust or some trust in central gvmt. officials %	0.75	0.75	0.03	0.99
Institutional Environment				
People in your town are favorable towards entrepreneurs %	0.68	0.60	0.08	0.33
Local government is favorable towards entrepreneurs %	0.82	0.70	0.03	0.00***
Regional government is favorable towards entrepreneurs %	0.78	0.76	0.04	0.74
Central government is favorable towards entrepreneurs %	0.81	0.90	0.05	0.10*
Private entrepreneurs pay bribes to avoid regulations %	0.50	0.54	0.05	0.57
Private entrepreneurs pay bribes to change rules %	0.40	0.50	0.11	0.39

(*Continued*)

Table 5.1 (Continued)

	Entrepreneurs' mean	*Non-entrepreneurs' conditional mean*	*Standard error for difference in means*	*p-value for difference in means*
Are businessmen subject to theft of property %	0.70	0.98	0.14	0.08*
Go to court against a business relation if cheated %	0.90	0.88	0.02	0.48
Go to court against a government official if abused %	0.80	0.73	0.01	0.00***
It is relatively easy to find money to start a business in town %	0.38	0.26	0.09	0.28
Very serious problem for business				
High taxes %	0.12	0.16	0.02	0.17
Complicated tax rules and hard tax forms %	0.10	0.28	0.02	0.00***
Competition %	0.10	0.36	0.04	0.00***
Rackets %	0.10	0.43	0.03	0.00***
Inflation and macroeconomic instability %	0.12	0.39	0.04	0.00***
Poor functioning of courts %	0.15	0.38	0.07	0.01**
Difficulty of raising outside finance %	0.25	0.42	0.05	0.01**
Government administrative regulations %	0.19	0.26	0.06	0.35
Unequal treatment of similar businesses by bureaucrats %	0.08	0.28	0.03	0.00***
Corruption %	0.17	0.48	0.09	0.01**
Crime %	0.09	0.45	0.04	0.00***
Bad public infrastructure %	0.04	0.26	0.03	0.00***
Poor public goods provision %	0.06	0.26	0.02	0.00***
Non-transparent 'rules of the game' %	0.21	0.29	0.07	0.30

Source: Authors' survey.

patterns; they spent less of their income on food, owned more consumer durables and were more likely to own a car.

In terms of their family background, the parents of entrepreneurs do not have a higher level of education than non-entrepreneurs but they were more likely to have been bosses or directors and were richer than average. Interestingly, while fathers of entrepreneurs were not more likely to have been members of the Communist Party, mothers were less likely to have been party members. An important difference between entrepreneurs and non-entrepreneurs relates to the number of entrepreneurs in the family or among childhood friends. Entrepreneurs had nearly three times more entrepreneurs in their family (parents, aunts or uncles, siblings and cousins) than non-entrepreneurs. Respondents were asked to name five childhood and adolescence friends and then to report on how many of these five became entrepreneurs. The difference in response for entrepreneurs and non-entrepreneurs was striking: the answer is 0.84 for childhood friends and 1.265 for adolescence friends among entrepreneurs compared to 0.55 and 0.44 for non-entrepreneurs.

Entrepreneurs also differed in terms of labour–leisure preferences. Respondents were asked whether they would retire if they received a windfall income of 100 or 500 or 5,000 times the annual per capita GDP of the country. Entrepreneurs were much less likely to respond positively than non-entrepreneurs. The main reason is that entrepreneurs want to earn more money (70 per cent of those who did not want to retire if earning above 5,000 times GDP per capita mentioned it as a motivation compared to 43 per cent for non-entrepreneurs who would not retire for the same amount). Among other motivations, entrepreneurs do not believe that their work serves a useful purpose compared to non-entrepreneurs but work satisfaction was cited as a motive by about three-quarters of all respondents, whether entrepreneurs or not. While entrepreneurs did not perceive themselves happier (92 per cent against 91 per cent), they considered that they were successful in life (64 per cent against 43 per cent).

Respondents were asked questions about values and beliefs. We did not find big differences with two important exceptions. Work was more important for entrepreneurs (80 per cent against 63 per cent) and they valued political freedom much more (73 per cent compared to 28 per cent for non-entrepreneurs). Answers to questions about social norms differ in some respects. Entrepreneurs consider bribing to be more justifiable. Intriguingly, they consider shirking at work more justifiable and wrongly think that other people should agree. Questions on trust did not deliver many different answers except for the – perhaps not surprising – result that entrepreneurs place greater trust in other businessmen and their subordinates.

Questions on the individual perceptions of institutional environment were also asked. Interestingly, controlling for city-level differences, entrepreneurs have a more positive perception of local government's attitude towards entrepreneurs than non-entrepreneurs, but this is reversed when it comes to the central government. Note, however, that about 80 per cent of entrepreneurs consider that different levels of government are favourable towards entrepreneurs. Entrepreneurs would also be more likely to go to court if abused by a government official. This reveals that entrepreneurs perceive in general government to be favourable towards entrepreneurship. If the institutional environment were the same for all (potential) firms in each city, this could be interpreted as evidence for the importance of perceptions for the choice to become an entrepreneur: those who have lower perceptions chose not go into entrepreneurship since we control for city-level variation. Interestingly, on perceptions of crime levels, when asked if business people are subject to theft of property, one has less positive answers among entrepreneurs.

We also asked questions related to problems in doing business. In general, entrepreneurs responded less pessimistically than non-entrepreneurs. The most serious problems cited by entrepreneurs were the difficulty of raising outside finance (mentioned by 25 per cent) followed by non-transparent rules of the game (21 per cent), government regulations (19 per cent) and corruption (17 per cent).

To summarize this section, the main differences we found between entrepreneurs and non-entrepreneurs is that entrepreneurs are more willing to take risks, have more entrepreneurs in their family and among childhood friends, value work highly and have high wealth aspirations. They also have in general a more positive opinion of local government's attitude towards entrepreneurs.

4 Determinants of entrepreneurship and business expansion

To understand the determinants of entrepreneurship, we focus on variables that can plausibly be considered exogenous to the decision to become an entrepreneur.

The first three columns of Table 5.2 present some multivariate probit regressions where the dependent variable takes a value of 1 if the respondent is an entrepreneur and 0 otherwise. We find again that the social network variables (having family members and childhood friends as entrepreneurs) are strongly associated with entrepreneurship. Making a causal claim about the effect of social interactions using cross-sectional survey data of this sort is problematic because of the likely omitted variables (for instance, external factors that influence various members of a social group). So we should interpret the results cautiously and do not claim more than a robust correlation at this stage. Note that risk-loving and greed are also significant. Having a mother who is a member of the Communist Party has a significant negative effect in columns 1 and 3. Note also the positive coefficient on height. In column 4, we use the number of years as entrepreneur as a dependent variable.

Table 5.2 Entrepreneurship and entrepreneurial experience

	Dependent variable			
	Entrepreneurship indicator variable, Probit			*Years as entrepreneur OLS*
Father had higher education	0.018	0.009	0.005	0.564
	[0.046]	[0.023]	[0.020]	[0.282]*
Father was a boss or director	0.06	0.011	0.011	0.111
	[0.036]*	[0.025]	[0.022]	[0.445]
Mother was a boss or director	0.07	0.091	0.081	0.498
	[0.045]	[0.059]	[0.059]	[0.337]
Mother was a party member	−0.047	−0.019	−0.021	−0.467
	[0.012]***	[0.012]	[0.012]*	[0.120]***
Family members entrepreneurs	0.041	0.013	0.012	0.566
	[0.006]***	[0.007]*	[0.007]*	[0.112]***
Friends entrepreneurs	0.036	0.029	0.031	0.564
(from the last place of study)	[0.008]***	[0.008]***	[0.010]***	[0.094]***
Cognitive test score	0.004	0.003	0.004	0.031
	[0.011]	[0.005]	[0.005]	[0.059]
Height	0.003	0.001	0.001	0.016
	[0.000]***	[0.001]**	[0.000]**	[0.011]
Risk-loving		0.077	0.078	0.661
		[0.007]***	[0.006]***	[0.141]***
Top 10% in secondary school		−0.007	−0.007	−0.012
(self-reported)		[0.010]	[0.010]	[0.118]
Greed		0.142	0.141	1.329
		[0.028]***	[0.027]***	[0.216]***
City population perceived favourable towards entrepreneurs			0.009	0.144
			[0.008]	[0.106]
Government perceived favourable towards entrepreneurs			0	−0.174
			[0.004]	[0.040]***
Observations	851	843	802	785
R-squared				0.2

We find essentially the same variables playing a significant role except that the father having a higher education enters positively and the experience as entrepreneur is negatively associated to the perceived attitude of government towards entrepreneurs.

Interestingly, the surveys carried out among non-entrepreneurs allowed us to sample former entrepreneurs and people who considered becoming an entrepreneur, but in the end decided not to do so. Note that in both cases, while social network variables remain significant (although family entrepreneurs were not significant for failed entrepreneurs), greed and risk-taking are not significant. This could suggest that social networks have an effect on the decision to become an entrepreneur but that risk-taking and greed are necessary for success and drive. Another reason why these regressions are interesting is that one might fear that the friend entrepreneur variable is endogenous since entrepreneurs who are in frequent contact with other entrepreneurs might first remember their entrepreneur friends. The positive coefficient of that variable in the regression for former entrepreneurs is reassuring from that point of view since their memory is less likely to be biased.

Another issue is that there are different types of business owners who became entrepreneurs to varying circumstances. We asked respondents questions about those circumstances. The two major categories that come out are what we call *entrepreneur by opportunity* and *entrepreneur by necessity*. The former became business owners because they seized a business opportunity. They are the true entrepreneurs in the Schumpeterian sense. The latter became business owners primarily because they lost their job or because of economic decline in their previous sector. Note that other motives for becoming entrepreneur such as having obtained money play a relatively minor role in the response to that question. Table 5.3 reports probit analysis as well as multinomial logit on these two different types of business owner. The results are much the same as for entrepreneurs in general with a few exceptions. Family is not significant for the entrepreneur as regards opportunity. The main variables are friends, risk-loving and greed. For the entrepreneur by necessity, the family variable is significant and the higher education of the father has a negative coefficient.

Table 5.4 looks at the sales growth of entrepreneurs' firms. Column 1 presents the results of a probit regression for those entrepreneurs who had a positive sales growth and the next three columns are simple OLS regressions of a discrete variable that equals 1 if past year's sales growth was below 0 per cent, 2 if it was between 0 and 5 per cent, 3 if it was between 6 and 10 per cent, 4 if 11 to 20 per cent, 5 if growth was above 20 per cent on a number of dependent variables. Apart from the variables used in previous tables, we also control for the sector and for size of business, measured by the log number of employees. We note that the family entrepreneur variable comes out significantly positive in all regressions. This is interesting because it shows not only that family matters for the choice to become an entrepreneur but also for enterprise expansion. The current survey instrument does not permit to find out the precise channels through which family matters. Family might not only influence values, transmit idiosyncratic skills for entrepreneurship, provide moral encouragement but also provide money to start and expand the enterprise.

Table 5.5 takes a more direct look at the sources of financing entrepreneurs and the obstacles to becoming an entrepreneur. We see from Table 5.5a that

Table 5.3 Failed and would be of entrepreneurs and entrepreneur by opportunity or necessity

	Probit				*Multinomial logit*	
	Was entrepreneur	*Thought about entrepreneurship*	*Entrepreneur by opportunity*	*Entrepreneur by necessity*	*Entrepreneur by opportunity*	*Entrepreneur by necessity*
Father had higher education	0.012	−0.003	0.02	−0.006	0.005	−0.004
	[0.030]	[0.081]	[0.035]	[0.002]***	[0.010]	[0.001]***
Father was a boss or director	0.007	0.006	−0.001	0.006	0.001	0.001
	[0.026]	[0.064]	[0.009]	[0.007]	[0.006]	[0.004]
Mother was a boss or director	0.008	0.191	0.101	−0.008	0.025	−0.007
	[0.066]	[0.151]	[0.106]	[0.002]***	[0.014]*	[0.005]
Mother was a party member	0	0.093	−0.014	0	−0.013	−0.003
	[0.045]	[0.069]	[0.011]	[0.005]	[0.012]	[0.003]
Family members entrepreneurs	0.03	0.065	0.008	0.003	0.004	0.002
	[0.023]	[0.018]***	[0.007]	[0.001]***	[0.004]	[0.001]***
Friends entrepreneurs	0.037	0.078	0.029	0.005	0.016	0.004
(from the last place of study)	[0.010]***	[0.023]***	[0.005]***	[0.002]**	[0.005]***	[0.002]**
Cognitive test score	−0.004	0.005	0.001	0.002	0.001	0.001
	[0.016]	[0.013]	[0.003]	[0.002]	[0.001]	[0.001]*
Height	−0.006	0.003	0	0	0	0
	[0.001]***	[0.002]	[0.000]	[0.000]	[0.000]	[0.000]
Risk-loving	0.038	−0.005	0.053	0.011	0.046	0.012
	[0.039]	[0.028]	[0.009]***	[0.004]***	[0.008]***	[0.003]***
Top 10% in secondary school	0.119	−0.018	0.003	0.003	−0.004	−0.001
(self-reported)	[0.053]**	[0.017]	[0.009]	[0.004]	[0.005]	[0.003]
Greed	0.016	0.032	0.1	0.026	0.043	0.015
	[0.029]	[0.047]	[0.023]***	[0.004]***	[0.009]***	[0.003]***
City population perceived	0.009	0.015	0.005	0.001	0.005	0.002
favourable towards entrepreneurs	[0.027]	[0.049]	[0.008]	[0.002]	[0.007]	[0.000]***
Government perceived	−0.048	−0.014	−0.004	−0.001	0	0
favourable towards entrepreneurs	[0.006]***	[0.017]	[0.001]***	[0.001]	[0.002]	[0.001]
Observations	456	392	718	718	782	782

Note: Robust standard errors in brackets.

Table 5.4 Enterprise growth and expansion

	Probit		*OLS*	
	Sales growth dummy	*Sales growth*	*Sales growth*	*Sales growth*
Father had higher education	−0.221	−0.328	−0.385	−0.308
	[0.077]***	[0.171]	[0.174]*	[0.169]
Father was a boss or director	−0.011	−0.156	−0.162	−0.213
	[0.090]	[0.172]	[0.176]	[0.162]
Mother was a boss or director	−0.167	−0.443	−0.453	−0.439
	[0.138]	[0.338]	[0.346]	[0.394]
Mother was a party member	−0.109	0.097	0.122	0.152
	[0.156]	[0.314]	[0.328]	[0.385]
Family members entrepreneurs	0.088	0.225	0.218	0.227
	[0.032]***	[0.066]**	[0.072]**	[0.086]**
Friends entrepreneurs	−0.004	−0.066	−0.054	−0.058
(from the last place of study)	[0.020]	[0.034]*	[0.033]	[0.045]
Cognitive test score	−0.031	−0.04	−0.041	−0.035
	[0.038]	[0.045]	[0.047]	[0.071]
Height	0.008	0.005	0.006	0.005
	[0.005]	[0.007]	[0.007]	[0.008]
Risk-loving	0.157		0.109	0.128
	[0.120]		[0.243]	[0.235]
Top 10% in secondary school	0.118		0.164	0.18
(self-reported)	[0.057]**		[0.099]	[0.100]
Greed	0.134		0.241	0.223
	[0.032]***		[0.109]*	[0.143]
City population perceived	−0.03			−0.121
favourable towards entrepreneurs	[0.092]			[0.244]
Government perceived	0.035			0.109
favourable towards entrepreneurs	[0.021]*			[0.024]***
Business size	0.08	0.163	0.176	0.184
	[0.013]***	[0.027]***	[0.031]***	[0.032]***
Observations	340	354	353	340
R-squared		0.19	0.2	0.22

Note: Robust standard errors in brackets.

the main source of financing for both start-ups and expansion of firms is retained earnings (respectively 57 per cent for the former and 70 per cent for the latter). Loans or investment from relatives play a role only for 12 per cent of start-ups and 5 per cent of expansions and loans from friends account for 6 per cent of start-ups and only 4 per cent of expansions. Note that while bank credit accounts for only 4 per cent of start-ups, it finances 13 per cent of expansions. This suggests strongly that liquidity constraints play a big role at the start-up level. Table 5.5b asks about the main reason

Table 5.5 Financing Chinese entrepreneurs

a. The main source of finance for start-ups and for expansion of existing business

	Start-ups (414 obs.)	*Expansion (198 obs.)*
Personal savings/retained earnings %	57	70
Loan or investment from relatives %	12	5
Loan or investment from friends %	6	4
Bank credit %	4	13
Government subsidy or grant %	0	1
Other sources %	21	8

b. What is the main reason why your thoughts did not realize in an actual business?

Did not find money %	58
Did not find a good project %	14
Too risky %	12
For personal reasons %	5
Bureaucratic constraints and corruption %	4
I had / found better paid job	2
Other	5

c. What is the main reason why you have never seriously thought of becoming an entrepreneur?

Would not have been about to find money %	29
Do not have appropriate skills %	24
Satisfied with current job %	21
Entrepreneurship is too risky %	15
For personal reasons %	4
Would not like entrepreneurship as an activity %	4
Unfavourable economic environment %	3
Entrepreneurship is not prestigious %	0

Notes: Table 5.5b covers respondents who seriously considered becoming entrepreneurs but faired to start a business (54 observations). Table 5.5c covers respondents who never considered becoming an entrepreneur (402 observations).

those who seriously thought of becoming an entrepreneur chose not to do so. By far the most important reason that comes up is that they did not find the money (58 per cent). Only 14 per cent responded that they did not find a good project and 12 per cent that too much risk was involved. In Table 5.5c, we asked non-entrepreneurs why they had never thought of becoming an entrepreneur. The most important reason mentioned was that they would not have been able to find the money (29 per cent) but it is closely followed by 'Do not have the appropriate skills' (24 per cent) and 'Satisfied with current job' (21 per cent). So, while liquidity constraints seem to play an important role for those who seriously considered becoming an entrepreneur, it was only one among others for other respondents.

5 Conclusions

Preliminary results suggest that the determinants of entrepreneurship in China are multiple. Chinese entrepreneurs like to take risks and are greedy. Social network effects – having entrepreneurs in the family and among one's friends – appear important for the decision to become an entrepreneur. Cultural differences do not seem to play a key role, even though there are some notable differences between entrepreneurs and non-entrepreneurs, including their self-expressed work ethic. Credit constraints appear to play an important role in discouraging people from starting or expanding an enterprise, but they are only one factor among others.

The current survey does not allow us to differentiate the precise channels through which social network effects influence the choice to become an entrepreneur. Could there be hidden characteristics in entrepreneurial families that produce a sorting effect to create clusters of social networks of entrepreneurs? Are there peer effects? To the extent that there are network effects, what are these about? Do they merely alleviate credit constraints? Do they serve to encourage and create herding effects? Are they the locus for the exchange of business information and skills that have significant value for entrepreneurs? We are refining our survey to give a better answer to those questions. In addition, the data from the Chinese pilot study were insufficient to evaluate the effect of institutional variables on entrepreneurship because of too few town-level observations. One of the tasks of the larger survey is to compare the importance of individual and institutional effects.

Notes

1. There exists a large literature on entrepreneurship in the management literature devoted mostly to advanced industrialized countries but it often lacks both theory and rigorous empirical analysis
2. It is important to note that all the main results from the comparison of means are robust to adding a control for the current wealth of the individual.

References

Acemoglu, D., J. Robinson and S. Johnson (2001) 'The Colonial Origins of Comparative Development: An Empirical Investigation', *American Economic Review*, vol. 91, pp. 1369–401.

Aghion, P. and P. Howitt (1997) *Endogenous Growth Theory* (Cambridge, MA: MIT Press).

Banerjee, A. and A. Newman (1993) 'Occupational Choice and the Process of Development' *Journal of Political Economy*, vol. 101, no. 2.

Besley, T. (1995) 'Property Rights and Investment Incentives: Theory and Evidence from Ghana', *Journal of Political Economy*, vol. 103, no. 5, pp. 903–37.

Che, J. and Y. Qian (1998) 'Insecure Property Rights and Government Ownership of Firms', *Quarterly Journal of Economics, May*, vol. 113, no. 2, pp. 467–96.

Cochran, T. (1971) 'The Entrepreneur in Economic Change', in *Entrepreneurship and Economic Development* (New York, NY: The Free Press).

De Soto, H. (2000) *The Mystery of Capital: Why Capitalism Triumphs in the West and Fails Everywhere Else* (New York, NY: Harper & Row).

Djankov, S., R. La Porta, F. Lopez de Silanez and A. Shleifer (2002) 'The Regulation of Entry', *Quarterly Journal of Economics*, vol. 117, no. 1, pp. 1–37.

Djankov, S., E. Miguel, Y. Qian and E. Zhuravskaya (2005) 'Who are Russia's Entrepreneurs?', *Journal of the Euopean Economic Association*, vol. 3, no. 2–3, pp. 587–97.

Frye, T. and E. Zhuravskaya (2000) 'Rackets, Regulation and the Rule of Law', *Journal of Law, Economics, and Organization*, vol. 16, no. 2 pp. 478–502.

Johnson, S., J. McMillan and C. Woodruff (2002) 'Property Rights and Finance', *American Economic Review*, vol. 92, no. 5, pp. 1335–56.

Lao, R.C. (1970) 'Internal–External Control and Competent and Innovative Behavior among Negro College Students', *Journal of Personality and Social Psychology*, vol. 14, pp. 263–70.

Liles, P.R. (1974) *New Business Ventures and the Entrepreneur* (Homewood, IL: Richard D. Irwin. Inc.).

McClelland, D. (1961) *The Achieving Society* (Princeton, NJ: D. Van Nostrand).

McGhee, P.E and V.C. Crandall (1968) 'Beliefs in Internal-External Control of Reinforcement and Academic Performance', *Child Development*.

Roland, G. (2000) *Transition and Economics: Politics, Markets and Firms* (Cambridge, MA: MIT Press).

Roland, G. and T. Verdier (2003) 'Law Enforcement and Transition', *European Economic Review*, vol. 47, pp. 669–85.

Schumpeter, J.A. (1934) *The Theory of Economic Development* (Cambridge, MA: Harvard University Press).

World Bank (2003) *Doing Business in 2004: Understanding Regulation* (Oxford, UK: Oxford University Press).

Young, F. W. (1971) 'A Macrosociological Interpretation of Entrepreneurship', *Entrepreneurship and Economic Development* (London: The Free Press).

6

A Gain with a Drain? Evidence from Rural Mexico on the New Economics of the Brain Drain*

Steve Boucher, Oded Stark, and J. Edward Taylor

1 Introduction

Recent theoretical work suggests conditions under which a positive probability of migration from a developing country stimulates human capital formation in that country and improves the welfare of migrants and non-migrants alike (Stark et al., 1997, 1998; Stark and Wang, 2002). This 'brain gain' hypothesis contrasts with the received, long-held 'brain drain' argument, which stipulates that the migration of skilled workers depletes the human capital stock and lowers welfare in the sending country (Usher, 1977; Blomqvist, 1986). The 'brain gain' view is that a strictly positive probability of migrating to destinations where the returns to human capital are higher than at origin creates incentives to acquire more human capital in migrant-sending areas.

If there are positive education externalities, as modeled by Stark and Wang (2002), then, in the absence of a prospect of migration, the optimal level of human capital that individuals choose to form falls short of the socially optimal level of human capital. In this case, migration could conceivably nudge the level of investment in human capital towards its socially optimal level.

A helpful step towards assessing the validity of the brain gain hypothesis is to conduct an empirical examination of the relationship between the probability of migration and education in migrant-sending areas. Using data from 37 developing countries, Beine et al. (2001) tested the hypothesis of Stark et al. (1997, 1998) and of Stark and Wang (2002) and found evidence that the migration of highly-educated individuals from developing countries has a positive impact on aggregate human capital formation in those countries. While providing some support for the brain gain hypothesis, the value of the study by Beine et al. is limited by the use of aggregate cross-sectional

* We are indebted to Walter Hyll, Ewa Kepinska, and Aaron Smith for helpful advice and enlightening comments.

data, which requires working with restrictive assumptions, as well as by its use of migration instruments to address migration endogeneity. To date, no study has tested the brain gain hypothesis either at the micro level or using a dynamic econometric model.

The objective of the present chapter is to help fill in this void using household data from rural Mexico. Specifically, we seek to test the hypothesis that, other things being equal, the average level of human capital of non-migrants is higher in villages from which a larger share of individuals have migrated to destinations in which the economic returns to schooling are higher than at origin. The received brain drain literature argues that the migration of relatively highly educated individuals depletes human capital stocks at origin. It neglects the consideration that high returns to schooling at migrant destinations may create incentives to invest in schooling at origin. If some of the individuals who respond to these incentives by acquiring more schooling end up not migrating, then the average level of schooling (human capital) at origin may rise. Workers respond to the expected returns that they face, rather than to certain returns, and the higher the expected returns, the higher the acquired education. When the state of nature unfolds, some workers usefully apply their acquired education at destination, others do not end up migrating, but all workers are aware of this ex post variety of possible outcomes when they elect to acquire education in the first place. A brain gain occurs if the 'gain' in human capital by those individuals who end up as non-migrants exceeds the migration-caused 'drain' of human capital.

In the theoretical work on the brain gain (Stark and Wang, 2002), the probability of successful migration is exogenous and is determined by government policy. Such, for example, is the case studied by McKenzie et al. (2006), in which Tongan immigrants to New Zealand are selected by a lottery. In Mexico, where migration policies are at best an imperfect deterrent to international migration and where there is no policy deterrent to internal migration, the ex ante probability of migration is unobservable to the researcher and is endogenous. In particular, it depends upon the networks that a community has developed through past migration (Massey et al., 2005; Munshi, 2003). Rural Mexico is an interesting laboratory setting to test the effect of migration on human capital formation, especially in view of the massive outflow of migrants in recent decades and the resulting concern that this migration is depleting the rural areas of valuable human resources. Rural Mexico has a dichotomy of migration flows (internal and international) for which the selectivity of migration and the signals that migrants send home regarding the returns to, hence the value of, their education are likely to differ.

Our empirical investigation has two components. First, we develop and estimate a dynamic model using village-level data on education and on international and internal migration. This approach is similar in spirit to a country-level study of the brain gain, but with a longitudinal dimension that is lacking in existing studies. The approach yields cautious but illuminating support for the brain gain hypothesis. We find that in rural Mexico, even though internal migrants are more educated than those who stay behind, average village schooling *increases* with internal migration. This finding is consistent with the hypothesis that the dynamic investment effect counteracts and even reverses the static, depletion effect of migration on schooling.

A brain gain explanation for this aggregate village finding implies that children in households with a positive probability of high-skill internal migration have a higher probability of being enrolled in school than do children in households where there is only a low probability of high-skill internal migration. The second component of our empirical strategy attempts to 'unpack' the effect of migration on schooling at a finer micro level, using data on households' access to high-skill internal migration networks and other variables that may influence schooling enrollment. Cross-section findings indicate that access to high-skill internal migration networks significantly increases the probability that children will attend school beyond the compulsory level, whereas access to low-skill internal networks does not. In contrast with internal migration, migration from rural Mexico to the United States does not select positively on schooling, and human capital formation is not higher in households that have high-skill migrants abroad. When there are no returns to schooling upon migration, migration does not encourage schooling. Low-skill international networks do have a modest positive effect on schooling investments. This effect can be attributed to remittances from Mexican migrants in the United States far outweighing remittances from internal (including skilled) migrants, and of schooling investment being a normal good.

Section 2 illustrates the brain gain argument. Section 3 describes the data. Findings from the dynamic model are presented in section 4. Section 5 presents the results of a micro cross-section analysis of school enrollment. Concluding remarks are provided in section 6.

2 Accounting for a brain gain

Let θ_t and θ_t^m denote, respectively, the average of schooling levels of stayers and of migrants, and let Δ_t be the change in the average level of human capital of stayers resulting from a new schooling investment at time t. For a community of origin that starts out at time $t-1$ with an average schooling level of θ_{t-1} and loses a share s_{t-1} of its population to migration, the resulting average human capital stock at period t, θ_t, is given by

$$\theta_t = \frac{\theta_{t-1} - s_{t-1}\theta_{t-1}^m}{1 - s_{t-1}} + \Delta_t. \tag{6.1}$$

Equation (6.1) shows that for a given migrants share of the population, s_{t-1}, the mean education level of the individuals remaining in the village, θ_t, is increasing in the level of their own average schooling investment, Δ_t, and decreasing in the average schooling level of the migrants, θ^m_{t-1}. Differentiation of equation (6.1) with respect to s_{t-1} decomposes the overall effect of migration on education at origin into two components:

$$\frac{\partial \theta_t}{\partial s_{t-1}} = \frac{\theta_{t-1} - \theta^m_{t-1}}{(1 - s_{t-1})^2} + \frac{\partial \Delta_t}{\partial s_{t-1}}. \quad (6.2)$$

The first term on the right-hand side of equation (6.2) is the static depletion effect, which results from migrants taking with them their average human capital. When migration selects positively on schooling, $\theta_{t-1} < \theta^m_{t-1}$, the static effect is negative. The second term is the dynamic investment effect, or the influence of migration on new investments in schooling by the stayers. The brain gain hypothesis is that this effect is positive; that is, if the returns to schooling are larger at destination than at origin, a positive probability of migrating (represented by s_{t-1}) creates an incentive to invest more in schooling at origin at time *t*. The net effect on the average schooling of the stayers depends upon which of these two effects dominates: a brain drain occurs when the average schooling of the migrants is higher than the average schooling of the non-migrants and the effect of investment in rural schooling is small or nil.[1] When the reverse holds, the result is a brain gain.

The effect of migration on average schooling at origin thus depends on two considerations. The first is whether migration selects positively on schooling. If it does not, then migration does not produce a brain drain, nor can it create the dynamic incentives that result in a brain gain.[2] If migration does select positively on schooling, then a second consideration is whether there is a positive investment effect and, if so, whether the ensuing brain gain is sufficient to counteract the negative depletion effect.

3 Data

The data used in our empirical analysis are taken from the Mexico National Rural Household Survey (*Encuesta Nacional a Hogares Rurales de Mexico*, or ENHRUM). The ENHRUM, carried out jointly by the University of California, Davis, and El Colegio de Mexico, Mexico City in 2003, provides retrospective data on migration by individuals from a nationally representative sample of rural households. The sample consists of between 22 and 25 households randomly selected in each of 80 villages. INEGI (*Instituto Nacional de Estadística, Geografía e Información*), Mexico's national census office, designed the sampling frame to provide a statistically reliable characterization of Mexico's population living in rural areas, defined by the Mexican government as communities with fewer than 2,500 inhabitants. For reasons of cost and tractability, individuals in hamlets or dispersed populations of fewer than 500 inhabitants were not included in the survey. The resulting sample is representative of more than 80 per cent of the population that INEGI considers to be rural.

The ENHRUM survey assembled complete migration histories from 1980 through 2002 in 65 of the 80 villages, and from 22 households in each of these villages.[3] For these 1,430 households, histories were constructed for: (i) the household head; (ii) the spouse of the household head; (iii) all the individuals who lived in the household for three months or more in 2002; and (iv) a random sample of sons and daughters of the head and of his/her spouse who lived outside the household for longer than three months in 2002. While the illustration in the preceding section implicitly assumes a single migrant destination, in real life individuals may migrate to different destinations with different returns to education. In our empirical analysis we consider two destinations: international and internal. Education is likely to have a different influence on migration to these two destinations. In the brain drain literature, it is assumed that international migration selects positively on education. However, in our case this is not so. Mora and Taylor (2005) find cross-section evidence that, for rural Mexicans, the association between schooling and migration probabilities is significant and positive for internal migration, but negative for migration to the United States, which usually entails unauthorized entry and work in low-skill jobs. Our findings using longitudinal village data, presented below, echo that evidence. Data from the migration histories make it possible to calculate the population shares of domestic and international migrants in each surveyed community and in each year from 1980 through 2002.

Information on education (years of completed schooling and number of repeated years) was collected for all family members. This information was used to reconstruct average levels of village schooling for each year from 1980 through 2002. Human capital in the source area at time t was calculated as the average level of schooling of all non-migrants. In total, there are $(65 \times 23 =)$ 1,495 village-year observations on migration and average education.[4] The retrospective migration and schooling data were also used in the cross-section analysis of school enrollment, presented in section 5.

4 Migration and schooling: a dynamic village model

As already noted, a brain gain arises if migration selects positively on schooling and the dynamic investment effect dominates the static depletion effect. If migration selects positively on schooling, there can be either a brain drain or a brain gain. If migration is positively selective with respect to productive attributes such as educational level, then villages with a better educated workforce tend to generate more migration than villages with a poorly educated workforce. Thus, we first study the effect of the selectivity of internal and international migration from rural Mexico on schooling. We then examine the net effect of internal and international migration on the average schooling level in the origin villages.

Our dynamic econometric model is in the spirit of cross-country models of brain drain and brain gain, but with a time dimension that is lacking in those models due to the absence of harmonized time series data on country human capital and migration. The village panel data from Mexico make it possible to estimate a dynamic rather than a cross-section model of the impact of migration on human capital at migrant origins, and to include fixed effects to control for unobserved variables that may confound cross-section estimates.

The village is a natural unit of analysis for contemplating educational spillover effects in rural areas, and is more fitting than smaller units (households, individuals) for the study of the effect of migration on the average level of human capital in migrant-sending areas. Villages also have the advantage of being intuitive units with respect to information and networks, which impact upon and shape migration flows. Many of the variables that determine the net benefits of migration are essentially village-level variables: infrastructure, land quality, distance to migrant destinations, and so on, vary more amongst rather than within villages. We can control for the influence of the village level variables using village fixed effects.

Using the longitudinal data provided by the ENHRUM, we estimate a dynamic, three equation village migration and schooling model of the following form:

$$s^I_{t,i} = \beta_{0,i} + \beta_1 s^I_{t-1,i} + \beta_2 s^N_{t-1,i} + \beta_3 \theta_{t-1,i} + \beta_4 t + \varepsilon^I_{t,i} \tag{6.3a}$$

$$s^N_{t,i} = \gamma_{0,i} + \gamma_1 s^I_{t-1,i} + \gamma_2 s^N_{t-1,i} + \gamma_3 \theta_{t-1,i} + \gamma_4 t + \varepsilon^N_{t,i} \tag{6.3b}$$

$$\theta_{t,i} = \alpha_{0,i} + \alpha_1 s^I_{t-1,i} + \alpha_2 s^N_{t-1,i} + \alpha_3 \theta_{t-1,i} + \alpha_4 t + \varepsilon^\theta_{t,i} \tag{6.3c}$$

where $s^I_{t,i}$ and $s^N_{t,i}$ are the shares of individuals from village i who are international migrants and internal migrants in year t, respectively, and $\theta_{t,i}$ and $\theta_{t-1,i}$ denote mean years of schooling of adults in the community of origin in year t and $t-1$, respectively. The regressors include the lagged dependent variables and a time trend, t. The parameters $\beta_{0,i}$, $\gamma_{0,i}$ and $\alpha_{0,i}$ are village fixed effects. The errors $\varepsilon^I_{t,i}$, $\varepsilon^N_{t,i}$ and $\varepsilon^\theta_{t,i}$ are assumed to be approximately normally and independently distributed across equations and over time. Effects of time-invariant unobserved village variables and time-varying variables affecting migration and human capital investment in a similar fashion across all villages are picked up by the fixed effects and trend coefficients, respectively. Because of this, no village-level instruments to control for the endogeneity of migration shares, the value placed on schooling, or other variables are needed or, indeed, can be included in this model. The coefficients β_1, γ_2, and α_3 represent the dynamic adjustments to exogenous shocks that divert the

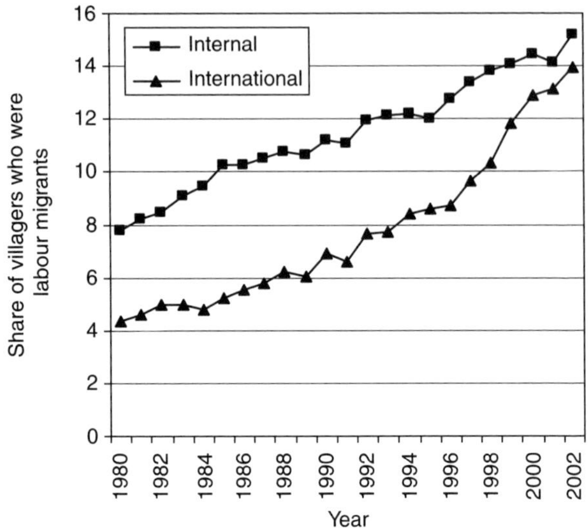

Figure 6.1 Trends in internal and international migration from rural Mexico, 1980–2002
Source: ENHRUM.

respective dependent variables from their trends. Stability of the dynamics requires that each of these coefficients is less than one.

Since equations (6.3a), (6.3b), and (6.3c) share the same right-hand side variables, there is no efficiency gain from estimating them as a system (cf., for example, Greene, 2003, p. 343). The lagged migration share and schooling variables are correlated with $\beta_{0,i}$, $\gamma_{0,i}$ and $\alpha_{0,i}$ because migration shares and schooling in a village are correlated with the village fixed effect in all periods. Thus, we estimate each equation in the model using the Generalized Method of Moments (GMM) estimator of Arellano and Bond (1991). This estimator is free from the bias that arises upon estimation of dynamic panel models by least squares dummy variable estimators.

The effect of the selectivity of migration on schooling

Figures 6.1 and 6.2 illustrate trends between 1980 and 2002 in the three dependent variables, using the retrospective data on migration and on schooling gathered in the ENHRUM. The clear upward trends evident in both figures reveal that migration to internal and international destinations increased sharply during this period, as did the average schooling of migrants and of non-migrants. Table 6.1 reports mean adult education levels and migration shares for the sample villages over the entire 22-year period. The average shares of international and internal migrants in total village populations were 7.8 per cent and 11.5 per cent, respectively. With the exception

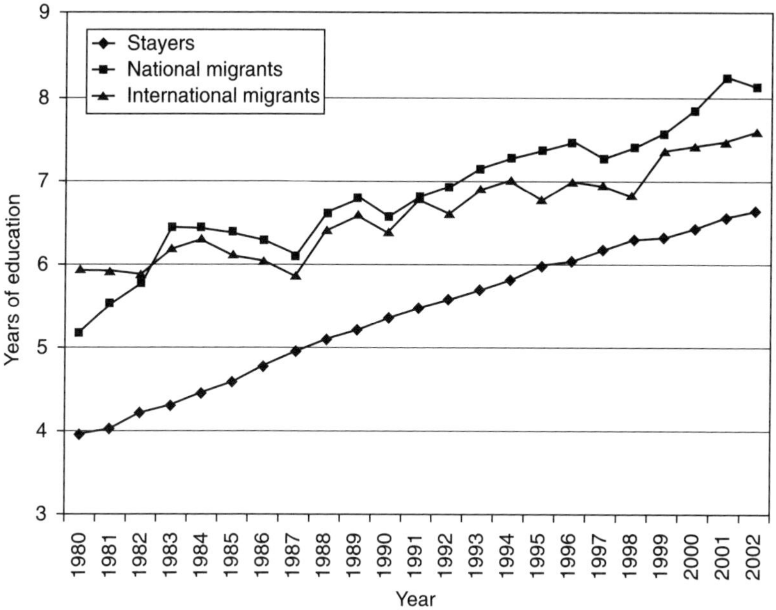

Figure 6.2 Mean education of migrants and stayers (excluding children under 18)
Source: ENHRUM.

of the first three years of the recall period, the average education of internal migrants ('National Migrants' in Figure 6.2) was slightly higher than that of international migrants. For the full 22-year period, the average completed schooling of internal migrants was 6.9 years, and of international migrants it was 6.7 years. The average completed schooling of adult stayers was only 5.4 years for the full 22-year period and was consistently and significantly below the average schooling levels of both migrant groups.

The parameter estimates for equations (6.3a) through (6.3c) are reported in Table 6.2. The results reveal that when we control for the other variables in equation (6.3a), international migration from rural Mexico does not select positively on schooling. The estimated coefficient on the lagged schooling variable in the international migration share equation (equation 6.3b) is −0.16, and is not significantly different from zero (first row of Panel (1)). It is likely that this finding reflects low returns to schooling for village migrants (who are mostly undocumented) in United States labour markets. We should not then expect international migration to result in a significant brain drain in the population represented in our data. Yet rewarding international migration by villagers with little human capital could negatively affect the incentive to invest in human capital by raising the opportunity cost of going to school. Alternatively, through remittances, this migration

Table 6.1 Mean education levels and migrant shares in the sample villages between 1980 and 2002

	Mean	*Standard deviation*
Completed years of schooling of:		
Adult international migrants	6.7	2.9
Adult internal migrants	6.9	2.9
Adult non-migrants	5.4	1.8
Share of villagers that were:		
International migrants	7.8	10.2
Internal migrants	11.5	10.4

Source: Authors' calculations using data from ENHRUM.

Table 6.2 Regression results for the dynamic migration and education model using the Arellano–Bond procedure

	Equation (1): Share of villagers at international destinations ($s^I_{t,i}$)		*Equation (2): Share of villagers at internal destinations ($s^N_{t,i}$)*		*Equation (3): Average schooling of stayers ($\theta_{t,i}$)*	
Variable	*Coefficient*	*z-statistic*	*Coefficient*	*z-statistic*	*Coefficient*	*z-statistic*
$\theta_{t-1,i}$	−0.16	−0.56	**1.54**	**5.23**	**0.89**	**27.81**
$s^I_{t-1,i}$	**0.71**	**21.36**	0.02	0.57	0.00	−0.03
$s^I_{t-2,i}$	**0.19**	**6.63**	0.01	0.18	0.00	0.90
$s^N_{t-1,i}$	−0.36	−1.29	**0.90**	**30.55**	**0.01**	**2.78**
T	**0.14**	**3.36**	**−0.16**	**−3.67**	0.01	0.95
Arellano–Bond m2 test (p-value)	0.52		0.88		0.39	
R-squared	0.94		0.93		0.98	
N (village-years)	1430					

Note: Each equation was estimated with village fixed effects.

could contribute to human capital formation by providing rural households with financial resources to invest in schooling.

By contrast, internal migration selects positively and significantly on schooling. Other things being equal, a 1-year increase in the average schooling of village adults in a given period is associated with an increase in migration to internal destinations of 1.54 percentage points in a subsequent period (the first row of Panel (2) in Table 6.2). Given that, on average, in 2002, 15 per cent of villagers were internal migrants, this amounts to a 10 per cent increase in internal migration.[5] In a static model, we could expect internal migration to considerably deplete human capital in rural areas. The question that we seek to answer is whether this static effect may be dampened or reversed as high returns to schooling from internal migration create incentives for human capital investment in villages.

Testing for a brain gain

Controlling for the underlying dynamics and village fixed effects, the brain drain hypothesis implies that $\alpha_2 < 0$. Given our finding that internal migration positively selects on schooling, a non-negative dynamic relationship between internal migration and average village schooling refutes the brain drain hypothesis and lends support to the hypothesis that internal migration creates incentives to invest in human capital that are powerful enough to at least cancel out the negative static effect of migration on the average level of the village human capital. To wit, if the dynamic investment effect more than compensates for the static human capital loss, the average village schooling level could even be higher with migration than without migration. No relationship is implied in the case of international migration, which does not select on schooling, however.

Panel 3 of Table 6.2 reports the parameter estimates of the schooling equation. As expected, international migration does not have a significant effect on the next period's average schooling of non-migrants. In contrast, internal migration has a small, but statistically significant, *positive* effect on the average schooling of non-migrants. This finding suggests that the dynamic incentive effect of internal migration on human capital formation more than offsets the static brain drain effect.

We might suspect that the positive effect of internal migration on schooling is the result of a relaxation of liquidity constraints via remittances instead of being the result of the incentive effect. While we do not have in hand longitudinal data on remittances which would enable us to distinguish empirically between these two effects, we believe that the latter effect does not drive the positive association between internal migration and schooling.[6] Remittances from internal migrants in the sample averaged US$83 in 2002. By contrast, as shown in Table 6.3, total per-pupil expenditures averaged US$171 for grades 1 through 6 (primary), US$307 for grades 7 through 9 (lower secondary), and US$821 for grades 10 through 12 (upper secondary, or high school). The higher schooling costs for secondary education are attributable primarily to transportation and to meals away from home. Due to the presence of elementary schools in all villages in the sample, transportation costs are minimal for primary students. The absence of high schools in most villages results in both transportation and meal costs being highest for grades 10 through 12. (Only 11 per cent of villages in the sample had a high school; 69 per cent had a lower secondary school.) Since the opportunity costs of attending school can be expected to increase as children grow older and become more productive on the farm or in family businesses, the overall cost of attending grades 10

Table 6.3 Average schooling expenditures per pupil, by schooling level in 2002 (US dollars)

Schooling expenditure	*Elementary (1–6)*	*Lower secondary (7–9)*	*Upper secondary (10–12)*
Lodging	3.16	10.46	80.56
Tuition and fees	11.05	22.01	115.23
Transportation	15.82	60.78	249.66
Meals	83.95	135.86	255.11
Uniforms	25.95	34.65	32.82
Supplies	21.16	28.84	49.56
Other	9.78	14.62	37.86
Total	170.87	307.23	820.79
Sample size (number of pupils)	1,287	502	304

Source: Authors' calculations using data from ENHRUM.

through 12 is even higher, and the discrepancy between this cost and the cost of attending lower grades is correspondingly larger.

The remaining results in Table 6.2 indicate that the village migration and schooling equations are stable (the estimated coefficients on each of the lagged-dependent variables are significantly less than 1.0). Nevertheless, there is strong persistence both in the migration equations and in the education equation. The trend variable is significant and positive for international migration, negative for internal migration, and insignificant for non-migrants' schooling. There are no cross-effects of lagged migration between the two migration equations.

5 Migration and school enrollment: an individual retrospective

The findings from the dynamic model suggest that the positive investment effect of internal migration on schooling is sufficiently strong to reverse the negative depletion effect. The brain gain hypothesis implies that, other things being equal, children in households with a positive probability of lucrative high-skill migration are more likely to be enrolled in school than children in households where there is only a low probability of such migration.

In this section, we use individual-level, retrospective data to test how the number of high-skill family migrants at internal destinations affects the likelihood of school enrollment in the *households* at origin. By using retrospective household information on migration and schooling of individuals, it is possible to estimate the impact of household migration networks, by skill level, on each child's enrollment status at time t, given that the child was enrolled in school at time $t-1$, and controlling for selected individual and household characteristics, as well as for village fixed effects.

A network can be construed as a set of individuals linked together by a web of social interactions. In the economic sphere, the network serves as a conduit of personal exchanges that pass on job-related information. This transmission shapes and expands the employment opportunities of members of the network and improves their labour market outcomes.

Migrant networks can affect the evaluation by a potential migrant (or the evaluation by a potential migrant's parent) of the returns to staying in school in at least two ways: access and information. Migrants holding high-skill jobs may facilitate access to, and placement in, such jobs by highly educated new arrivals, in a way that migrants holding low-skill jobs may not. Because of this access effect, we predict that children in households with high-skill migrant networks will be more likely to enroll in school than children in households who lack such high-skill migrant networks. In addition, migrant networks convey information about the earnings of relatively educated workers employed in high-skill jobs in migrant destinations. High-skill networks are likely to convey this information more accurately and more effectively than low-skill networks. A low variance associated with the information signal from high-skill networks, in and by itself, will tend to reinforce the positive access and placement effect.

Let E_{jht} denote the enrollment status of child j in household h at time t. The variable E_{jht} takes on the value of 1 if the child is enrolled, and 0 otherwise. The child is enrolled if the net benefits of enrollment, B_{jht}, are positive. This general formulation is akin to other models of schooling investment, including Todd and Wolpin's (2006) matching estimators of program effects, and the grade progression models of Cameron and Heckman (2001). Net benefits from enrollment have a deterministic (b_{jht}) as well as a random (v_{jht}) component; that is, $B_{jht} = b_{jht} + v_{jht}$. The probability of observing enrollment is then

$$\Pr[B_{jht} > 0] = \Pr[-v_{jht} < b_{jht}] = F(b_{jht}), \tag{6.4}$$

where F is the cumulative distribution function of $(-v_{jht})$. The deterministic component of net benefits depends on individual and household characteristics, Z_{jht}, that may vary over time. Our hypotheses center on how the destination (d = internal, international) and skill level (s = high, low) of the household level migration networks of child j at time t, NET_{jhtds}, affect the enrollment decision via their influence on the net benefits of schooling. Therefore,

$$b_{jht} = \alpha + Z_{jht}\beta + \sum_{d,s} NET_{jhtds}\gamma_{ds} + \delta t + G_{t-1}\phi \tag{6.5}$$

where G_{t-1} is a vector of dummy variables indicating the grade in which the child was enrolled at time $t-1$, and ϕ is a vector of parameters measuring the net benefits of continuing enrollment at each grade level. The null hypothesis that the skill composition of networks does not affect the net benefits of enrollment is H_0: $\gamma_{ds} = \gamma_{ds'}$ for $s \neq s'$. The null hypothesis that the effects of networks of different skill levels do not differ across migrant destinations is $H_0 : \gamma_{ds} = \gamma_{d's}$ for $d \neq d'$.

The variables measuring the skill level of migration networks include the number of family members with low (grades 0–9) and high (10 or greater) school completion levels at internal and international migrant destinations in the year prior to the year in which the successive enrollment decision is observed.[7] Variables in the vector Z_{jht} include the child's grade level at $t-1$; the number of school-aged children in the household; the child's gender; and the child's grade-point average in the final year at school, a proxy for intellectual ability. The child's age in 2002 is used to control for t. The model also controls for the maximum level of schooling obtained by either the household head or his or her spouse. In addition, the model includes a dichotomous variable equal to 1 if at least one of the child's maternal grandparents was literate and zero otherwise, and an identical variable measuring paternal-grandparent literacy. These variables control for unobserved parental characteristics such as attitudes towards schooling or the role model effect of parents regarding schooling. We also control for the gender of the household head (1 if male, 0 if female), and we include a dichotomous variable equal to 1 if an indigenous language is spoken in the household, and zero otherwise. Because income data are only available for 2002 and the enrollment data cover a 23-year period (from 1980 to 2002), income could not be included in the regression. The inclusion of determinants of income other than parental education and family size, including landholdings and wealth measured in 2001, did not alter any of the key findings presented below, nor did the use of village migration instruments, including village participation in the Bracero programme, or the incorporation of dummies indicating whether or not the village sample had at least one United States migrant in 1980, in lieu of the village fixed effects.[8]

School attendance in Mexico is compulsory through grade 9.[9] Logit estimates of equation (6.5) using a sample of all children between the ages of 6 (potential first graders) and 17 (potential 12th graders), and controlling for grade level at time $t-1$, revealed no significant relationship between any of the migration variables and the likelihood of enrollment. Figure 6.3 summarizes the probability of enrollment at time t by grade level of children enrolled at time $t-1$ during the 1980–2002 period. It reveals that the probability of enrollment is high and nearly flat up through grade 6, decreases between the 6th and 7th grades, and decreases again, more sharply, between the 9th and 10th grades. The trends depicted in Figure 6.3 mirror those presented in Sadoulet and de Janvry (2004) who draw on a large, government-generated PROGRESA data set.

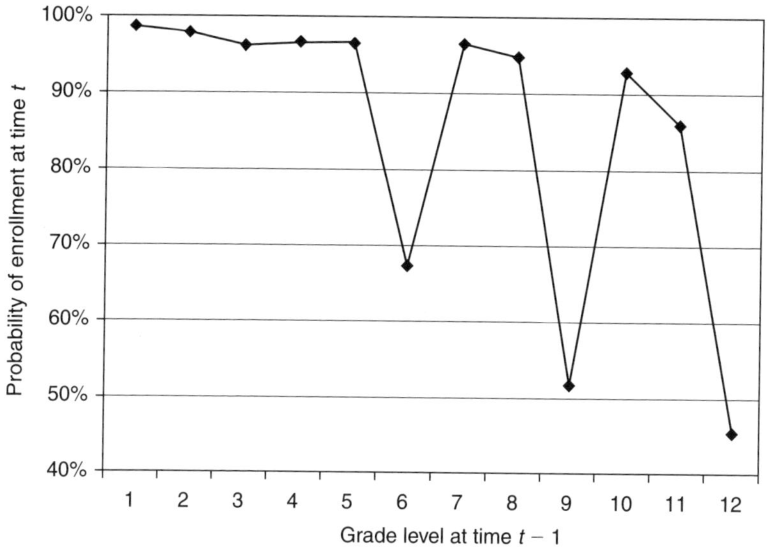

Figure 6.3 Probability of school enrollment of rural Mexican children aged 6 to 18 at time t, by grade level of enrollment at time $t-1$, 1980–2002[12]
Source: ENHRUM.

Table 6.4 presents the results of the logit estimation when we restrict our sample to include only children who were in the 9th grade at time $t-1$. We find that high-skill internal migrant networks significantly *increase* the likelihood of high-school enrollment at time t (significant at below the 0.05 level).[10] In contrast, low-skill internal and high-skill international migrant networks have no significant effect on enrollment probabilities.[11] Apparently, the network effect on additional schooling in international high-skill migration is weak. We return to this finding shortly. McKenzie and Rapoport (2006) and Hanson and Woodruff (2003) find significant cross-section effects of household United States migration experience on grade-years of schooling, negative in the first case and positive in the second. These studies do not consider the effect on schooling attainment of the skill composition of migrant networks or of the potentially heterogeneous effect of internal versus international migrant networks. Consistent with their estimates, we find that parent (household head) levels of school completion have a significant positive influence on schooling investment. Intellectual ability, proxied by grade point average in the final year at school, also has a significant positive effect.

It might be argued that a positive effect of networks on school enrollment is due, at least in part, to a positive income effect of remittances that loosens the financial constraints on investment in schooling. If this

Table 6.4 Logit estimation of students' probability of continuing their education after the ninth grade

Variable definition	*Variable mean*	*Standard deviation*	*Coefficient estimate*	*z-statistic*
Age in 2002	22.80	5.80	−0.062	4.26[a]
Sex (1 = male)	0.50	0.50	−0.202	1.45
No. of school-age children in household	3.2	1.62	−0.229	4.68[a]
GPA (out of 10)	8.3	0.87	0.298	3.55[a]
Education of household head	6.4	1.62	0.158	5.53[a]
Sex of the household head (1 = male)	0.88	0.33	0.509	2.41[b]
Indigenous (indicator)	0.13	0.34	−0.059	0.19
Paternal grandparents can read and write (indicator)	0.71	0.46	0.218	1.15
Maternal grandparents can read and write (indicator)	0.59	0.49	−0.310	1.65[c]
International migration network-low education	0.14	0.48	0.483	3.06[a]
International migration network-high education	0.04	0.27	−0.044	0.16
Internal migration network-low education	0.16	0.50	−0.097	0.66
Internal migration network-high education	0.04	0.22	1.059	2.49[b]
Village fixed effects	N/A	N/A	N/A	included
Sample Size[d]	1,259			

Notes: [a] significant at 1%, [b] significant at 5%, [c] significant at 10%.
[d] This sample includes all household members who are not household heads (or spouses of household heads), and the random sample of sons and daughters of either the head or his/her spouse living outside the household who were chosen for the detailed survey, so that the GPA variable could be included. A similar regression was performed that included the children living outside the household not chosen for the detailed survey, which increases the sample to 1829. The significance increases for all the variables of interest, but the results to not change.

were the case, we would expect the largest network effect to be associated with the largest remittance-generating migrant destination. Table 6.5 compares average annual remittances from (relatively) highly-educated migrants and little-educated migrants at internal and international destinations, using the 2002 cross-sectional data. Remittances from highly-educated internal migrants are 25 per cent higher than remittances from little-educated internal migrants. However, remittances from international migrants, both little-educated and highly-educated, are 1,500 per cent higher than remittances from highly-educated internal migrants. In addition to suggesting that remittances from United States migrants are not sensitive to migrants' schooling,

Table 6.5 Remittances by education level of internal and international migrants (US dollars)

Migrant destination	*Annual remittances*	*Schooling level of migrant*		*All migrants*
		0–9 Years	*>9 Years*	
Internal	Mean	81	100	83
	Standard deviation	375	300	366
	Sample size	1,463	222	1,685
International	Mean	1,504	1,505	1,504
	Standard deviation	3,082	3,068	3,078
	Sample size	729	98	827
Total	Mean	554	530	551
	Standard deviation	1,923	1,829	1,911
	Sample size	2,192	320	2,512

Source: Authors' calculations using data from ENHRUM.

these findings demonstrate that international migration is vastly superior to internal migration in terms of generating income that *could* be used to finance school expenditures. Although international high-skill networks do not promote human capital investment, low-skill networks have a modest positive effect that is consistent with a financial constraints argument. The finding that high-skill networks do not have this effect suggests that educated family members who migrate abroad remit not only money, but also a signal that discourages schooling investment, and this negative signal is sufficiently large to counteract any positive financial effect that remittances might have.

Strictly speaking, it is high-skill migrant networks that lead to high-skill jobs, and not high-skill migrant networks as such, that should be presumed to create an incentive for human capital formation in the village. Suppose, though, that we were to find that belonging or being linked to a high-skill migrant network did *not* increase the likelihood of school enrollment. We would then suspect that such a network did not convert skill endowments into skilled jobs. Conversely, if we were to find that belonging to a high-skill network did entail an increased likelihood of school enrollment, we would suspect that the network was effective as a skilled-jobs network. Otherwise, the network association would have indicated that skill acquisition was useless. Put differently, it would not be logical to expect that the effect of a high-skill network on *skill acquisition* was positive if the network connection led to jobs that were independent of skill. Furthermore, if a systematic relationship between skill acquisition and skill network affiliation is governed by an unobserved familial trait, such as a taste for or tendency to acquire skills, we would not expect the relationship to be present in one context (say, internal migrant networks) yet absent in another (say, international migrant networks).

Even though internal migration is relatively inefficient as a generator of remittance income for rural households, past migration by skilled family members to internal destinations, where the returns to schooling are high, appears to send an enticing signal that has the effect of increasing rural households' demand for schooling above and beyond the compulsory level. The picture that emerges is that it is not the amount of remittances that determines investment in schooling. A dollar remitted from a poorly educated family migrant in the United States does not convey the same appeal as a 'dollar' remitted by a skilled family migrant in Mexico. One dollar of remittances turns out not to be equal to another dollar of remittances.

Our findings echo those of Kochar (2004), who reports that in India in the period 1983–94, the urban rate of return to schooling affects the incidence of rural schooling, especially among the rural households most likely to seek urban employment. Kochar found that among rural households likely to engage in rural-to-urban migration – that is, landless as opposed to land-owning households – the urban rate of return to schooling made it significantly more likely that children will complete rural middle school. This effect was larger than the corresponding effect for landowning households. Our findings link educational levels in the wake of migration to the human capital content of family migration networks.

6 Conclusions

The analysis of data from rural Mexico leads us to reject the brain drain hypothesis, both for international migration and for internal migration. Relatively highly educated villagers are selected into internal migration. However, controlling for the underlying dynamics of human capital formation in rural areas, the effect of (lagged) internal migration propensities on average schooling of non-migrants is positive. The returns to – and the continued possibility of – internal migration appear to create incentives for investment in schooling which, in turn, reverse the static, human capital depleting effect of internal migration. International migration from rural Mexico does not select on schooling and has no significant effect on the average education of non-migrants.

Cross-section grade-progression analysis suggests that, *controlling for other household and village characteristics*, the presence of high-skill family migration networks at internal destinations significantly increases the likelihood that a child will be enrolled beyond the compulsory (9th grade) level. In contrast, low-skill internal networks and high-skill international networks have no significant effect on school enrollment. That high-skill international migration does not have a significant positive effect on schooling is not inconsistent with the brain gain hypothesis advanced by Stark and Wang. The brain gain model *assumes* that the returns to schooling are high in a foreign developed country compared to the sending developing country. Yet among the rural Mexican population, migration to the United States does not significantly select on schooling since the returns to schooling for unauthorized migrants are low.

Rural Mexico, with its poorly educated population, presents a particularly challenging setting in which to test a brain gain model. Both our static estimations and dynamic estimations lend support to the brain gain hypothesis in the case of internal migration. Internal migrants are significantly better educated than non-migrants (7.5 versus 5.5 years of completed schooling in 2002, a 36 per cent disparity), and the effect of schooling on internal migration is positive and statistically significant. In a static world, given the large magnitude of migration to internal destinations, such migration could have depleted rural human capital stocks. The fact that it *increases* the schooling of non-migrants is consistent with the existence of a positive incentive effect of gainful internal migration on rural human capital formation. The finding that high-skill internal migration networks increase the probability of enrollment in post-compulsory (high-school) education provides further evidence that the probability of migration encourages investment in schooling in rural Mexico.

Notes

1. If migration competes with schooling by raising the opportunity cost of attending school, the investment effect could be negative. However, this will probably occur upon low-skill international migration, that is, upon migration for which $\theta_{t-1} < \theta^m_{t-1}$.
2. Obviously, migration by relatively low-skill individuals could, in and by itself, raise the average schooling of those left behind. This increase in average does not occur as a result of enhanced formation of human capital.
3. In 15 of the 80 villages, the migration recall module of the survey was not applied to the children of household heads who were no longer living in the household. Those villages are not included in our empirical analysis.
4. In the regression analysis, one year per village is lost due to the use of lagged education and lagged migration variables. Thus, the sample size becomes 1,430. The sample is balanced in the sense that each of the villages appears in each of the 22 years of the panel.
5. Arellano and Bond's m_2 test rejects the null hypothesis of no serial correlation in the international migration equation with a single lag. When a second lag is included, its coefficient is significant and the m_2 test no longer rejects the null of serial correlation. Adding the second lag does not substantially affect any of the parameter estimates in the internal migration equation.
6. Remittance data are available only in the 2002 cross-section.
7. For example, if a household had 1 family member with low schooling and 3 family members with high schooling at an internal migrant destination, then

the low- and high-skill internal migrant variables would take on the values of 1 and 3, respectively. Family members include: the household head, the spouse of the household head, all individuals living in the household for at least three months in 2002, and all children of either the head or his/her spouse who lived outside the household for longer than three months in 2002.

8. Landholdings changed little during this time period because most were *ejido*, or reform-sector lands that could not be bought or sold until recent (Article 27) reforms.
9. As in other contexts and settings, laws are not necessarily enforced.
10. This estimation controls for village fixed effects. However, for individuals in the same household who completed the 9th grade, there were not sufficient observations of successive enrollment to estimate this model-controlling for household fixed effects. Of course, it is not possible to control for individual fixed effects while restricting the sample to individuals in a given grade level.
11. We repeated this procedure considering only children who were in the 6th grade in 2001, but none of the network variables was found to be significant.
12. The horizontal axis measures the child's observed grade level in 2001, the year prior to the survey year. The vertical axis measures the probability of enrollment (at the next grade level) in 2002.

References

Arellano, Manuel and Stephen R. Bond (1991) 'Some Tests for Specification of Panel Data: Monte Carlo Evidence and an Application to Employment Equations', *Review of Economic Studies* 58: 277–97.

Beine, Michel, Frédéric Docquier, and Hillel Rapoport (2001) 'Brain Drain and Economic Growth: Theory and Evidence', *Journal of Development Economics* 64(1): 275–89.

Blomqvist, Ake G. (1986) 'International Migration of Educated Manpower and Social Rates of Return to Education in LDCs', *International Economic Review* 27(1): 165–74.

Cameron, Stephen V. and James J. Heckman (2001) 'The Dynamics of Educational Attainment for Black, Hispanic and White Males', *Journal of Political Economy* 109(3): 455–99.

Greene, William H. (2003) *Econometric Analysis*, 5th edition. Upper Saddle River, NJ: Prentice Hall.

Hanson, Gordon H. and Christopher Woodruff (2003) Emigration and Educational Attainment in Mexico. Mimeo, University of California at San Diego.

Kochar, Anjini (2004) 'Urban Influences on Rural Schooling in India', *Journal of Development Economics* 74: 113–36.

Massey, Douglas S., Joaquin Arango, Graeme Hugo, Ali Kouaouci, Adela Pellegrino and J. Edward Taylor (2005) *Worlds in Motion: Understanding International Migration at the End of the Millennium*. New York: Oxford University Press.

McKenzie, David, John Gibson and Steven Stillman (2006) 'How Important is Selection? Experimental Versus Non-experimental Measures of the Income Gains from Migration', The World Bank Policy Research Working Paper Number 3906.

McKenzie, David and Hillel Rapoport (2006) 'Can Migration Reduce Educational Attainment? Evidence from Mexico', The World Bank Policy Research Working Paper Number 3952.

Mora, Jorge and J. Edward Taylor (2005) 'Determinants of Migration, Destination, and Sector Choice: Disentangling Individual, Household, and Community Effects', in

Çaglar Özden and Maurice Schiff (eds), *International Migration, Remittances, and the Brain Drain*. New York: Palgrave Macmillan.

Munshi, Kaivan (2003) 'Networks in the Modern Economy: Mexican Migrants in the US Labor Market', *Quarterly Journal of Economics* 18(2): 549–99.

Sadoulet, Elisabeth and Alain de Janvry (2004) 'Making Conditional Cash Transfer Programs More Efficient: Designing for Maximum Effect of the Conditionality', *The World Bank Economic Review* 20(1): 1–29.

Stark, Oded, Christian Helmenstein, and Alexia Prskawetz (1997) 'A Brain Drain with a Brain Gain', *Economics Letters* 55: 227–34.

Stark, Oded, Christian Helmenstein, and Alexia Prskawetz (1998) 'Human Capital Depletion, Human Capital Formation, and Migration: A Blessing or a "Curse"?', *Economics Letters* 60: 363–7.

Stark, Oded and Yong Wang (2002) 'Inducing Human Capital Formation: Migration as a Substitute for Subsidies', *Journal of Public Economics* 86: 29–46.

Todd, Petra E. and Kenneth I. Wolpin (2006) 'Assessing the Impact of a School Subsidy Program in Mexico: Using a Social Experiment to Validate a Behavioral Model of Child Schooling and Fertility', *American Economic Review* 96: 1384–417.

Usher, Dan (1977) 'Public Property and the Effects of Migration upon Other Residents of the Migrants' Countries of Origin and Destination', *Journal of Political Economy* 85(5): 1001–20.

7

The Brain Drain, 'Educated Unemployment', Human Capital Formation, and Economic Betterment*

Oded Stark and C. Simon Fan

1 Introduction

Labour migration has long been a topic of intense interest in population research in general and in development economics in particular. The topic has been gaining added appeal in the era of globalization. The received wisdom has been that such migration results in a detrimental brain drain for the developing countries (for a systematic review see Bhagwati and Wilson, 1989).[1] A recent and growing literature argues that the brain drain is accompanied by a beneficial brain gain.[2] The new writings contend that compared with a closed economy, an economy open to migration differs not only in the opportunities that workers face but also in the structure of the incentives that they confront; higher prospective returns to human capital in a foreign country impinge favourably on human capital formation decisions at home.

We seek to synthesize and extend the two strands of the received literature, and to analyze both the positive and the negative impact of migration in a unified framework. The basic analytical construct of this chapter is delineated in Fan and Stark (2007), who show that the prospect of international migration results not only in a brain drain but also in 'educated unemployment', which is an important feature of the labour market in many developing countries.[3] In this chapter we conduct our analysis in the framework of a 'threshold externality' of human capital, which enables us to analyze the negative and the positive impact of migration in different periods, and to make welfare comparisons.

We extend the received literature of 'harmful brain drain' by showing that in the short run international migration can result in 'educated

* We are indebted to Nicola Fuchs-Schündeln, to two anonymous referees, to Katarzyna Saczuk, and to Anna Zylicz for helpful advice and constructive suggestions. Financial Support from the Humboldt Foundation, the Sohmen Foundation, and the International Centre for the Study of East Asian Development is gratefully acknowledged.

unemployment' and in overeducation, as well as in a brain drain. Specifically, in contrast to the literature that views the brain drain as the only negative consequence of international migration of skilled workers, we identify *three* possible negative short-run consequences. First, consistent with the 'traditional' view, migration leads to a reduction in the 'stock' of better-educated individuals, which in turn reduces the average income in the developing country. Second, since some educated individuals who would otherwise have taken jobs are lured into further education only to end up unemployed, output shrinks. Third, since the possibility of migration induces individuals in a developing country to acquire higher education, when some of these individuals end up remaining in the country, the returns from their education could be less than its costs. From their perspective, they are overeducated.[4] If the country's economy cannot 'take off', then these individuals' overeducation is socially inefficient (in the short run). Moreover, the simulation shows that the costs of the two new negative consequences of migration introduced in this chapter, namely 'educated unemployment' and overeducation, can amount to significant losses for the individuals affected, who may constitute a substantial proportion of the educated individuals. On the other hand, in per capita terms, the direct cost of a brain drain can be relatively small if the proportion of the educated individuals in the economy is small.

However, we next demonstrate that in the long run (one generation down the road), the legacy of a relaxation in migration policy prompts a 'take-off' of the economy. Drawing on the studies by Azariadis and Drazen (1990) and Galor and Stark (1994) that link the long-run growth in a country's output with the average level of the country's human capital, we emphasize the role of a 'threshold externality' of human capital in economic development. (Azariadis and Drazen (1990) and Pritchett (1997) provide evidence in support of the assumption of a threshold externality, and Fan (2004) offers an explanation for the existence of the threshold externality in economic development by showing that a poor economy will engage in international trade, which will accelerate its growth, if and only if its average level of human capital is sufficiently high.) In a dynamic framework we show that the brain drain is accompanied by a 'brain gain'; that the ensuing 'brain gain' can result in a higher average level of human capital in the home country; that the higher average level of human capital can prompt the 'take-off' of the economy; and that the 'take-off' can bite into the unemployment rate. In such a setting, overeducation can become dynamically efficient (due to the intergenerational externality effect of human capital) even though it may be statically inefficient. Thus, we depict a setting in which rather than being to blame for human capital drain and output contraction, the migration of educated workers is the harbinger of human capital gain and output growth. An analysis of the entire dynamics associated with the response of educated workers to the prospect of migration therefore raises the intriguing possibility that what at first sight appears to constitute a curse is, in fact, a blessing in disguise. Our results are more dramatic than those reported in the received literature because in our present framework the prospect of migration is taken to entail both depletion of human capital and unemployment of human capital, which stacks the cards more firmly against viewing migration as a catalyst for growth.

Our analytical predictions appear to be in line with some empirical observations. For example, from 1960 to 1980, countries characterized by high rates of migration of skilled labour (such as India and Ireland) were among those countries that experienced the lowest rates of economic growth (Summers and Heston, 1991). However, since the late 1980s (that is, after approximately one generation), both India and Ireland have experienced rapid economic growth, which to a large extent has been due to an expansion of their skill-intensive information technology sector.[5] Thus, by analyzing and synthesizing both the 'traditional' and the new views of migration, we present a framework that is in line with some intertemporal evidence.

In section 2 we set up the basic analytical framework. Section 3 investigates the negative and the positive impact of migration in the framework of a 'threshold externality' of human capital and of a rational-expectations equilibrium. Section 4 contains the welfare analysis. Section 5 presents simulations aimed at illustrating how the channels described in the model in the preceding sections could operate in reality. Section 6 presents complementary simulations. Section 7 offers conclusions.

2 The basic analytical framework

The basic analytical framework of this chapter draws on Fan and Stark (2007). Consider a world that consists of two countries: Home, H, and Foreign, F. Country H is developing and is poorer than the developed country F. Due to a policy of selective migration by F, only educated individuals (say university graduates) of H have a chance of working in, hence migrating to, F. An educated individual makes decisions in (at most) three stages.

1. When an individual graduates from a university, the individual participates in a draw that results in probable work in F. If the individual obtains a winning ticket, his income will be a constant w^f. The probability of being selected to work in F is p.
2. An individual who graduates and fails to secure work in F faces the following choices: to work or to wait for another draw. For example, if the individual were to work, little time (and energy) would be available for preparing applications and, in addition, the individual's academic qualifications could depreciate, thereby lowering the probability of being picked up for work in F. For simplicity, it is assumed that if the individual works, he cannot participate in any additional draw so that the probability of his ending up working in F is zero. If the individual does not work and

awaits another draw, his chance of going abroad is p', where

$$p' = p(1 + \alpha)$$

and α is a fixed parameter. To ensure that $0 < p' < 1$, we assume that $-1 < \alpha < \frac{1}{p} - 1$.

3. If an individual wins this draw, he will go abroad. Otherwise, he will work at home, receiving the home country's mean wage rate.

The job offers in the second and the third stages follow an independently identical distribution. The cumulative distribution function of the wage offer, $\widetilde{w}$, is $F(\cdot)$. We assume that $F(\cdot)$ is differentiable, that

$$\widetilde{w} \in [w^l, w^h],$$

and that the density function, $\frac{dF(w)}{dw} \equiv F'(w)$, is strictly positive in its domain. The expected income of the (risk-neutral) individuals in the third stage is

$$(1 - p')\overline{w} + p'w^f \tag{7.1}$$

where $\overline{w}$ is the mean wage in H, namely,

$$\overline{w} = \int_{w^l}^{w^h} w dF(w).$$

In the second stage, if the individual receives a wage offer w at H, he will accept it if and only if

$$w > \frac{1}{1+r}[(1 - p')\overline{w} + p'w^f], \tag{7.2}$$

where r is the individual's discount rate.

We define

$$w^c \equiv \frac{1}{1+r}[(1 - p')\overline{w} + p'w^f]. \tag{7.3}$$

Then, the individual will accept the wage offer at H if and only if

$$w > w^c.$$

Further simplifying, we assume that

$$w^l \geq \frac{1}{1+r}\overline{w}; \tag{7.4}$$

'educated unemployment' will not exist in the absence of an additional possibility of migration (that is, when $p'=0$). Clearly, equation (7.4) will be satisfied if r is large enough.

Then, the fraction of the educated who are unemployed is

$$u \equiv P(\widetilde{w} \leq w^c) = F(w^c). \tag{7.5}$$

Clearly,

$$\begin{aligned}\frac{du}{dp'} &= \frac{du}{dw^c}\frac{dw^c}{dp'} \\ &= F'(w^c)\frac{w^f - \overline{w}}{1+r}.\end{aligned} \tag{7.6}$$

Note that the assumption that F is developed and H is developing naturally implies that $w^f > \overline{w}$. Since $F'(w^c) > 0$,

$$\frac{du}{dp'} > 0. \tag{7.7}$$

In addition, noting that $w^c \equiv \frac{1}{1+r}[\overline{w} + p'(w^f - \overline{w})]$,

$$\frac{du}{d(w^f - \overline{w})} = F'(w^c)\frac{p'}{1+r} > 0. \tag{7.8}$$

In summary, we have the following results:

1. The unemployment rate for university graduates in a developing country will increase as the probability of migration rises.
2. The unemployment rate of university graduates in a developing country will increase as the wage gap between the developed country and the developing country increases.

The benefit that education without migration confers is simply H's mean wage rate of educated workers,

$$\overline{w}.$$

When migration is a possibility, the expected payoff from the three stages described above is

$$\begin{aligned}V &\equiv pw^f + (1-p)\left\{\int_{w^c}^{w^h} w dF(w) + F(w^c)\left[\frac{p'w^f + (1-p')\overline{w}}{1+r}\right]\right\} \\ &= pw^f + (1-p)\left[\int_{w^c}^{w^h} wF'(w)dw + F(w^c)w^c\right].\end{aligned} \tag{7.9}$$

We further assume that

$$w^f > w^h. \tag{7.10}$$

To rule out the unreasonable possibility that all the educated are unemployed, we assume that

$$w^c < w^h. \tag{7.11}$$

We next incorporate the cost of acquiring education. Our idea is that individuals differ in their abilities and family background, hence in the cost of their education. We normalize the size of the (pre-migration) population of H to be Lebesgue measure 1. Suppose that the cost of an individual's education, c, follows the following uniform distribution

$$\widetilde{c} \in [0, \Omega].$$

We assume that the (lifetime) income of an uneducated individual is constant, and we denote it by Φ. Then, recalling the assumption that only individuals with university degrees have any chance of migrating, an individual will choose to acquire a university education if and only if

$$V - c \geq \Phi. \tag{7.12}$$

Let us define

$$c^* \equiv V - \Phi. \tag{7.13}$$

It follows that an individual will obtain a university education if and only if the cost of his education maintains

$$c \leq c^*.$$

Since $\widetilde{c}$ follows a uniform distribution and the population size of the economy is of Lebesgue measure 1, both the proportion and the number of educated individuals are given by

$$\frac{c^*}{\Omega}. \tag{7.14}$$

With these building blocks on site, we obtain the following lemma.

Lemma 1: *There exists a positive level of p at which the number of university graduates remaining in the developing country is higher than the number of university graduates in the developing country when $p=0$, for any given α, if $w^f > (3+\alpha)\overline{w}$.*

Proof: See Fan and Stark (2007).

Lemma 1 implies that a developing country may end up with more university graduates despite the brain drain of university graduates. Noting that there is a reduction in the population in the wake of migration, the lemma also implies that the developing country may end up with a higher proportion of educated individuals, despite the brain drain of university graduates.

3 A short-run loss versus a long-run gain

In this section we will show that in the short run, a relaxation of migration, which leads to a brain drain and to 'uneducated unemployment', could result in a reduction in per-capita output. Yet in the longer run (in the next generation), the legacy of a relaxed migration policy will prompt a 'take-off' of the economy. The latter result will be derived in a framework of rational expectations equilibrium.

Our analysis draws on the work of Azariadis and Drazen (1990), who emphasize the role of a 'threshold externality' in economic development.[6] They argue forcefully that the average level of human capital is a key factor for an economy's 'take-off'.[7] Specifically, we assume that

$$\text{wage of the educated in the home country} = \begin{cases} \beta\widetilde{w} & \text{if } e \geq e^c \\ \widetilde{w} & \text{if } e < e^c \end{cases}$$

where $\beta > 1$,[8] and e denotes the proportion of the educated in the home country. Note that e^c is the critical value that characterizes the 'threshold externality' of average human capital. With labour being the only factor of production in the economy, an increase in the wage rate is tantamount to 'take-off' of the economy. Since our modeling of the externality effect of human capital is different from the corresponding modeling in related literature (Mountford, 1997; Stark and Wang, 2002), our model complements the received literature.

Since the number of individuals undertaking education is a function not only of the probability of migration, p, but also of the wage rate that awaits educated workers, we define

$$\xi = \begin{cases} \beta & \text{if } e \geq e^c \\ 1 & \text{if } e < e^c. \end{cases}$$

We then note that c^* is a function of V and hence of p and ξ, so we define

$$c^* \equiv c(p, \xi). \tag{7.15}$$

Then, when there is a prospect of migration, the number of educated individuals *remaining* in the home country is

$$\frac{c(p,\xi)}{\Omega} - \left[p\frac{c(p,\xi)}{\Omega} + (1-p)p'\frac{c(p,\xi)}{\Omega}F(w^c)\right]$$
$$= c(p,\xi)[(1-p)(1-p(1+\alpha)F(w^c))]/\Omega. \tag{7.16}$$

Note that the size of the population remaining in the home country, which we denote by $n(p,\ \xi)$, decreases when $p>0$ in comparison with the case when $p=0$. Also, recall that to begin with, the size of the population of the economy is of Lebesgue measure 1. Then,

$$n(p,\xi) = 1 - \left[p\frac{c(p,\xi)}{\Omega} + (1-p)p'F(w^c)\frac{c(p,\xi)}{\Omega}\right]$$
$$= 1 - \frac{c(p,\xi)}{\Omega} + \frac{c(p,\xi)}{\Omega}(1-p)\left[1-p(1+\alpha)F(w^c)\right]. \tag{7.17}$$

From equation (7.16), we know that the fraction of educated individuals in the population remaining in the home country is

$$e(p,\xi) \equiv \frac{c(p,\xi)(1-p)[1-p(1+\alpha)F(w^c)]}{n(p,\xi)\Omega}. \tag{7.18}$$

Then, 'take-off' of H can be sustained (or achieved) by a rational expectations equilibrium if and only if

$$e(p,\beta) \geq e^c. \tag{7.19}$$

If equation (7.19) can be satisfied by a careful choice of p, then 'take-off' can occur in the current period. Yet even if equation (7.19) cannot be satisfied in the current period, it may be satisfied in the next period upon a careful choice of p in the current period, which increases the number of educated parents in the next period.[9]

In the following exposition we will use the subscript t to denote the current period, the subscript $t-1$ to denote the preceding period, and the subscript $t+1$ to denote the next period. When ξ takes the value 1, we will not write ξ explicitly unless the omission could cause confusion. (For example, to denote $c(p,\ 1)$, we will write $c(p)$.)

Resorting to an assumption which appears to have gained wide adherence – that the cost of acquiring education decreases with parental human capital (that is, the number of parents who have acquired a university education), we write

$$\frac{d\Omega_{t+1}}{de_t} < 0. \tag{7.20}$$

The importance of parental human capital for an individual's educational attainment has been consistently confirmed in the empirical literature. (For a helpful survey see Hanushek, 1996.)

We are now in a position to state and prove the following proposition.

Proposition 1: *(1) If equation (7.19) cannot be satisfied so that 'take-off' does not occur in the current period, the prospect of migration entails a decline in the economy's per capita output in the short run. (2) However, a careful choice of p in both the current period and the next period can facilitate 'take-off' of the economy in the next period.*

Proof: (1) If 'take-off' does not occur in the current period, the prospect of migration will result in a loss of average (per-capita) output.

To facilitate a comparison between the case in which $p > 0$ and the case in which $p = 0$, we divide the individuals into three distinct categories (for the case in which $p > 0$):

(i) Individuals who do not acquire education;
(ii) Individuals who acquire education and fail to secure work abroad;
(iii) Individuals who acquire education and migrate.

(i) Individuals of the first type do not acquire education when $p > 0$. From the analysis in the preceding section we know that they would not have acquired education when $p = 0$. Thus, the prospect of migration has no impact on their (net) earnings which, in either case, are equal to the wage of the uneducated, Φ.

(ii) As to individuals of the second type, the prospect of migration results in some of them receiving lower net earnings than the earnings that they would have received when $p = 0$. This comes about through two channels: (a) the prospect of migration prompts 'too many' individuals to acquire education; (b) the prospect of migration causes 'educated unemployment'.

(a) When there is no prospect of migration, the number of educated individuals is $\frac{c(0)}{\Omega}$. When $p > 0$, the number of educated individuals is $\frac{c(p)}{\Omega}$. The number of educated individuals who would not choose to be skilled without the prospect of migration is then

$$\frac{c(p)}{\Omega} - \frac{c(0)}{\Omega}.$$

Note that the proportion of these individuals who do not migrate is

$$(1-p)[1-p'F(w^c)] = (1-p)[1-p(1+\alpha)F(w^c)].$$

Thus, when there is a prospect of migration, the number of educated individuals remaining in the home country who have acquired a higher education 'wrongly' is not less than

$$\left[\frac{c(p)}{\Omega} - \frac{c(0)}{\Omega}\right](1-p)[1-p(1+\alpha)F(w^c)]. \tag{7.21}$$

For these individuals, the cost of their education is in the domain $[c(0), c(p)]$, and the distribution of that cost in this domain is uniform. Thus, the average cost of education for these individuals is

$$\frac{c(0)+c(p)}{2}. \tag{7.22}$$

The (expected) benefit of education (in comparison with no education) for any individual who remains in the home country is less than[10] or equal to $\overline{w} - \Phi$. (Since the number of individuals is a continuum, the expected value is equal to the average value.)

When $p=0$, $V=\overline{w}$. Hence, from equation (7.13) and the definition $c^* = c(p)$,

$$c(0) = V - \Phi = \overline{w} - \Phi. \tag{7.23}$$

Thus, the average net loss per individual is not less than

$$\frac{c(0)+c(p)}{2} - (\overline{w} - \Phi) > c(0) - (\overline{w} - \Phi) = 0. \tag{7.24}$$

(b) From equation (7.4), no educated individual will choose to be unemployed if he has no prospect of migration. Therefore, the (discounted) income of some of the educated individuals remaining in the home country would have been higher had they not chosen to be unemployed (in the sense of an *ex post* consideration). From the above description and analysis, we can see that the total number of unemployed educated individuals before the second lottery of migration occurs (that is, in Stage 2) is $F(w^c)\frac{c(p)}{\Omega}(1-p)$. Therefore, the number of these unemployed educated individuals who remain in the home country is

$$F(w^c)\frac{c(p)}{\Omega}(1-p)[1-p(1+\alpha)]. \tag{7.25}$$

If these individuals had worked rather than been unemployed, their average income would have been

$$E(w|w^l \leq w \leq w^c) = \frac{\int_{w^l}^{w^c} w dF(w)}{F(w^c)}, \tag{7.26}$$

where E is the expectation operator.

However, because they chose to wait, their expected earnings are

$$\frac{\overline{w}}{1+r}. \tag{7.27}$$

(Again, note that the number of individuals is a continuum, hence the expected value is equal to the average value.)

Thus, the average loss per individual is

$$E(w|w^l \leq w \leq w^c) - \frac{\overline{w}}{1+r} > w^l - \frac{\overline{w}}{1+r} \geq 0, \tag{7.28}$$

where the inequality sign in equation (7.28) arises from equation (7.4).

The preceding discussion shows that for the set of individuals who remain in the home country when $p > 0$, that is, individuals of types (i) and (ii), some receive lower net earnings than when $p = 0$, while others receive the same net earnings. Thus, the average earnings of type (i) and type (ii) individuals when $p > 0$ are lower than when $p = 0$. We next show that the departure of educated individuals further reduces the average income.

(iii) Had $p = 0$, the individuals who would have acquired an education as a fraction of the individuals who would have acquired education had $p > 0$ is

$$\frac{c(0)/\Omega}{c(p)/\Omega} = \frac{c(0)}{c(p)}.$$

When $p = 0$, the average income of type (iii) individuals who would have acquired education, net of the education cost, would have been $\overline{w} - \frac{c(0)}{2}$. Recall that the earnings of the uneducated are Φ. Thus, when $p = 0$, the average income of individuals of type (iii) is

$$\frac{c(0)}{c(p)}\left[\overline{w} - \frac{c(0)}{2}\right] + \left[1 - \frac{c(0)}{c(p)}\right]\Phi. \tag{7.29}$$

When $p = 0$, the average income of all individuals is

$$\frac{c(0)}{\Omega}\left[\overline{w} - \frac{c(0)}{2}\right] + \left[1 - \frac{c(0)}{\Omega}\right]\Phi. \tag{7.30}$$

Because $\Omega > c(p)$, and $\overline{w} - \frac{c(0)}{2} > \overline{w} - c(0) = \Phi$ (recall equation (7.4)), we have that

$$\frac{c(0)}{c(p)}\left[\overline{w} - \frac{c(0)}{2}\right] + \left[1 - \frac{c(0)}{c(p)}\right]\Phi > \frac{c(0)}{\Omega}\left[\overline{w} - \frac{c(0)}{2}\right] + \left[1 - \frac{c(0)}{\Omega}\right]\Phi.$$

Thus, the average income of the individuals whom the home country loses through migration would have been higher than the national average when

$p=0$. Thus, when $p=0$, the average income of individuals of type (i) and type (ii) is lower than the average income of individuals of type (i), type (ii), and type (iii). Therefore, the loss of educated individuals through migration further reduces the average income in the economy.

(2) Note that from equation (7.18),

$$\frac{de_t(p_t, \xi)}{d\Omega_t} < 0 \tag{7.31}$$

for any given p_t and ξ. Since, recalling equation (7.20),

$$\frac{d\Omega_t}{de_{t-1}} < 0,$$

it follows that

$$\frac{de_t(p_t, \xi)}{de_{t-1}} > 0. \tag{7.32}$$

Thus, when p_{t-1} is chosen in such a way that $p_{t-1}=p^o>0$ and $e(p^o, 1)>e(0, 1)$, noting equation (7.32), we have

$$e_t(p_t^*, \beta)|_{p_{t-1}=p^o} \geq e_t(p_t^{**}, \beta)|_{p_{t-1}=p^o} > e_t(p_t^{**}, \beta)|_{p_{t-1}=0} \tag{7.33}$$

where the notation $e_t(p_t^*, \beta)|_{p_{t-1}=p^o}$ means the fraction of the population remaining in the home country who are educated when $p_{t-1}=p^o$ and $p_t=p_t^*$, and where

$$p_t^* = \arg\max e_t(p_t, \beta)|_{p_{t-1}=p^o}$$

and

$$p_t^{**} = \arg\max e_t(p_t, \beta)|_{p_{t-1}=0}.$$

Hence, when e^c is in the region

$$e_t(p_t^*, \beta)|_{p_{t-1}=p^o} > e^c > e_t(p_t^{**}, \beta)|_{p_{t-1}=0} \tag{7.34}$$

'take-off' is possible in period t in a framework of rational expectations equilibrium only if migration was allowed in the preceding period so that more parents chose to become educated. Q.E.D.

Proposition 1 analyzes the negative and the positive welfare implications of migration by skilled individuals in a unified framework. In the short run, we encounter three possible negative consequences: migration leads to a reduction in the 'stock' of better-educated individuals, which in turn reduces average income; when a fraction of the educated individuals who otherwise would have worked are lured to form human capital only to end up unemployed, output shrinks; since the possibility of migration motivates individuals to acquire higher education, when some of them remain in the home country, the returns to their education will turn out to fall short of the costs of their education. Unless the economy 'takes off', these individuals' overeducation is socially inefficient in the short run.

However, we next demonstrate that in the long run (one generation down the road), the legacy of a relaxed migration policy prompts 'take-off' of the economy. Our results are derived in a framework of rational expectations equilibrium: the brain drain is accompanied by a 'brain gain'; the ensuing 'brain gain' can result in a higher average level of human capital in the home country; the higher average level of human capital can prompt 'take-off' of the economy. In such a setting, overeducation can become dynamically efficient (due to the intergenerational externality effect of human capital) even though it may be statically inefficient. Thus, Proposition 1 implies that a relaxation in migration policy in both periods is conducive to achieving the benefit of long-run growth.

4 The prospect of a welfare gain

In this section we examine the welfare implications of 'take-off' in the next period. We use L^s to denote the short-run loss in terms of average income arising from the prospect of migration, and G^l to denote the benefit measured in terms of the average income in the next period arising from the prospect of migration less the average income that would have obtained with no such prospect. We thus define the social welfare function as follows:

$$-L^s + \rho G^l \tag{7.35}$$

where ρ is the social discount rate across generations. Then, we have the following proposition.

Proposition 2: *Suppose that the economy takes off in the next period if and only if migration is allowed. If β is sufficiently large such that*

$$\beta > \frac{0.5[(1-p)(c(p))^2 - (c(0))^2] + \Phi(c(p) - c(0))}{\rho c(0)\overline{w}} + \frac{r + \rho + r\rho}{\rho(1+r)}, \tag{7.36}$$

migration of educated individuals will confer a welfare gain to the individuals remaining in the home country.

Proof: See the Appendix.

Proposition 2 implies that in spite of the additional costs of migration for a developing country, the insight that the brain drain can confer a benefit to the country is still retained. Rather than causing human capital drain and output contraction, the migration of educated workers entails human capital gain and output growth. An analysis of the entire dynamics associated with the response of educated workers to the prospect of migration therefore raises the intriguing possibility that the devil is, in fact, an angel. The results are more powerful than those reported early on since the prospect of migration is taken to entail both depletion of human capital and unemployment of human capital, which renders it more difficult to hold migration as a catalyst for growth.

In addition, when 'take-off' occurs, we have the following proposition.

Proposition 3: *After 'take-off', the unemployment rate of the educated is lower than that prior to 'take-off'.*

Proof: Prior to 'take-off' we know, following equations (7.3) and (7.5), that the unemployment rate of the educated is

$$u^b \equiv F(w^c) = F\left[\frac{(1-p')\overline{w}}{1+r} + \frac{p'w^f}{1+r}\right]. \tag{7.37}$$

After 'take-off', the fraction of the educated who are unemployed is

$$u^a \equiv P(\beta\widetilde{w} \leq w^{cc}) = F\left(\frac{w^{cc}}{\beta}\right) \tag{7.38}$$

where w^{cc} is the equivalent of w^c in (2.3), that is,

$$w^{cc} \equiv \frac{1}{1+r}\left[(1-p')\beta\overline{w} + p'w^f\right]. \tag{7.39}$$

Thus,

$$\begin{aligned} u^a &= F\left(\frac{w^{cc}}{\beta}\right) \\ &= F\left(\frac{[(1-p')\beta\overline{w} + p'w^f]}{(1+r)\beta}\right) \\ &= F\left[\frac{(1-p')\overline{w}}{1+r} + \frac{p'w^f}{(1+r)\beta}\right]. \end{aligned} \tag{7.40}$$

Comparing equations (7.37) and (7.40) and noting that $\beta > 1$ and $F' > 0$, we have

$$u^b > u^a. \tag{7.41}$$

Q.E.D.

Proposition 3 states that 'take-off' bites into the unemployment rate of the educated. The intuition is straightforward. After 'take-off', the domestic wage rate of educated workers increases. Hence, the relative benefit of waiting for overseas employment decreases. This reduces the unemployment rate of the educated.

5 Simulation

We conduct simulation exercises aimed at fleshing out the channels that were identified in the analysis undertaken in the preceding sections. We divide this section into 5 subsections. Subsection 5.1 specifies the parameters. In relation to the proof of Proposition 1, subsection 5.2 analyses the cost of 'educated unemployment'; subsection 5.3 examines the cost of overeducation; subsection 5.4 discusses the direct cost of a brain drain; subsection 5.5 investigates the brain gain.

5.1 Parameter specifications

We specify the parameters as follows:

$$\alpha = 0, w^l = 1, w^h = 2, w^f = 5, r = 0.5\%, \Phi = 1.2 \tag{7.42}$$

$\widetilde{w}$ follows a uniform distribution over the domain [1, 2]. Therefore we get

$$\overline{w} = 1.5. \tag{7.43}$$

This implies that the wage rate in F is approximately 3.3 times the average wage rate for the skilled in H. Also, note that it is possible that $\Phi > w^l$ since schooling involves an opportunity cost of not working. Moreover, we specify that the (initial) value of Ω, the upper bound of the cost of acquiring education, is 3.

From equations (7.42) and (7.43), and recalling equation (7.3), we get

$$w^c = \frac{1}{1+r}[(1-p')\overline{w} + p'w^f] = 1 + \frac{7}{3}p. \tag{7.44}$$

Since $w^c < w^h$, we assume that

$$1 + \frac{7}{3}p < 2$$

namely that

$$p < \frac{3}{7}. \tag{7.45}$$

From equation (7.44), we get

$$F(w^c) = \int_1^{1+\frac{7}{3}p} dw = \frac{7}{3}p. \tag{7.46}$$

Inserting equations (7.42), (7.44), and (7.46) into (7.9), we get

$$\begin{aligned} V &= pw^f + (1-p)\left[\int_{w^c}^{w^h} wF'(w)dw + F(w^c)w^c\right] \\ &= \frac{3}{2} + \frac{7}{2}p + \frac{49}{18}p^2 - \frac{49}{18}p^3. \end{aligned} \tag{7.47}$$

Then, from equation (7.13), we have

$$c(p) = V - \Phi = \frac{3}{10} + \frac{7}{2}p + \frac{49}{18}p^2 - \frac{49}{18}p^3.$$

Then, recalling equation (7.16), when there is a prospect of migration, the number of the educated individuals, say university graduates, *remaining* in the developing country is

$$\begin{aligned} R(p) &\equiv \frac{c(p)}{\Omega} - \left[p\frac{c(p)}{\Omega} + (1-p)p'\frac{c(p)}{\Omega}F(w^c)\right] \\ &= \left(\frac{3}{10} + \frac{7}{2}p + \frac{49}{18}p^2 - \frac{49}{18}p^3\right)\left[(1-p)\left(1 - \frac{7}{3}p^2\right)\right]/\Omega. \end{aligned} \tag{7.48}$$

Since the number of uneducated individuals (who do not migrate) is $1 - \frac{c(p)}{\Omega}$, the total number of individuals remaining in H is

$$R(p) + 1 - \frac{c(p)}{\Omega}. \tag{7.49}$$

5.2 The cost of 'educated unemployment'

Inserting equations (7.42), (7.44), (7.46), and $\Omega = 3$ into equation (7.25), we get that the number of the unemployed educated individuals who remain in the home country is

$$\begin{aligned} U(p) &\equiv (1-p)F(w^c)\frac{c(p)}{\Omega}(1-p) \\ &= \frac{7}{9}p(1-p)^2\left(\frac{3}{10} + \frac{7}{2}p + \frac{49}{18}p^2 - \frac{49}{18}p^3\right). \end{aligned} \tag{7.50}$$

The proportion of these individuals as a percentage of the total number of individuals who remain in the home country is

$$U(p) \equiv \frac{U(p)}{R(p) + 1 - \frac{c(p)}{\Omega}}. \tag{7.51}$$

Also, as discussed in section 2, a simple indicator of the unemployment rate among the educated individuals is $F(w^c)$.

From (7.28), we know that the average loss for these individuals is

$$E(w|w^l \leq w \leq w^c) - \frac{\overline{w}}{1+r} = \frac{1+1+\frac{7}{3}p}{2} - \frac{\frac{3}{2}}{1+\frac{1}{2}} = \frac{7}{6}p. \tag{7.52}$$

This earnings loss in terms of the percentage of these individuals' average earnings in the absence of unemployment is then

$$l^u = \frac{\frac{7}{6}p}{E(w|w^l \leq w \leq w^c)} = \frac{\frac{7}{6}p}{1+\frac{7}{6}p} = \frac{7p}{6+7p}. \tag{7.53}$$

Then, we have the following Table:

Table 7.1 The short-run cost of 'educational unemployment'

p(%)	l^u(%) (average cost of 'educated unemployment')	$F(w^c)$ (%) (unemployment rate of the educated)	u(%) (total unemployment rate)
1	1.15	2.33	0.26
2	2.28	4.67	0.56
3	3.38	7.00	0.90
4	4.46	9.33	1.28
5	5.51	11.67	1.71
6	6.54	14.00	2.17
7	7.55	16.33	2.66
8	8.54	18.67	3.20
9	9.50	21.00	3.77
10	10.45	23.33	4.37

From Table 7.1 we see that as the probability of migration increases, both the unemployment rate of the educated and the average loss for these unemployed individuals increases. For example, if $p = 10$ per cent, then the unemployment rates among the educated and among the entire population are, respectively, 23.33 per cent and 4.37 per cent, and the average (percentage) loss for these unemployed individuals is 10.45 per cent.

5.3 The cost of overeducation

From equations (7.21) and (7.48), we know that when there is a prospect of migration, the number of educated individuals remaining in the home country who have acquired a higher education 'wrongly' is not less than

$$O(p) \equiv R(p) - R(0). \tag{7.54}$$

The proportion of these individuals as a percentage of the educated individuals who remain in the home country is

$$\lambda(p) \equiv \frac{O(p)}{R(p)}; \tag{7.55}$$

the proportion of these individuals as a percentage of the total number of individuals who remain in the home country is

$$\eta(p) \equiv \frac{O(p)}{R(p) + 1 - c(p)/\Omega}. \tag{7.56}$$

From (7.24), we know that for these individuals, the average net loss per individual is not less than

$$\frac{c(0) + c(p)}{2} - (\overline{w} - \Phi). \tag{7.57}$$

If an individual does not acquire an education, his net earnings are Φ. Thus, the percentage loss is not less than

$$l^o \equiv \frac{\frac{c(0)+c(p)}{2} - (\overline{w} - \Phi)}{\Phi} = \frac{c(0) + c(p) - 0.6}{2.4}. \tag{7.58}$$

Then, we have the following Table:

Table 7.2 The short-run cost of overeducation

p(%)	l^o(%) *(average cost of overeducation)*	$\lambda(p)$(%) *(the proportion of the overeducated among the educated)*	$\eta(p)$(%) *(the proportion of the overeducated among the entire population)*
1	1.47	9.59	1.06
2	2.96	17.43	2.12
3	4.47	23.92	3.16
4	6.01	29.38	4.19
5	7.56	34.03	5.20
6	9.13	38.01	6.20
7	10.73	41.46	7.19
8	12.33	44.46	8.16
9	13.96	47.09	9.11
10	15.60	49.40	10.04

From Table 7.2 we see that as the probability of migration increases, the proportion of overeducated individuals increases no matter whether the proportion is measured as a percentage of the educated individuals who remain in the home country or as a percentage of the total number of individuals who remain in the home country. For example, if $p = 10$ per cent, the proportion of overeducated individuals is close to 50 per cent of the educated individuals who remain in the home country, and about 10 per cent of the entire population. Also, as the probability of migration increases, the average net loss of overeducated individuals increases. For example, if $p = 10$ per cent, then the average loss of overeducation is 15.60 per cent.

5.4 The direct cost of a brain drain

Suppose that a certain number of educated individuals migrate from H to F, which results in a brain drain. The *direct* cost of the brain drain is measured as the difference between the average income when no migration is allowed and the (maximal) average income when a certain number of educated individuals migrate. Specifically, we proceed in two steps. (i) We calculate the average net income when migration is not allowed. We denote this average income by Z^1. Clearly,

$$Z^1 = \frac{c(0)}{\Omega}\left[\overline{w} - \frac{c(0)}{2}\right] + \left[1 - \frac{c(0)}{\Omega}\right]\Phi. \tag{7.59}$$

(ii) From the preceding analysis we know that the number of individuals who migrate is

$$\begin{aligned} M(p) &\equiv \frac{c(p)}{\Omega}p + p'(1-p)\frac{c(p)}{\Omega}F(w^c) \\ &= \left(\frac{3}{10} + \frac{7}{2}p + \frac{49}{18}p^2 - \frac{49}{18}p^3\right)\left[p + (1-p)\frac{7}{3}p^2\right] / \Omega. \end{aligned} \tag{7.60}$$

For the remaining individuals, if they could anticipate that they would stay in H, then neither 'educated unemployment' nor overeducation would occur. In this hypothetical scenario, we calculate the average income for the remaining individuals (educated and uneducated) in H, which we denote by Z^2. Note that this calculating procedure eliminates the influence of 'educated unemployment' and overeducation, which allows us to calculate the direct cost of the brain drain. Then, the *direct* loss from the brain drain, which is denoted by D, is

$$D \equiv Z^1 - Z^2.$$

To calculate Z^2, we first calculate what the average income of those individuals who migrate would have been had they stayed at home (in the hypothetical scenario that they anticipate $p = 0$). We denote this average income by $I(p)$, and we get

$$I(p) \equiv \frac{c(0)}{c(p)}\left[\overline{w} - \frac{c(0)}{2}\right] + \left[1 - \frac{c(0)}{c(p)}\right]\Phi. \tag{7.61}$$

Recall that the total number of individuals in H in the absence of migration is one. Then, we know that the total income of the remaining individuals (in this hypothetical scenario) is

$$1Z^1 - M(p)I(p) = Z^1 - M(p)I(p). \tag{7.62}$$

Thus,

$$Z^2 = \frac{Z^1 - M(p)I(p)}{1 - M(p)}. \tag{7.63}$$

Then, the *direct* loss from the brain drain in percentage terms is

$$d \equiv \frac{Z^1 - Z^2}{Z^1}. \tag{7.64}$$

Then, we have the following Table:

Table 7.3 The direct cost of a brain drain in the short run

p(%)	Z^1	*M(p) (% of total population)*	Z^2	*d(%) (average direct cost of migration)*
1	1.215	0.11	1.2149	0.011
2	1.215	0.26	1.2147	0.023
3	1.215	0.44	1.2146	0.034
4	1.215	0.65	1.2144	0.046
5	1.215	0.89	1.2143	0.058
6	1.215	1.18	1.2141	0.070
7	1.215	1.50	1.2140	0.082
8	1.215	1.86	1.2139	0.094
9	1.215	2.27	1.2137	0.107
10	1.215	2.72	1.2136	0.119

From Table 7.3 we see that d increases with the probability of migration. However, d is only 0.119 per cent even when $p = 10$ per cent, which implies that the direct cost of migration is quite small. The intuition is that most of the population in a developing country is uneducated, and it is this uneducated population that mainly determines the average income in the country. Thus, even if a significant proportion of the educated migrate, the impact on the average income of the developing country can be relatively small.

In summary, the simulation conducted thus far shows that the cost of the two new negative consequences of migration introduced in this chapter, namely 'educated unemployment' and overeducation, can amount to significant losses for the individuals affected, who may constitute a substantial proportion of the educated individuals. In addition, in per capita terms, the cost of a brain drain may be relatively small if the proportion of educated individuals in the economy is small.

5.5 The brain gain

In this subsection, we calculate the proportions of university graduates in the developing country in both the preceding period and the current period. As analyzed in section 3, an individual's decision to acquire education depends on the domestic wage rate as well as on the probability of working abroad, which implies that, in particular, the decision depends on whether the economy can 'take off'.

For simplicity, we slightly modify a previously made assumption, considering now a setting wherein 'take-off' is possible in the current period, but not in the preceding period. Hence, from equations (7.48) and (7.49), we know that in the preceding period, the proportion of university graduates *remaining* in the developing country as a percentage of the total number of individuals who remain in the country is

$$k(p) \equiv \frac{R(p)}{R(p) + 1 - c(p)/\Omega}. \tag{7.65}$$

Then, we have the following Table:

Table 7.4 The brain gain

p(%)	$\frac{c(p)}{\Omega}$ *(% of individuals who choose to be educated)*	$k(p)$ *(% of individuals who choose to be educated and remain in H)*
0	10.00	10.00
1	11.18	11.07
2	12.37	12.14
3	13.58	13.20
4	14.81	14.25
5	16.05	15.29
6	17.31	16.32
7	18.58	17.34
8	19.87	18.35
9	21.17	19.34
10	22.48	20.32

From Table 7.4 we see that as p increases from 0 per cent to 10 per cent, the proportion of university graduates *remaining* in the developing country more than doubles.

Now we specify

$$\Omega_t = \Omega_{t-1} - 15(k_{t-1} - 0.1) \tag{7.66}$$

where k_{t-1} is the value of $k(p)$ at time $t-1$. As in Section 3, we refer to time $t-1$ as the preceding period, and to time t as the current period. We make the following specifications:

$$\beta = 1.2, e^c = 33\%. \tag{7.67}$$

There is now a need to calculate two Nash equilibria. The first equilibrium is derived under the belief that $\xi = 1$, the second equilibrium is derived under the belief that $\xi = \beta = 1.2$. Then, if $e(p_t, 1) < 33\%$, the first equilibrium is a self-fulfilling rational-expectations equilibrium; if $e(p_t, 1) \geq 33\%$, the second equilibrium is a self-fulfilling rational-expectations equilibrium. When there are two equilibria, for simplicity, we will refer only to the equilibrium under the belief $\xi = \beta = 1.2$ (that is, under the belief that the economy will 'take off').

Under the belief that $\xi = \beta = 1.2$, we have that

$$w^l = 1.2, w^h = 2.4 \tag{7.68}$$

with $\widetilde{w}$ following a uniform distribution over the domain [1.2, 2.4]. Then, akin to section 5.1, we obtain the following items. (Note that we use the subscript β to indicate that the items are derived under the belief that $\xi = \beta = 1.2$.)

$$\overline{w}_\beta = 1.8. \tag{7.69}$$

$$w^c_\beta = \frac{1}{1+r}[(1-p')\overline{w} + p'w^f] = 1.2 + 2.13p. \tag{7.70}$$

$$F_\beta(w^c) = \int_{1.2}^{1.2+2.13p} \frac{1}{1.2} dw = 1.78p. \tag{7.71}$$

$$\begin{aligned} V_\beta &= pw^f + (1-p)\left[\int_{w^c}^{w^h} wF'_\beta(w)dw + F_\beta(w^c)w^c\right] \\ &= 1.8 + 3.2p + 1.9p^2 - 1.9p^3. \end{aligned} \tag{7.72}$$

$$c_\beta(p) = V_\beta - \Phi = 0.6 + 3.2p + 1.9p^2 - 1.9p^3.$$

$$\begin{aligned} R_\beta(p) &\equiv \frac{c_\beta(p)}{\Omega} - \left[p\frac{c_\beta(p)}{\Omega} + (1-p)p'\frac{c_\beta(p)}{\Omega}F_\beta(w^c)\right] \\ &= (1.8 + 3.2p + 1.9p^2 - 1.9p^3)[(1-p)(1-1.8p^2)]/\Omega. \end{aligned} \tag{7.73}$$

$$k_\beta(p) \equiv \frac{R_\beta(p)}{R_\beta(p) + 1 - c_\beta(p)/\Omega}. \tag{7.74}$$

For simplicity, we assume that the government of the home country can only set $p = 5$ per cent in the current period. Then, if $k_\beta(0.05) \geq 33$ per cent, the proportion of university graduates *remaining* in the developing country as a percentage of the total number of individuals who remain in the country is $k_\beta(0.05)$; if $k_\beta(0.05) < 33$ per cent, the proportion of university graduates *remaining* in the developing country as a percentage of the total number of individuals who remain in the country is $k(0.05)$. Noting Table 7.4 and drawing upon the preceding analysis and calculations, we have the following Table:

Table 7.5 The brain gain and economic betterment in the long run

$p_t(\%)$	$p_{t-1}(\%)$	$k_{t-1}(\%)$ *(the proportion of the educated in the preceding period)*	$k_t(\%)$ *(the proportion of the educated in the current period)*
5	0	10.00	15.29
5	1	11.07	16.17
5	2	12.14	17.15
5	3	13.20	18.24
5	4	14.25	19.47
5	5	15.29	33.40
5	6	16.32	35.96
5	7	17.34	38.93
5	8	18.35	42.38
5	9	19.34	46.42
5	10	20.32	51.26

From Table 7.5 we see that 'take-off' will occur in the current period if and only if 'k_{t-1}' (that is, $k(p) \times 100$ in the preceding period) is greater than or equal to 15.29, that is, correspondingly, the home country's government sets $p_{t-1} \geq 5$ per cent in the preceding period. We also see that when k_{t-1} increases (slightly) from 14.25 per cent to 15.29 per cent, k_t increases substantially from 19.47 per cent to 33.40 per cent. This is so because when $k_{t-1} = 14.25$ per cent, then under the belief that $\xi = \beta = 1.2$, we would get $k_t = 31.15$ per cent. Since 31.15 per cent < 33 per cent, the belief that $\xi = \beta = 1.2$ cannot be sustained by rational expectations and hence, only the belief that $\xi = 1$ is self-fulfilling, which yields $k_t = 19.47$ per cent.

Thus, the simulation shows that a relaxation in migration policy in both the current period and the preceding period can facilitate 'take-off' in a developing economy in the current period.

6 Complementary simulations

We conduct additional simulations aimed at assessing the sensitivity of the results that were obtained above. To this end, we fix p at 5 per cent but allow the value of the wage in F, w^f, to vary. Also, we make a different assumption regarding the evolution of Ω. The specifications of the remaining parameters are the same as those in section 5, namely,

$$\alpha = 0, w^l = 1, w^h = 2, p = 0.05, r = 0.5\%, \Phi = 1.2, \Omega = 3. \qquad (7.83)$$

Then, $\widetilde{w}$ follows a uniform distribution over the domain [1, 2], which implies $\overline{w} = 1.5$.

Varying w^f

The logic of the analysis is essentially the same as that in section 5. The only difference is that the variables will be a function of w^f instead of p. We then derive the following Table:

Table 7.6 Complementary simulations with alternative foreign country – home country wage gaps

w^f	l^u	$F(w^c)$	u	l^o	λ	η	M	d
2	0.83	1.67	0.16	1.05	2.79	0.29	0.55	0.05622
3	2.44	5.00	0.57	3.17	15.84	1.90	0.66	0.05693
4	4.00	8.33	1.08	5.35	25.96	3.53	0.77	0.05755
5	5.51	11.67	1.71	7.56	34.03	5.20	0.89	0.05808
6	6.98	15.00	2.44	9.82	40.60	6.91	1.02	0.05853
7	8.40	18.33	3.30	12.12	46.07	8.64	1.16	0.05888
8	9.77	21.67	4.27	14.47	50.68	10.41	1.30	0.05914
9	11.11	25.00	5.38	16.86	54.62	12.21	1.45	0.05931
10	12.41	28.33	6.61	19.30	58.02	14.05	1.61	0.05937
11	13.67	31.67	7.98	21.78	60.99	15.92	1.78	0.05934
12	14.89	35.00	9.49	24.30	63.61	17.83	1.96	0.05920

Table 7.6 shows that when the wage gap between the foreign country and the home country widens, there will be a higher level of educated unemployment and a higher level of overeducation. For example, when $w^f = 12$ such that the income gap is $\frac{12}{1.5} = 8$, then the unemployment rate among the educated is 35 per cent and the proportion of the overeducated is 63.61 per cent, even though $p = 5$ per cent. Meanwhile, as the wage gap between the foreign country and the home country widens, the average cost of educated unemployment, and that of overeducation, will also increase. However, we note that an increase in the wage gap between the foreign country and the home country has little impact on the direct cost of migration or on the

number of migrants. This is so because p is at a fixed level no matter what the foreign wage is. Also, as the foreign wage rises, individuals with lower qualifications (for whom the cost of education is higher) will receive education. Consequently, the migrants will increasingly include less qualified individuals. Losing these individuals through migration may not even have a negative impact on the average income in the home country.

The brain gain

Now we rewrite equation (7.66) as

$$\Omega_t = \Omega_{t-1} - \pi(k_{t-1} - 0.1) \tag{7.84}$$

where π is a positive parameter. In this part, we specify $p_{t-1} = 0.05$ and $w^f = 5$. Then, from section 5, we know that

$$k_{t-1} = 0.1529.$$

Also, we specify $p_t = 0.05$. In addition, as in Section 5, we make the following specifications: $\beta = 1.2$, $e^c = 33$ per cent. From an analysis similar to that of section 5.5, we derive the following Table:

Table 7.7 The brain gain under alternative intergenerational externality effects of human capital

π	9	10	11	12	13	14	15	16	17	18	19	20
k_t(%)	18.21	18.60	19.02	19.45	19.90	20.37	33.40	34.23	35.11	36.04	37.01	38.04

Table 7.7 shows that the results obtained in Table 7.5 are quite robust.

7 Conclusions

Extending both the 'harmful brain drain' literature and the 'beneficial brain gain' literature, this chapter analyzes both the negative and the positive impact of migration by skilled individuals in a unified framework. The chapter extends the received literature on the 'harmful brain drain' by showing that in the short run, international migration can result in 'educated unemployment' and in overeducation in developing countries, as well as in a brain drain from these countries. Adopting a dynamic framework, it is then shown that due to the positive externality of the prevailing, economy-wide endowment of human capital on the formation of human capital, a relaxation in migration policy in both the current and the preceding period can facilitate 'take-off' of a developing country in the current period. Thus, it is suggested that while controlled migration by skilled individuals may reduce the social welfare of those who stay behind in the short run, it improves it in the long run.

The reason we resort to the 'educated unemployed' assumption is that we seek to track the implications of the removal of workers from gainful employment in their home country, a separation that occurs because they have the prospect of employment abroad. Our argument does not hinge then on workers being unemployed at home; if workers who failed to secure employment abroad while remaining at home were then to migrate and seek employment while living abroad, and then, if unsuccessful, were to return and take up work at home, the result would be the same – as long as seeking employment while abroad did not make it more likely to succeed. It is the removal of workers from employment, not their location when seeking work abroad, that matters.

At the heart of our analysis is the idea that allowing some individuals to work abroad implies not only a brain drain and 'educated unemployment' at home, but also, because the prospect of migration raises the expected returns to higher education, a 'brain gain': the developing country ends up with a higher proportion of educated individuals. Indeed, the brain drain is a catalyst for a 'brain gain'. Since, as already noted, due to the positive externality of the prevailing endowment of human capital on the formation of human capital a relaxation in migration policy in both the current period and the preceding period can facilitate 'take-off' in a developing economy in the current period, our analysis points to a new policy tool that could yield an improvement in the well-being of the population of a developing economy: controlled migration by educated workers. Somewhat counterintuitively, it is the departure of human capital that sets in motion a process of acquisition of human capital which, in turn, may well lead to economic betterment for all.

We conduct our analysis in the framework of partial equilibrium, assuming away a detailed analysis of the determination of the wage rate. Although an analysis based on a general-equilibrium framework will constitute a useful extension, we contend that such an extension will not change the qualitative results of our analysis. For example, if we are interested in exploring significant economy-wide repercussions of migration, would it not be appropriate for us to assume, as in basic textbook reasoning, that the departure of workers raises wages at home and lowers wages abroad? Not really. The essence of our argument is that a small probability of working abroad could trigger large repercussions such as the ones to which we allude. As such, the limited migration that takes place need not be accompanied by any discernible changes in wage rates either at home or abroad. Moreover, there are two main repercussions to the formation of human capital that tend to impact in opposite directions, and hence could cancel each other out: on the one hand, an increased supply of human capital at home could lower the returns to human capital at home; on the other hand, the increased supply of human capital could confer positive externalities, and hence raise the returns to human capital. The partial equilibrium setting could then be akin to that which would be yielded by a general equilibrium configuration.

Two additional comments in support of the robustness of our analysis are in order. First, it might be argued that if a fraction of the educated workers exit the home economy and if educated workers withdraw their labour from the home economy, then the wage paid to educated workers could be expected to rise. We have, however, already pointed out that such a wage change may not occur since these two responses coincide with the remainder of the educated workforce being more educated, an occurrence that is in direct response to the prospect of migration. Furthermore if, contrary to our assumption, the said two responses do indeed entail an increase in the home-economy's wage for the educated, then the effect of the enhancement of expected earnings through the prospect of migration will only be amplified by the higher home-country wage, and our claim that the prospect of migration impacts favourably on human capital formation will become even more compelling. Second, the assumption of a homogenous workforce eases our exposition. In related work, Stark and Wang (2002) have shown, albeit at the cost of some mathematical complexity, that incorporating the alternative assumption of a heterogeneous workforce yields results akin to those derived upon assuming a homogeneous workforce.

8 Appendix

Proof of Proposition 2

From the proof of Proposition 1, recalling equation (7.30), we know that when $p=0$, the average income of all the individuals is

$$\frac{c(0)}{\Omega}\left[\overline{w}-\frac{c(0)}{2}\right]+\left[1-\frac{c(0)}{\Omega}\right]\Phi.$$

When $p>0$, and recalling equation (7.16), the number of educated individuals remaining in the home country is,

$$(1-p)[1-p(1+\alpha)F(w^c)]\frac{c(p)}{\Omega},$$

and the number of uneducated individuals is $1-\frac{c(p)}{\Omega}$. Therefore, for all the individuals remaining in the home country, *if* no one had chosen to be unemployed, the total (net) income would have been

$$(1-p)[1-p(1+\alpha)F(w^c)]\frac{c(p)}{\Omega}\left[\overline{w}-\frac{c(p)}{2}\right]+\left[1-\frac{c(p)}{\Omega}\right]\Phi. \quad (7.75)$$

Furthermore, from equation (7.25), we know that the number of the individuals who become unemployed and remain in the home country is

$$F(w^c)c(p)(1-p)[1-p(1+\alpha)]/\Omega.$$

The average income of these individuals, had they chosen to work rather than become unemployed, would have been $E(w|w^l \leq w \leq w^c)$, whereas, recalling equation (7.27), their average income when choosing unemployment is $\frac{\overline{w}}{1+r}$. Since, recalling equation (7.28), the average net cost is

$$E(w|w^l \leq w \leq w^c) - \frac{\overline{w}}{1+r},$$

the total cost is

$$\left[E(w|w^l \leq w \leq w^c) - \frac{\overline{w}}{1+r}\right]F(w^c)c(p)(1-p)[1-p(1+\alpha)]/\Omega. \qquad (7.76)$$

Thus, when $p > 0$, for all the individuals remaining in the home country, their total income (income if all were employed less the income lost due to unemployment) is equal to

$$\Lambda \equiv (1-p)[1-p(1+\alpha)F(w^c)]\frac{c(p)}{\Omega}\left[\overline{w} - \frac{c(p)}{2}\right] + \left[1 - \frac{c(p)}{\Omega}\right]\Phi$$
$$- \left[E(w|w^l \leq w \leq w^c) - \frac{\overline{w}}{1+r}\right]F(w^c)c(p)(1-p)[1-p(1+\alpha)]/\Omega. \qquad (7.77)$$

For expositional simplicity, we define $\Gamma \equiv (1-p)[1-p(1+\alpha)F(w^c)]$. Since $\Gamma > (1-p)[1-p(1+\alpha)]$, total income is

$$\Lambda > \Gamma\frac{c(p)}{\Omega}\left[\overline{w} - \frac{c(p)}{2}\right] + \left[1 - \frac{c(p)}{\Omega}\right]\Phi$$
$$- \left[E(w|w^l \leq w \leq w^c) - \frac{\overline{w}}{1+r}\right]F(w^c)c(p)\Gamma/\Omega$$
$$\geq \Gamma\frac{c(p)}{\Omega}\left[\overline{w} - \frac{c(p)}{2}\right] + \left[1 - \frac{c(p)}{\Omega}\right]\Phi$$
$$- \left[E(w|w^l \leq w \leq w^h) - \frac{\overline{w}}{1+r}\right]F(w^h)c(p)\Gamma/\Omega$$
$$= \frac{\overline{w}}{1+r}\Gamma\frac{c(p)}{\Omega} - \Gamma\frac{(c(p))^2}{2\Omega} + \left[1 - \frac{c(p)}{\Omega}\right]\Phi. \qquad (7.78)$$

Assuming that the condition, $w^f > (3+\alpha)\overline{w}$, is satisfied, we know from Lemma 1 that

$$\Gamma\frac{c(p)}{\Omega} = (1-p)\left[1-p(1+\alpha)F(w^c)\right]\frac{c(p)}{\Omega} > \frac{c(0)}{\Omega}.$$

Therefore, we have

$$\Lambda > \frac{c(0)}{\Omega}\frac{\overline{w}}{1+r} - \Gamma\frac{(c(p))^2}{2\Omega} + \left[1-\frac{c(p)}{\Omega}\right]\Phi.$$

Note that since the entire population is normalized to be one, the total number of the individuals remaining in the home country is less than one. Noting that $\Gamma < 1-p$, we know that the average net income of these individuals is greater than

$$\frac{c(0)}{\Omega}\frac{\overline{w}}{1+r} - \Gamma\frac{(c(p))^2}{2\Omega} + \left[1-\frac{c(p)}{\Omega}\right]\Phi > \frac{c(0)}{\Omega}\frac{\overline{w}}{1+r} - (1-p)\frac{(c(p))^2}{2\Omega} + \left[1-\frac{c(p)}{\Omega}\right]\Phi. \quad (7.79)$$

When $p=0$, recalling (7.30), the average income of all individuals is

$$\frac{c(0)}{\Omega}\left[\overline{w}-\frac{c(0)}{2}\right] + \left[1-\frac{c(0)}{\Omega}\right]\Phi.$$

Thus, the short-run loss in terms of average income arising from the migration prospect is less than

$$\begin{aligned} L \equiv {} & \frac{c(0)}{\Omega}\left[\overline{w}-\frac{c(0)}{2}\right] + \left[1-\frac{c(0)}{\Omega}\right]\Phi - \frac{c(0)}{\Omega}\frac{\overline{w}}{1+r} \\ & + (1-p)\frac{(c(p))^2}{2\Omega} - \left[1-\frac{c(p)}{\Omega}\right]\Phi \\ = {} & \frac{rc(0)}{(1+r)\Omega}\overline{w} + \frac{(1-p)(c(p))^2-(c(0))^2}{2\Omega} + \frac{\Phi}{\Omega}(c(p)) - c(0)). \end{aligned} \quad (7.80)$$

Consider now the gain to the home country if 'take-off' occurs in the next period. We first note that a feasible scenario is for the government to set $p=0$ after the economy takes off. Hence, the maximal average income of the economy when p is optimally chosen is not less than that when $p=0$. Next, we note that when $p=0$ and after the economy takes off, the number of individuals who choose to be skilled is greater than the corresponding number before the economy takes off, $\frac{c(0)}{\Omega}$. This increase in the number of educated individuals will increase average national income, since the gain from receiving education is greater than the cost of acquiring education. Thus, after the economy takes off, average income in the economy is greater than that when $p = 0$ and $\frac{c(0)}{\Omega}$ fraction of individuals receive higher education, namely

$$\frac{c(0)}{\Omega}\left[\beta\overline{w} - \frac{c(0)}{2}\right] + \left[1 - \frac{c(0)}{\Omega}\right]\Phi.$$

Then, the benefit measured in terms of the average income in the next period arising from the prospect of migration less the average income that would have obtained in the absence of such a prospect is greater than

$$\begin{aligned} G &\equiv \frac{c(0)}{\Omega}\left[\beta\overline{w} - \frac{c(0)}{2}\right] + \left[1 - \frac{c(0)}{\Omega}\right]\Phi - \frac{c(0)}{\Omega}\left[\overline{w} - \frac{c(0)}{2}\right] - \left[1 - \frac{c(0)}{\Omega}\right]\Phi \\ &= (\beta - 1)\frac{c(0)}{\Omega}\overline{w}. \end{aligned} \tag{7.81}$$

Thus, the long-run gain is greater than the short-run loss if

$$-L + \rho G > 0, \tag{7.82}$$

where ρ is the social discount rate across generations.

Inserting equations (7.80) and (7.81) into (7.82), we get

$$-\frac{rc(0)}{(1+r)\Omega}\overline{w} - \frac{(1-p)(c(p))^2 - (c(0))^2}{2\Omega} - \frac{\Phi}{\Omega}(c(p) - c(0)) + \rho(\beta - 1)\frac{c(0)}{\Omega}\overline{w} > 0,$$

namely

$$\beta > \frac{0.5[(1-p)(c(p))^2 - (c(0))^2] + \Phi(c(p) - c(0))}{\rho c(0)\overline{w}} + \frac{r + \rho + r\rho}{\rho(1+r)}.$$

In other words, if the condition (7.36) is satisfied, then (7.82) will be satisfied. Q.E.D.

Notes

1. As noted by Stark (2004), this view has become so entrenched that it is regularly echoed by the informed press.
2. See, for example, Stark, Helmenstein, and Prskawetz (1997, 1998), Mountford (1997), Beine, Docquier, and Rapoport (2001), Stark and Wang (2002), Stark (2005), Stark *et al.* (2006), and Boucher, Stark, and Taylor (2008).
3. See, for example, the empirical observations with regard to 'educated unemployment' in Fan and Stark (2007).

4. There is an interesting literature in labour economics on 'overeducation' which is defined somewhat differently than in our setting (Sicherman, 1991). Interestingly, using American data, Sicherman shows that overeducation can be partly explained by the mobility patterns of educated workers. In our setting, overeducation is explained by the prospect of migration for educated workers.
5. See, for example, Kapur and McHale (2003) on the link between migration and the growth of the IT sector in these countries.
6. The assumption has been used widely in the literature (see, for example, Galor and Stark, 1994; and Galor and Tsiddon, 1996). The 'beneficial brain drain' literature has so far drawn on a single-period model or on a long-run steady state analysis, and hence is not suitable for the unraveling of the complete set of the dynamic costs and benefits, presumably tilting the analysis in favour of a more sympathetic view of the consequences of the migration of skilled workers.
7. The concept and phenomenon of a 'take-off' have been emphasized frequently in the development literature and are at the heart of many analyses by economic historians of the stages of economic growth (Rostow, 1960).
8. The 'big push' theory (for example, Murphy, Shleifer and Vishny, 1989) and the argument of a skill-induced technological change (for example, Acemoglu, 1998) both explain the endogenous determination of β.
9. Since a larger β implies higher returns to education, we would expect $e(p, \beta)$ to be an increasing function of β. In addition, if $e(0, \beta) < e^c$, a careful choice of p (>0) can reverse this inequality.
10. It can be less because some individuals may choose to become unemployed, yet the unemployment is *ex post* inefficient if they fail to go abroad.

References

Acemoglu, D. (1998) 'Why Do New Technologies Complement Skills? Directed Technical Change and Wage Inequality', *Quarterly Journal of Economics* 113, 1055–89.

Azariadis, C. and A. Drazen (1990) 'Threshold Externalities in Economic Development', *Quarterly Journal of Economics* 105, 501–26.

Beine, M., F. Docquier, and H. Rapoport (2001) 'Brain Drain and Economic Growth: Theory and Evidence', *Journal of Development Economics* 64, 275–89.

Bhagwati, J. and J. D. Wilson (1989) *Income Taxation and International Mobility* (Cambridge, MA: MIT Press).

Boucher, S., O. Stark, and J. E. Taylor (2008) 'A Gain with a Drain? Evidence from Rural Mexico on the New Economics of the Brain Drain', in this volume.

Fan, C. S. (2004) 'Quality, Trade, and Growth', *Journal of Economic Behavior and Organization* 55, 271–91.

Fan, C. S. and O. Stark (2007) 'International Migration and 'Educated Unemployment', *Journal of Development Economics* 83, 76–87.

Galor, O. and O. Stark (1994) 'Migration, Human Capital Formation, and Long-Run Output', in H. Sibert (ed.), *Migration: A Challenge for Europe* (Tübingen: Mohr).

Galor, O. and D. Tsiddon (1996) 'Income Distribution and Growth: The Kuznets Hypothesis Revisited', *Economica* 63, S103–17.

Hanushek, E. (1996) 'Measuring Investment in Education', *Journal of Economic Perspectives* 10, 9–30.

Kapur, D. and J. McHale (2003) 'Sojourns and Software: Internationally Mobile Human Capital and High-Tech Industry Development in India, Ireland, and Israel', Harvard University, mimeo.

Mountford, A. (1997) 'Can a Brain Drain Be Good for Growth in the Source Economy?', *Journal of Development Economics* 53, 287–303.

Murphy, K., A. Shleifer and R. Vishny (1989) 'Industrialization and the Big Push', *Journal of Political Economy* 97, 1003–26.

Pritchett, L. (1997) 'Divergence, Big Time', *Journal of Economic Perspectives* 11, 3–17.

Rostow, W. W. (1960) *The Stages of Economic Growth* (Cambridge: Cambridge University Press).

Sicherman, N. (1991) ' "Overducation" in the Labor Market', *Journal of Labor Economics* 9, 101–22.

Stark, O. (2004) 'Rethinking the Brain Drain', *World Development* 32, 15–22.

Stark, O. (2005) 'The New Economics of the Brain Drain', *World Economics* 6, 137–40.

Stark, O., A. Casarico, C. Devillanova and S. Uebelmesser (2008) 'International Migration, Human Capital Formation, and the Setting of Migration Control Policies: Mapping the Gains', in this volume.

Stark, O., C. Helmenstein and A. Prskawetz (1997) 'A Brain Gain with a Brain Drain', *Economics Letters* 55, 227–34.

Stark, O., C. Helmenstein and A. Prskawetz (1998) 'Human Capital Depletion, Human Capital Formation, and Migration: A Blessing or a "Curse"?', *Economics Letters* 60, 363–7.

Stark, O. and Y. Wang (2002) 'Inducing Human Capital Formation: Migration as a Substitute for Subsidies', *Journal of Public Economics* 86, 29–46.

Summers, R. and A. Heston (1991) 'The Penn World Table (Mark 5): An Expanded Set of International Comparisons, 1950–1988', *Quarterly Journal of Economics* 106, 327–68.

8

An Optimal Selective Migration Policy in the Absence of Symmetric Information, and in the Presence of Skill Formation Incentives*

Oded Stark, Alessandra Casarico, and Silke Uebelmesser

1 Introduction

In this chapter we study the selection policy of incoming migrant workers when the receiving country's own welfare guides the formation of policies, when selection is made under asymmetric information, and when workers differ in terms of their level of human capital. Informational asymmetry arises when employers in the receiving country (in contrast to employers in the sending country) cannot decipher the true skill level of individual workers (who, however, know well their own skill levels). Selection is achieved via levying a proportional tax on migrants' earnings. (An equivalent way of conceptualizing the selection tool is to think of it as an entry fee to be paid in the form of a tax on earnings.[1]) We calculate the optimal tax when human capital is fixed – 'a fixed human capital framework' – and in the presence of a human capital formation incentive – 'an adjustable human capital framework'.

We find that in the presence of a behavioural response by potential migrants, there is a trade-off between selecting high-skill migrant workers and reaping tax revenues on the one hand, and the detrimental reaction with respect to the incentive to invest in skill acquisition, as a consequence of the tax, on the other hand. Human capital responses at origin tie the taxing hand at destination. Such is not the case in the absence of an incentive to invest in skill acquisition. The absence or presence of a skill formation response matters also for establishing the impact of a selection policy on the welfare of the natives of the sending country. In the adjustable human capital framework, we find that there are instances in which the sending country experiences an aggregate increase in welfare compared to a closed economy,

* We are indebted to Thomas Piketty, Marcin Jakubek, and Anna Zylicz for insightful comments and very helpful advice.

even though the tax is selected in order to maximize the welfare of the natives of the receiving country.

Migration policies have occupied the center stage of policy debates in both developing and developed countries. In particular, countries in Europe have recently exhibited an increasing tendency to formulate policies targeted at attracting skilled workers. France has been coming up with corresponding legislation ('Loi relative à l'immigration et à l'intégration'); Germany is discussing similar policies; the UK has recently introduced a point system akin to the systems already in place in Canada, Australia, and New Zealand, and the European Union has come forward with the 'blue card' initiative which targets exclusively skilled workers, and which allows such workers free mobility across the member countries. All of these moves are aimed at enticing the skilled, and keeping out the unskilled.

As early as the 1980s, the economics literature yielded several elegant studies of the management of migration flows by the receiving countries (examples of such studies include Ethier, 1986, and Djajic, 1989). Recently, Bianchi (2006) has analyzed the interplay between immigration restrictions and migrants' skill composition in a framework in which migrants are positively self-selected, and resorting to alternative welfare functions, Benhabib and Jovanovic (2007) asked which migration policy (skill-neutral or skill-biased) maximizes world welfare.

In this chapter we identify a country-of-destination tool for achieving selection, and we show how the tool should be wisely applied by that country. Moreover, given a natural concern that 'creaming off' policies could inflict harm on the sending countries, we further show that, quite unexpectedly, the receiving countries' gain need not come about at the expense of the sending countries' pain.

2 The basic model

We consider a two-country setting: a sending country, S, and a receiving country, R.[2] Workers differ in their skill level. We assume that the level of human capital of the unskilled workers, $\underline{\vartheta}$, is exogenously given, and that it is the same in the two countries and the two frameworks. The level of human capital of the skilled workers in country i is ϑ^i, $i = S, R$.

Let the average level of human capital in country i be $\overline{\vartheta}^i$. In a closed economy setting, the gross earnings of a skilled worker (h) and the gross earnings of an unskilled worker (u) are, respectively,

$$f_h^i = \psi^i \beta^i \ln(\vartheta^i + 1) + \eta \ln(\overline{\vartheta}^i + 1) \tag{8.1}$$

$$f_u^i = \beta^i \ln(\underline{\vartheta} + 1) + \eta \ln(\overline{\vartheta}^i + 1). \tag{8.2}$$

Thus, we assume that f_j^i, $j = h, u$, depends on the level of the individual's human capital (ϑ^i or $\underline{\vartheta}$), and on the average level of human capital ($\overline{\vartheta}^i$), viz. a human capital externality effect. Countries differ in their technologies. While, for the sake of simplicity, we assume that social returns, η, are the same in both countries, private returns differ. The superior technology of an advanced, developed country renders the application there of a given level of human capital more productive than in the sending developing country. Consequently, we assume that $\beta^R > \beta^S$. The term ψ^i is an idiosyncratic productivity parameter that applies to skilled workers. It reflects their productivity edge when compared to the productivity of unskilled workers, for any given level of human capital. We assume that ψ^i pertains only to the receiving country where more advanced technologies are applied, that is, we assume that $\psi^R > \psi^S = 1$.

We assume that in the open economy setting, workers of skill level j in the sending country face an exogenous probability m_j, $j = h, u$, of migrating to the receiving country with $m_u = m_h = m < 1$ in the absence of selection. The total number of migrants will then be $M = mN^S = m_h H^S + m_u(N^S - H^S)$, where N^S is the total native population in the sending country, and H^S is the number of skilled workers in the sending country.

Given our interest in the selection procedure of the receiving country, we assume that $\vartheta^S > \overline{\vartheta}^R$, which implies that in an open economy environment, the receiving country has an incentive to attract skilled migrants who will have a positive impact on the average level of human capital there. We also assume that $\overline{\vartheta}^R > \overline{\vartheta}^S$, viz. if the receiving country allows in a mixture of sending-country workers whose average skill is the same as that which obtains in the sending country, the productivity of its native workers will suffer.

The government of the receiving country exercises selection via levying a proportional tax γ on the earnings of the incoming migrants. The tax is set so as to maximize the welfare of the native citizens, whose welfare function is

$$\Phi = H^R \beta^R \psi^R \ln(\tilde{\vartheta}^R + 1) + (N^R - H^R)\beta^R \ln(\underline{\vartheta} + 1) + N^R \eta \ln(\tilde{\overline{\vartheta}}^R + 1) + M\gamma \tilde{f}_M^R. \quad (8.3)$$

H^R and N^R indicate the number of skilled workers and the total native population in the receiving country, respectively; a tilde denotes open economy variables; and $\tilde{f}_M^R$ denotes the earnings of the migrants. A higher average level of human capital at R contributes to higher incomes and welfare there.

When selection is successful, $m_u = 0$; only skilled migrants enter. The number of migrants is then $M = m_h H^S$, where $m_h = m\frac{N^S}{H^S} > m$. We assume that H^S is large enough so as to ensure that $M < H^S$.

When establishing the equilibrium conditions under which the receiving country successfully selects in only skilled migrants, the behavioural responses of skilled workers in S turn out to be of paramount importance.

To see this we analyze first the fixed human capital framework and, then, the adjustable human capital framework.

2.1 A fixed human capital framework

Obviously, for equilibrium to hold in which only skilled workers migrate, the unskilled workers will have to find it disadvantageous to migrate, while the skilled workers will have to find it attractive to migrate. If unskilled workers were to migrate, then we assume that in the presence of asymmetric information every migrant worker will be paid the same wage, $\hat{\tilde{f}}^R$, based on the average productivity in R of the group of skilled and unskilled migrants

$$\hat{\tilde{f}}^R = \frac{H^S}{N^S}\tilde{f}_h^R + \frac{N^S - H^S}{N^S}\tilde{f}_u^R, \tag{8.4}$$

where a hat indicates the absence of selection policies, and where the proportions of skilled workers and unskilled workers in the migrant population are the same as their proportions in the population of the country of origin. We assume that the actual wage paid is equal to $\hat{\tilde{f}}^R$, and that the wage determination rule is known to all workers prior to their possible migration. For selection to be successful, the following twin conditions need to hold:

$$(1-\gamma)\hat{\tilde{f}}^R < \tilde{f}_u^S \rightarrow \gamma > 1 - \frac{\tilde{f}_u^S}{\hat{\tilde{f}}^R} \equiv \gamma_{\min}, \tag{8.5}$$

$$(1-\gamma)\tilde{f}_h^R > \tilde{f}_h^S \rightarrow \gamma < 1 - \frac{\tilde{f}_h^S}{\tilde{f}_h^R} \equiv \gamma_{\max}. \tag{8.6}$$

In (8.5), we have a condition that the unskilled do not find it advantageous to migrate. If the unskilled do not migrate, then the skilled, if they were to migrate, would be paid their group-specific wage $\tilde{f}_h^R$. The condition in (8.6) states that for the skilled workers to find it advantageous to migrate if the unskilled workers are weeded out, the skilled workers will need to have earnings in R, net of the tax, that are higher than their earnings in S in the closed economy setting. For an equilibrium with selection to obtain, the prevailing tax rate γ needs then to observe $\gamma_{\min} < \gamma < \gamma_{\max}$.[3]

2.1.1 *The optimal tax*

When (8.5) and (8.6) hold, $M = m_h H^S$, and thus $\tilde{f}_M^R = \tilde{f}_h^R$, that is, given that only skilled workers migrate, these workers earn in the receiving country their group-specific wage. The objective function to be maximized in order to determine the optimal tax rate is therefore, following (8.3),

$$\Phi = M\gamma\tilde{f}_M^R = m_h H^S \gamma \tilde{f}_h^R. \tag{8.7}$$

The reason for this simple objective function is that only the last term in (8.3) depends on γ. Differentiating (8.7) with respect to γ, we obtain

$$\frac{d\Phi}{d\gamma} = m_h H^S \tilde{f}_h^R > 0 \tag{8.8}$$

which, from (8.6), implies a corner solution to the maximization problem. Consequently, the optimal tax is

$$\gamma^* = \gamma_{\max} - \varepsilon \tag{8.9}$$

where ε is an infinitesimally small number.

Under a γ^*-based selection policy, the unskilled workers will not have an incentive to migrate since $\gamma^* = \gamma_{\max} - \varepsilon > \gamma_{\min}$. Once the skilled workers are sorted away from the unskilled workers, they are taxed so as to skim off all but a tiny amount of their extra earnings in R.

2.2 An adjustable human capital framework

We consider next the case in which the human capital investment decision of the skilled workers in S responds to the employment prospect in R, a prospect of which R's tax rate is a component. As in the fixed human capital framework, we seek to characterize the equilibrium condition under which the receiving country selects successfully. The following condition then needs to be satisfied:

$$(1-\gamma)\hat{\tilde{f}}^R < \tilde{f}_u^S(\gamma) \tag{8.10}$$

where, while 'recycling' the notation of (8.5), it is to be understood that the earnings can differ across the two frameworks, and where we write $\tilde{f}_u^S(\gamma)$, since $\tilde{f}_u^S$ depends on γ, albeit indirectly, via the resulting change in the average level of human capital in S. This dependence arises because the earnings landscape in the sending country is affected by the tax choices of the receiving country, and these choices, in turn, impact on the investment decisions of the skilled workers including those who end up not migrating. (This consideration will be elucidated further momentarily.) We define $\gamma_{\min}$ as the tax rate that solves $(1-\gamma_{\min})\hat{\tilde{f}}^R - \tilde{f}_u^S(\gamma_{\min}) = 0$.

When unskilled workers are deterred from migrating, the gross wage awaiting skilled workers upon migrating is, again, their group-specific wage $\tilde{f}_h^R(\gamma)$. In this setting, a skilled worker in S chooses the optimal level of his investment in human capital by maximizing his expected net earnings, $\tilde{w}_h$, which are given by

$$\tilde{w}_h = m_h(1-\gamma)\tilde{f}_h^R(\gamma) + (1-m_h)\tilde{f}_h^S(\gamma) - k\tilde{\vartheta}^S, \tag{8.11}$$

where $k > 0$ is the cost of acquiring a unit of human capital. Drawing on (8.1) and (8.2), a substitution of $\tilde{f}_h^R(\gamma)$ and $\tilde{f}_h^S(\gamma)$ enables us to rewrite (8.11) as

$$\tilde{w}_h = m_h(1-\gamma)\Big\{\beta^R\psi^R\ln(\tilde{\vartheta}^S+1)+\eta\ln(\tilde{\bar{\vartheta}}^R+1)\Big\} + (1-m_h)\Big\{\beta^S\ln(\tilde{\vartheta}^S+1)+\eta\ln(\tilde{\bar{\vartheta}}^S+1)\Big\} - k\tilde{\vartheta}^S. \quad (8.12)$$

The maximization of $\tilde{w}_h$ yields $\tilde{\vartheta}^{S*}$, the optimal level of investment in human capital when *R*'s selection policy is in place,

$$\tilde{\vartheta}^{S*} = \frac{\beta^S}{k} - 1 + \frac{m_h}{k}[\beta^R\psi^R(1-\gamma)-\beta^S]. \quad (8.13)$$

When $m_h = 0$, we have that $\tilde{\vartheta}^{S*} = \vartheta^{S*}$ (where $\vartheta^{S*} = \frac{\beta^S}{k} - 1$ is the optimal level of investment in human capital in the closed economy setting, assuming of course that $\beta^S > k$). When $m_h > 0$, however, $\tilde{\vartheta}^{S*} > \vartheta^{S*}$ as long as $\beta^R\psi^R(1-\gamma) > \beta^S$.[4] We know that $\beta^R\psi^R > \beta^S$. Therefore, the optimal policy of the government of *R* has to be such that the tax rate that it chooses will not trigger a process that will bring the average level of human capital in *R* below the level which obtains in *R* in the closed economy setting (unless such a decline will be compensated by tax revenues), *if R* is to admit skilled migrant workers from *S* at all. (Clearly, the government of *R* never needs to worry about not being able to 'protect' its welfare from a migration-induced erosion since it can always select a γ which curtails migration altogether.)

From equation (8.13) we see that there is a positive relationship between the optimal level of the human capital that skilled workers elect to form and the probability of migration, and a negative relationship between the optimal level of human capital that skilled workers elect to form and the tax rate.

In order for the skilled workers to find it advantageous to migrate, the tax rate γ has to obey the following condition:

$$(1-\gamma)\tilde{f}_h^{R*}(\gamma) - k\tilde{\vartheta}^{S*}(\gamma) > f_h^{S*} - k\vartheta^{S*}, \quad (8.14)$$

where $\tilde{f}_h^{R*}(\gamma)$ and f_h^{S*} denote, respectively, the gross earnings of skilled workers in the receiving country with selection, and the gross earnings of skilled workers in the sending country in the closed economy setting, evaluated in both cases at the individually optimal levels of investment, and where we highlight the dependency of the open economy variables on the selection policy by expressing each of these variables as a function of the tax rate. We define γ_{max} as the tax rate such that $(1-\gamma_{max})\tilde{f}_h^{R*}(\gamma_{max}) - k\tilde{\vartheta}^{S*}(\gamma_{max}) - [f_h^{S*} - k\vartheta^{S*}] = 0$.

2.2.1 *The optimal tax*

Mindful of the decision-making rule of the skilled workers in S, the government of R determines the optimal γ by maximizing the objective function (8.3) subject to the constraints (8.10) and (8.14), which jointly guarantee that the tax γ can indeed deliver an equilibrium with selection.[5] The objective function (8.3) reduces to

$$\Phi = N^R \eta \ln(\bar{\tilde{\vartheta}}^R + 1) + M\gamma \tilde{f}_M^R = N^R \eta \ln(\bar{\tilde{\vartheta}}^R + 1) + m_h H^S \gamma \tilde{f}_h^{R*}(\gamma). \tag{8.15}$$

The first term on the most right-hand side of (8.15) captures the impact that skilled migrants have on the average level of human capital in the receiving country. The second term on the most right-hand side of (8.15) is the tax revenue.

The optimal tax rate is determined by differentiating (8.15) and using

$$\bar{\tilde{\vartheta}}^R = \frac{N^R \overline{\vartheta}^R + m_h H^S \tilde{\vartheta}^{S*}(\gamma)}{N^R + m_h H^S}, \tag{8.16}$$

to obtain

$$\frac{\partial \Phi}{\partial \gamma} = \eta N^R \frac{1}{(\bar{\tilde{\vartheta}}^R + 1)} \frac{m_h H^S}{N^R + m_h H^S} \frac{\partial \tilde{\vartheta}^{S*}}{\partial \gamma} + m_h H^S \tilde{f}_h^{R*} \left[1 + \underbrace{\frac{\gamma}{\tilde{f}_h^{R*}} \frac{\partial \tilde{f}_h^{R*}}{\partial \tilde{\vartheta}^{S*}} \frac{\partial \tilde{\vartheta}^{S*}}{\partial \gamma}}_{\zeta} \right] \tag{8.17}$$

where $\zeta < 0$ can be interpreted as the elasticity of the gross earnings with respect to the tax rate.

Even though levying the tax allows selection of the skilled workers, and even though, as $m_h H^S \tilde{f}_h^{R*} > 0$ in (8.17) indicates, a higher tax rate bears positively on the tax revenue, we see that there is a trade-off that has to be taken into account. As (8.13) shows, raising the tax rate has a negative effect on the optimal level of human capital formed by migrants. This bears directly and negatively on the natives' welfare, as shown by the first term in (8.17), and additionally negatively via the reduction in the tax base, as shown by the second term in square brackets in (8.17).

The equilibrium tax rate, γ^*, is therefore

$$\gamma^* = \begin{cases} \gamma_{\min} & \text{if } \left.\frac{\partial \Phi}{\partial \gamma}\right|_{\gamma=\gamma_{\min}} \leq 0 \\ \gamma \in (\gamma_{\min}, \gamma_{\max} - \varepsilon) & \text{if } \frac{\partial \Phi}{\partial \gamma} = 0 \\ \gamma_{\max} - \varepsilon & \text{if } \left.\frac{\partial \Phi}{\partial \gamma}\right|_{\gamma=\gamma_{\max}} \geq 0 \end{cases}. \tag{8.18}$$

When the negative effect dominates at $\gamma_{\min}$, it is optimal for the receiving country to set γ at the minimal level of taxation that is compatible with the entry of only skilled migrants. When the positive effect dominates at $\gamma_{\max}$, it is optimal to choose the highest possible level of taxation that is compatible with the entry of skilled migrants. An intermediate tax rate γ is also possible, with that rate defined implicitly by setting (8.17) equal to 0.

2.3 A comparison of the two frameworks

The different reaction possibilities of skilled workers in terms of their investment in human capital map into different optimal tax policies by the receiving country.

Proposition 1: *In the fixed human capital framework, the government of the receiving country will maximize welfare by levying the maximal tax γ^* compatible with migration by only skilled workers, $\gamma^* = \gamma_{\max} - \varepsilon$. In the adjustable human capital framework, the government of the receiving country will maximize welfare by levying the tax $\gamma^* \in [\gamma_{\min}, \gamma_{\max} - \varepsilon]$. If a selection equilibrium does not exist, that is, if $\gamma_{\min} \geq \gamma_{\max}$, the government of the receiving country will set the tax $\gamma^* \geq \gamma_{\min}$ such that a closed economy regime obtains.*

In the fixed human capital framework, when migration is of skilled workers, the government of the receiving country serves the welfare interests of its native population by maximizing the tax proceeds, conditional on the tax 'honouring' the incentive compatibility constraint for the skilled migrants who have to find it advantageous to migrate.

In the adjustable human capital framework, however, the presence of a positive effect of a higher tax rate on revenue does not necessarily imply that it is optimal for the receiving country to increase the tax to the highest possible level. The interaction between the level of human capital of the migrants and the tax proceeds may be such that the natives' welfare is maximized at a lower tax rate. The taxman at destination must thus be sensitive to the calculus of the skilled workers at origin.

3 The welfare of the sending country

What is the impact of a selection policy by the government of R on the welfare of S? In this section we compare the level of welfare of the sending country when a selection policy by the receiving country is in place, with the level of welfare of the sending country when that country's economy is closed. Does the 'creaming off' policy of the receiving country necessarily come at the expense of the sending country's welfare, when the welfare of the sending country is the sum total of the welfare of all its natives, migrants and non-migrants alike?

In the fixed human capital framework, under the optimal taxation policy $\gamma^* = \gamma_{\max} - \varepsilon$, the welfare of the sending country is lower than in the closed economy setting: the non-migrants stand to lose since in the wake of the departure of skilled workers, the average level of human capital in the sending country is lowered, while the migrants fare about equally as their extra earnings are taxed away (but for a tiny amount).

In the adjustable human capital framework, the welfare effects pertaining to the sending economy are not that straightforward, however. While the skilled migrants are clearly benefiting from migration, assessing the welfare effects for the non-migrants (the skilled and the unskilled) is more involved. The change in welfare of the unskilled workers is intimately related to the change in the average level of human capital in the sending country. This level *increases* if the heightened incentive of the skilled workers to invest in human capital is not overcompensated by a reduction in the average level of human capital due to the departure of some of them. As to the skilled non-migrants, they also stand to benefit from an increase in the average level of human capital. However, they suffer a loss due to their overinvestment, given that, for them, the migration opportunity did not materialize.[6] The total welfare effect for the natives of the sending country depends therefore on the relative magnitude of the welfare changes for each of the three groups, and on the relative size of these groups. As we show next, this effect may very well be positive.

4 Simulations

In order to identify the optimal tax and assess whether selection is associated with a higher level of welfare for the sending country than the level of welfare that it would have experienced if it were closed, we resort to a simulation. We proceed as follows.

We begin with a concrete example. We represent our assumptions by means of specific magnitudes of the parameters. This yields what we refer to as the 'benchmark' simulation. We subsequently study the robustness of the results of the benchmark simulation under alternative magnitudes of the parameters.

In order to construct the benchmark simulation, we make the following assumptions regarding the magnitude of the parameters: the populations of the receiving country and the sending country are of equal size, $N^S = N^R$; the share of skilled workers in the sending country, denoted by α^S, represents 0.15 of the country's workforce; and the migration probability for the sending country's workers, m, is 0.03. Consequently, the probability of migration for the skilled workers, if the receiving country implements a selection policy (admitting only $0.03N^S$ workers who are skilled) is $m_h = 0.03/0.15 = 0.20$.[7] Regarding the parameters of the production function, we assume that $\beta^R = 2\beta^S$; $\psi_h^R = 4$; $\eta = 0.2\beta^S$, and $k = 0.5\beta^S$.[8] As a normalization rule, we set $\beta^S = 1$. We also fix $\overline{\vartheta}^R = 0.8$, and $\underline{\vartheta} = 0.2$.

4.1 Taxation policy

Given these parameter values, we find, using (8.18), that the maximization problem for the receiving country yields as a solution a tax rate of $\gamma^* = \gamma_{\min} = 0.811$ (with $\gamma_{\max} = 0.868$) in the adjustable human capital case, and, using (8.6) and (8.9) (and setting aside the epsilon), a tax rate of $\gamma^* = \gamma_{\max} = 0.868$ in the fixed human capital case. Thus, the optimal tax rate in the adjustable human capital case is *lower* than the optimal tax rate in the fixed human capital case; the human capital formation response in the sending country bites into the tax rate, it prompts the government of the receiving country to choose a milder tax.

4.2 The average level of human capital, and the level of welfare

We consider the case of an adjustable human capital. While our interest is in assessing the situation in the sending country, for the sake of completeness we first briefly attend to the situation in the receiving country.[9] We find that

$$\overline{\vartheta}^R = 0.800 < \tilde{\bar{\vartheta}}^R = 0.812 \qquad (8.19)$$

where $\tilde{\bar{\vartheta}}^R$ is defined in (8.16). The inequality in (8.19) reaffirms that selection via taxation under an adjustable human capital raises the average level of human capital in *R* above the average level of human capital that would have obtained in *R* if *R*'s economy had been closed. Equation (8.19) also yields a ranking of the welfare levels for the receiving country where, to recall, under selection, and as opposed to the closed economy setting, the welfare in *R* is enhanced not only by the elevated average level of human capital, but also by the revenues collected via the tax-based selection policy.

Looking at the sending country, and calculating the average level of human capital there, we find that in the case of adjustable human capital

$$\tilde{\bar{\vartheta}}^S = 0.324 > \overline{\vartheta}^S = 0.320. \qquad (8.20)$$

This is an interesting result: in comparison with the incentive to invest in human capital that would have prevailed had the sending country been immune to migration, the opportunity to migrate strengthens the incentive to invest, thereby *increasing* the average level of human capital in the sending country. This repercussion follows in spite of the sending country losing some of its skilled workers.[10] In and by itself, and as already noted, establishing that the average level of human capital in the presence of selection is higher than the average level of human capital in the closed economy setting does not guarantee that welfare in the sending country increases. Unskilled workers are surely better off, since the change in their welfare is determined by the change in the average level of human capital. Skilled migrants are better off as their very decision to move makes clear. While skilled non-migrants benefit from the increased level of average human capital, they are hurt by their overinvestment. Taking all these effects into consideration, in our benchmark simulation, the welfare of the sending country is higher (by 0.109) when the receiving country selects, compared to when the 'sending' economy is closed.[11]

4.3 Sensitivity of the results to alternative magnitudes of the parameters

We next analyze the robustness of our results to shifts in the parameters. We are particularly interested in finding out what happens to the welfare of the natives of the sending country in comparison with the benchmark configuration of parameters. With regard to the receiving country, since the very purpose of the selective migration policy is to raise the welfare of its natives, for all our variations of the parameters there is, indeed, a non-negative welfare effect for the receiving country, compared to the closed economy setting. In fact, and as already noted, if the receiving country cannot implement a policy with a positive impact on the welfare of its natives, it will choose such a tax that the closed-economy regime obtains, with no changes in welfare one way or the other. What, however, is more revealing is that, as we show next, the receiving country selecting confers welfare gains upon the sending country compared to the closed economy setting for most of the cases that we happened to consider.

We proceed by modifying, first, one parameter at a time, and within a selected interval. We find that changes in the relative size of the native population in the sending country, N^S, with respect to N^R, and variations in η, k, $\overline{\vartheta}^R$ and $\underline{\vartheta}$ do not affect the signs of the welfare effects; they impact only on their magnitudes.[12] The productivity gap between countries as captured by the values of ψ or β^R relative to β^S, the probability of migration m, and the share of the skilled workers in the native population of the sending country α^S, are crucial to assessing the impact of the selection policy on the welfare of the sending country. Tables 8.1–8.4 display the optimal tax rates (presented in bold in the columns $\gamma^*, \gamma_{\min}$ and $\gamma_{\max}$); a ranking of the average level of human capital in the sending country (a "Yes" indicates that in the open economy setting the sending country enjoys a higher average level of human capital than it experiences in the closed economy setting); and the welfare change in the sending country – that is, the difference between the open economy level of welfare with a selection by R, and the closed economy level of welfare (where a positive value indicates that selection increases welfare in the sending country as compared with the closed economy level). The lines preceded by a star replicate the results of the benchmark simulation. The first line in Table 8.1 and the last line in Table 8.4 – these two lines are displayed

Table 8.1 Variation of ψ, the idiosyncratic productivity parameter of skilled workers

ψ	γ^*	$\gamma_{\min}$	$\gamma_{\max}$	Av. human capital in *S*: selection vs. closed	Welfare in *S*: selection vs. closed
1.0	*0.987*	*0.629*	*0.502*		
2.0	0.787	0.718	**0.741**	No	−0.029
3.0	0.732	**0.773**	0.825	No	0.065
*4.0	0.710	**0.811**	0.868	Yes	0.109
5.0	0.700	**0.839**	0.894	Yes	0.139
6.0	0.695	**0.860**	0.911	Yes	0.160

Table 8.2 Variation of β^R, the individual productivity parameter in the receiving country

β^R	γ^*	$\gamma_{\min}$	$\gamma_{\max}$	Av. human capital in *S*: selection vs. closed	Welfare in *S*: selection vs. closed
1.0	0.787	0.650	**0.741**	No	−0.029
1.5	0.732	**0.754**	0.825	Yes	0.101
*2.0	0.710	**0.811**	0.868	Yes	0.109
3.0	0.695	**0.872**	0.911	Yes	0.114
4.0	0.692	**0.904**	0.933	Yes	0.112
5.0	0.693	**0.924**	0.946	Yes	0.108
6.0	0.695	**0.937**	0.955	Yes	0.103

Table 8.3 Variation of m, the probability of migration

m	m_h	γ^*	$\gamma_{\min}$	$\gamma_{\max}$	Av. human capital in *S*: selection vs. closed	Welfare in *S*: selection vs. closed
0.01	0.067	1.035	0.811	**0.868**	No	−0.009
0.02	0.133	0.787	**0.811**	0.868	Yes	0.074
*0.03	0.200	0.710	**0.811**	0.868	Yes	0.109
0.04	0.267	0.674	**0.811**	0.868	Yes	0.143
0.05	0.333	0.655	**0.813**	0.868	No	0.175
0.06	0.400	0.643	**0.813**	0.868	No	0.204

Table 8.4 Variation of α^S, the share of skilled workers in the sending country

α^S	m_h	γ^*	$\gamma_{\min}$	$\gamma_{\max}$	Av. human capital in *S*: selection vs. closed	Welfare in *S*: selection vs. closed
0.05	0.60	0.626	**0.689**	0.870	Yes	0.485
0.10	0.30	0.663	**0.764**	0.869	Yes	0.234
*0.15	0.20	0.710	**0.811**	0.868	Yes	0.109
0.20	0.15	0.761	**0.843**	0.867	No	0.033
0.25	0.12	0.814	**0.865**	0.866	No	–0.019
0.30	*0.10*	*0.868*	*0.882*	*0.865*		

in italics – delineate cases in which $\gamma_{\min} > \gamma_{\max}$, and thus the closed economy regime obtains.

With the exception of four cases, the values in the last columns of Tables 8.1–8.4 are positive. In this majority of cases, the increase in welfare typically coincides with an increase in the average level of human capital in the sending country, in line with the benchmark simulation.

The highest welfare gains to *S* accrue for parameter configurations which represent a high share of skilled migrants relative to the skilled population, that is when m, and thereby m_h, is large, or α^S is small, or for a high increase in the individual productivity of the skilled workers upon migration, viz. when ψ is large. This is to be expected, however, since in these cases the incentive of the skilled workers to invest in human capital is quite powerful. When m is large or when α^S is small (as can be seen by looking at Tables 8.3 and 8.4), the increase in the average level of human capital is significant; this impact makes it 'easier' to confer a welfare gain for all those who stay behind. Note, however, that (cf. Table 8.3) if m – or if correspondingly m_h – exceeds a certain threshold, the average level of human capital in *S* becomes lower with selection than when the sending economy is closed: the number of skilled workers who migrate is too large or, correspondingly, the number of skilled workers who remain in *S* is too small to compensate with their additional human capital investment for the outflow of human capital.[13] In addition, when ψ is large, the skilled workers benefit a great deal when moving to *R* compared to what the unskilled workers could gain. This implies that the tax does not have to increase by too much for successful selection to bite.

As is evident, however, from our simulations, an increase in the average level of human capital in the sending country is sufficient, but not necessary for a welfare gain to materialize there: in Tables 8.1, 8.3 and 8.4, several of the 'No' measures in the last but one column appear together with positive numbers in the last column. Of course, if the average level of human capital in the sending country *decreases* upon selection, the welfare of the natives of

Table 8.5 Variation of m and ψ: welfare in S, selection vs closed economy

		ψ					
		1	2	3	4	5	6
m	0.01	$\gamma_{\min} \geq \gamma_{\max}$	**−0.009**	**−0.009**	**−0.009**	**−0.010**	**0.010**
	0.02	$\gamma_{\min} \geq \gamma_{\max}$	**−0.018**	**−0.018**	0.074	0.094	0.109
	0.03	$\gamma_{\min} \geq \gamma_{\max}$	**−0.029**	**0.065**	*0.109	0.139	0.160
	0.04	$\gamma_{\min} \geq \gamma_{\max}$	**−0.002**	**0.086**	0.143	0.182	0.208
	0.05	$\gamma_{\min} \geq \gamma_{\max}$	**−0.004**	**0.104**	**0.175**	0.221	0.251
	0.06	$\gamma_{\min} \geq \gamma_{\max}$	**−0.007**	**0.121**	**0.204**	0.257	0.289

Note: Bold indicates cases where the average level of human capital in the sending country is larger in the closed economy setting than in the open economy with selection. The benchmark case is denoted by *.

S can rise only if the gain to the migrants is weighty enough to compensate for the losses to those who stay behind in the sending country. This is indeed what happens when the welfare effects are positive whilst the ranking, in terms of the average level of human capital, is such that the average level of human capital is higher in the closed economy.

When the productivity gap between countries is lower than in the benchmark simulation, as epitomized by a low value of ψ, or by a low value of β^R relative to β^S, the average level of human capital in the open economy setting in the sending country is lower than the average level of human capital there in the closed economy setting. This is a case in which the incentives to invest in human capital are not sufficiently strong. Depletion is followed by dilution. A similar reasoning applies if the probability of migration, m, is very small (which implies a small probability of migration for the skilled workers, m_h), or if the share of high-skill workers in the native population of the sending country, α^S, is rather large (which again implies that m_h is small for a given m, as can easily be discerned from Table 8.4). In these two cases, the migration expectations of the skilled are too weak to lead to much (additional) investment in human capital.

Finally, we evaluate the welfare changes for cases where variations in the most significant parameters, as revealed by the preceding analysis, occur two at a time. We present results for a simultaneous change in m and ψ. Table 8.5 shows that when m increases, smaller values of the idiosyncratic productivity parameter ψ suffice to 'deliver' a welfare increase. By the same token, when ψ increases, lower values of m suffice to increase the level of welfare in the sending country in comparison with the closed economy setting. This result is not all that surprising. Recall, from (8.13), that the optimal level of investment in human capital by a skilled worker in the case of an open economy with selection is rising in both m and ψ. Therefore, the average level of human capital in S will correspondingly be higher. And, as we have already noted, this increase in average is closely positively associated with S registering a welfare gain.

5 Conclusions

We considered the optimal selection policy of migrants by the government of a receiving country when migrants differ in their skills, and when the maximization of the welfare of the natives of the receiving country guides the government's hand. Heterogeneity of the skill levels of the workers in the sending country, hence of potential migrants, the production technology in the receiving country, and informational constraints prompt the receiving country to resort to instruments of selection. We studied closely one such instrument – a proportional tax on earnings. We found that when incentives to invest in human capital are prevalent, the level of this tax is sensitive to the calculus of the human capital formation of workers in the sending country. We conducted a simulation that showed that in the case of adjustable human capital, the sending country can experience an aggregate welfare gain upon selection by the receiving country, as opposed to the aggregate loss that its natives will be subjected to upon selection in the case of fixed human capital. This result turned out to be fairly robust to considerable shifts of the relevant parameters. The constraint that the receiving country faces in the adjustable human capital setting can translate into a welfare gain for the sending country. Somewhat surprisingly, then, it may not be only in the interest of the receiving country to resort to a selection policy; so resorting could also be advantageous to the sending country.

Notes

1. Indeed, the proportional tax that we analyze in this chapter is akin to the entry fee recently suggested by Freeman (2006).
2. While the structure of our basic model follows closely the structure of the model developed by Stark and Wang (2002), it is formulated from the perspective of the receiving country, as in Stark, Casarico, Devillanova, and Uebelmesser in this volume.
3. If $\gamma_{\min} \geq \gamma_{\max}$, the government of the receiving country cannot select skilled workers. At the minimal level of the tax, such that the unskilled workers do not find it advantageous to migrate, the skilled workers too find it advantageous to stay behind. Obviously, this is not the case that we seek to analyze here. (In section 4 we simulate an equilibrium with selection.)
4. Since the natives of the receiving country have no incentive to migrate to the sending country, it follows that in the receiving country $\tilde{\vartheta}^{R*} = \vartheta^{R*}$.
5. We cannot identify parameter restrictions such that (8.10) and (8.14) are jointly satisfied, because we cannot solve explicitly for γ. We therefore assume that the migration equilibrium exists, cf. the numerical example in section 4.

6. Stark and Wang (2002) establish sufficient conditions under which welfare in the selection framework is higher than in the closed economy in a model where there is no asymmetric information, and the sending country determines the out-migration of its natives by selecting the migration probability m_h. See also the simulations reported in Stark and Fan in this volume.
7. Stark and Wang (2002) resort to a probability of migration for the sending country's workers of 0.02. In addition, our parameter values are in line with data presented by Docquier and Marfouk (2006) who report a share of skilled workers among the residents in lower-middle and upper-middle income countries of 0.130 and 0.142, respectively, and an overall rate of migration for these two groups of countries of 0.032 and 0.042, respectively.
8. Freeman (2006) reports data according to which the increases in earnings upon migration is more pronounced for high-skill than for low-skill occupations ($\psi_h^R \beta^R$ versus β^R).
9. We do not make here a comparison in terms of the average level of human capital and of welfare in the fixed human capital case since this comparison was settled unambiguously in the theoretical model, both for the sending country and for the receiving country. (Recall sections 2.3 and 3.)
10. This is in line with the analytical and empirical results reported in Stark and Wang (2002), and with other observations, for example those of Beine, Docquier and Rapoport (2008). The latter examine the impact of migration on human capital formation in the sending country for a cross-section of developing countries, and identify the economic environment which favors an increase in the total quantity of human capital, which they define as a brain gain. In general, countries characterized by relatively low levels of human capital and low migration rates of skilled workers are likely to experience a brain gain.
11. This increase in welfare does not constitute, however, a strict Pareto improvement since the skilled non-migrants experience a loss.
12. The results are available from the authors upon request.
13. By contrast, when m_h is large because α^S is small rather than because m is large, we still observe an increase in the average level of human capital in S. When assessing the welfare repercussions for S, it makes a difference whether the skilled relative to the unskilled are many or few (whether α^S is high or low), not only whether a large or a small share of the skilled migrate (whether m_h is small or large).

References

Beine, Michel, Docquire, Frédéric and Rapaport, Hillel (2008) 'Brain Drain and Human Capital Formation in Developing Countries: Winners and Losers', *The Economic Journal* 118, 631–52.

Benhabib, Jess and Jovanovic, Boyan (2007) 'Optimal Migration: A World Perspective', NBER Working Paper No. 12871.

Bianchi, Milo (2006) 'Immigration Policy and Self-Selecting Migrants', SSE/EFI Working Paper No. 627.

Djajic, Slobodan (1989) 'Skills and the Patterns of Migration: The Role of Qualitative and Quantitative Restrictions on International Labor Mobility', *International Economic Review* 30, 795–809.

Docquier, Frédéric and Marfouk, Abdeslam (2006) 'International Migration by Education Attainment, 1990–2000', in Caglar Özden and Maurice Schiff (eds), *International Migration, Brain Drain and Remittances*. New York: Palgrave Macmillan, 151–99.
Ethier, Wilfred J. (1986) 'Illegal Immigration – The Host Country Problem', *American Economic Review* 76, 56–71.
Freeman, Richard B. (2006) 'People Flows in Globalization', *Journal of Economic Perspectives* 20, 145–70.
Stark, Oded, Casarico, Alessandra, Devillanova, Carlo and Uebelmesser, Silke (2008) 'International Migration, Human Capital Formation, and the Setting of Migration-Control Policies: Mapping the Gains', in this volume.
Stark, Oded and Fan, Simon C. (2008) 'The Brain Drain, "Educated Unemployment", Human Capital Formation, and Economic Betterment', in this volume.
Stark, Oded, and Wang, Yong (2002) 'Inducing Human Capital Formation: Migration as a Substitute for Subsidies', *Journal of Public Economics* 86, 29–46.

9

International Migration, Human Capital Formation, and the Setting of Migration-Control Policies: Mapping the Gains*

Oded Stark, Alessandra Casarico, Carlo Devillanova, and Silke Uebelmesser

1 Introduction

Recent research has identified conditions under which migration of human capital (skilled workers) from a developing (sending) country to a developed (receiving) country enhances human capital formation and improves wellbeing within the sending country (Mountford, 1997; Stark, Helmenstein, and Prskawetz, 1997, 1998; Stark and Wang, 2002; Fan and Stark, 2007; Stark and Fan, 2007, 2008). In contrast to earlier writings on the brain drain (for example, Patinkin, 1968; Bhagwati and Wilson, 1989), the recent contributions cast migration as a harbinger of human capital gain rather than a cause of human capital drain.

The above research considers a setting in which an individual's productivity is determined by his own human capital, as well as by a human capital externality. Other key assumptions are that the only migration policy instrument available to the sending country is the choice of the migration probability/quota that confers upon it the maximal benefit, and that this choice is cost free. However, in considering migration policies, it is plausible to assign an active role to the receiving country, and it is reasonable to postulate that the

* Earlier versions of this chapter were presented at the conference 'Advanced Perspectives on Migration and Mobility', University of Bonn, 2004; the Royal Economic Society Meeting, University of Nottingham, 2005; the CESifo Area Conference on Employment and Social Protection, Munich, 2005; the EALE Annual Meeting, San Francisco, 2005; the ESPE Annual Conference, Paris, 2005; and in seminars held at Tilburg University, at the Instituto de Análisis Económico (CSIC), Barcelona, at the University of Tübingen, and at the Free University of Berlin. We are indebted to Galina Zudenkova, to Katarzyna Saczuk, and to conference and seminar participants for helpful comments and suggestions. Stark gratefully acknowledges partial financial support from the Sohmen Foundation and the International Centre for the Study of East Asian Development. Casarico and Devillanova gratefully acknowledge financial support from Miur and Ricerca di Base, Università Bocconi.

implementation of any restrictive migration policy is anything but cost free. When such doses of realism are added in, do the main results of the recent research continue to hold?

To address this question we build on the work of Stark and Wang (2002), yet go beyond that work. We explore alternative distributions of the power to set migration policies between the sending country and the receiving country when migration controls are costly. We study a setting in which the country with the policy-formation power determines the migration probability which, for a given country size, is equivalent to fixing a migration quota. Unlike in Stark and Wang, we do not assume that the migration policy is necessarily determined by the sending country. Various tools are used to implement migration policies. While screening policies are used quite often, migration quotas too are prevalent. A striking example of setting a migration probability is the Green Card lottery in the USA: visas are randomly issued to prospective migrants on the basis of a computer-generated draw. Migration quotas are also common in European Union (EU) countries, as recently documented by Boeri and Bruecker (2005). A study of this type of a policy instrument invites the assumption of a homogeneous migrants framework. The framework that we develop is more general, however, since it can be used to study mechanisms that operate through the average level of human capital of heterogenous migrants. While these mechanisms are the result of both selection and quotas, we focus in this chapter only on the latter.

We find that the prevalence of a welfare gain to the sending country, as claimed by the recent research, is retained in a setting in which controlling migration is costly, and in which both the sending country and the receiving country wield the power to set migration policy. Moreover, when we allow for the possibility of sharing the migration-control costs in the form of transfers from the receiving country to the sending country, side-payments arise as a welfare-improving device, and once again the sending country stands to reap a welfare gain from its workers' prospect of migration.

2 A simple model

In this section we present our basic model. We draw on the model developed by Stark and Wang (2002). We consider a homogeneous-worker two-country world in which individuals in both the sending country and the receiving country decide how much human capital to acquire in the presence of human capital externalities. There is a continuum of homogeneous workers in the sending country S, which we denote by N^S, and in the receiving country R, which we denote by N^R. Workers produce a single commodity the price of which is normalized at 1. We first consider (in section 2.1) a closed-economy setting in which the investment in human capital depends only on the returns available within the country, and then (in section 2.2) consider human capital formation in an open-economy setting in which, when individuals decide how much human capital to acquire, they respond to the prevailing migration policy, which they take as given.

The basic model enables us to study three alternative regimes: the sending country has the exclusive migration policy-setting power, whereas the receiving country does not play any policy-formation role (section 3.1); the receiving country wields the exclusive migration policy-setting power whereas the sending country does not play any policy-formation role (section 3.2); a regime where both countries exercise decision power in the setting of migration policy (section 4). Section 5 concludes.

2.1 Human capital acquisition: the closed-economy case

Let the gross earnings of a worker f^j in country $j = S, R$, depend on the level of the worker's human capital, ϑ^j, with a productivity parameter weight of $\beta^j > 0$ (private returns), and on the average level of human capital, $\overline{\vartheta}^j$, with a productivity parameter weight of $\eta > 0$ (social returns):

$$f^j(\vartheta^j) = \beta^j \ln(\vartheta^j + 1) + \eta \ln(\overline{\vartheta}^j + 1) \tag{9.1}$$

Labour is the only production input. Thus, gross earnings per worker are equal to output per worker. To allow us to concentrate on essentials, we assume that the social returns are the same in each country, whereas the private returns differ between countries. Two features of the earnings function (9.1) merit comment. First, upon including the economy-wide average level of human capital, we incorporate a measure of externality that captures spillover effects that accrue within the national economy.[1] This is a common assumption in the theoretical literature on endogenous economic growth, and it has recently been adopted to address the relationship between migration, human capital accumulation, and growth, as alluded to in section 1.[2]

Second, the chosen functional form relies on constant private (and social) return parameters. This assumption is employed to facilitate tractability, and we discuss it further at the end of section 3.3.

The workers seek to maximize their net earnings, that is, their gross earnings minus the cost of forming human capital, $k\vartheta^j$, where $0 < k < \beta^j$ is a constant:

$$W^j(\vartheta^j) = \beta^j \ln(\vartheta^j + 1) + \eta \ln(\overline{\vartheta}^j + 1) - k\vartheta^j \tag{9.2}$$

When individuals choose their optimal level of human capital, they take the private returns to human capital and the costs of acquiring human capital into account, but they do not factor in the repercussions of their choices on the productivity of others. This disregard of the social returns to human capital results in underinvestment in human capital from a social point of view. Since

$$\frac{\partial W^j(\vartheta^j)}{\partial \vartheta^j} = \frac{\beta^j}{\vartheta^j + 1} - k \tag{9.3}$$

the optimal level of human capital acquired by an individual in country j is:[3,4]

$$\vartheta^{j*} = \frac{\beta^j}{k} - 1 \tag{9.4}$$

We assume, quite naturally, that the private returns to human capital are higher in the receiving country than in the sending country, that is, we assume that $\beta^R > \beta^S$. When countries differ in their technologies, and when technologies are country-specific, the superior technology of an advanced, developed country renders the application of a given level of human capital in that country more productive than in the developing country.

Given this assumption, it follows from (9.4) that $\vartheta^{S*} < \vartheta^{R*}$.

2.2 Human capital acquisition: the open-economy case

In an open-economy setting, migration is possible. Given the productivity differential between the two countries, migration will only be from the developing country to the developed country. Using a tilde to denote the level of a variable in the open-economy setting, we then have that for workers in the developed receiving country $\tilde{\vartheta}^{R*} = \vartheta^{R*}$. Migration opportunities affect the calculus of only the workers in the sending country who now have an attractive outside option available to them. To simplify, we assume that migration entails no cost of movement.[5]

Let m denote the probability of migration. The function of the expected net earnings of the workers in the sending country then becomes:

$$\begin{aligned}\widetilde{W}^S(\tilde{\vartheta}^S) &= m\left[\beta^{mR}\ln(\tilde{\vartheta}^S + 1) + \eta\ln\left(\tilde{\bar{\vartheta}}^R + 1\right)\right] \\ &\quad + [1-m]\left[\beta^S\ln(\tilde{\vartheta}^S + 1) + \eta\ln\left(\tilde{\bar{\vartheta}}^S + 1\right)\right] - k\tilde{\vartheta}^S \end{aligned} \tag{9.5}$$

where $\beta^{mR} \in (\beta^S + \eta, \beta^R]$ denotes the private returns to migrants in the receiving country and where the explicit form of $\tilde{\bar{\vartheta}}^R$ will be provided in section 3.2. The assumption that $\beta^{mR} \leq \beta^R$ allows for different remuneration between natives and migrants. It enables us to capture, in a simplified manner, the imperfect transferability of human capital between countries. Still, the degree of transferability is large enough to preserve the positive private return differential between the receiving and the sending country. The assumption $\beta^{mR} > \beta^S + \eta$ is clarified below following Proposition 1. Differentiating (9.5) with respect to $\tilde{\vartheta}^S$ yields:

$$\frac{\partial\widetilde{W}^S(\tilde{\vartheta}^S)}{\partial\tilde{\vartheta}^S} = \frac{m\beta^{mR}}{\tilde{\vartheta}^S + 1} + \frac{[1-m]\beta^S}{\tilde{\vartheta}^S + 1} - k = \frac{m(\beta^{mR} - \beta^S) + \beta^S}{\tilde{\vartheta}^S + 1} - k$$

Hence, the optimal level of human capital of individuals in country S, in the presence of a possibility to migrate, is:[6]

$$\widetilde{\vartheta}^{S*} = \frac{m(\beta^{mR} - \beta^{S}) + \beta^{S}}{k} - 1 \tag{9.6}$$

For an $0 < m < 1$, the level of human capital in S in an open-economy setting exceeds the corresponding level in S in a closed-economy setting, that is, $\widetilde{\vartheta}^{S*} > \vartheta^{S*}$, yet it still falls short of the level prevailing in the receiving country, $\widetilde{\vartheta}^{S*} < \vartheta^{R*}(= \widetilde{\vartheta}^{R*})$.[7] This simple observation is important since, as we elucidate later, it points to a possible drawback, from the receiving country's point of view, of opening up to migration: the admittance of migrant workers lowers the average level of human capital in the receiving country.

3 Migration policy

The extent of migration and how it affects the welfare of individuals in both countries depend on their migration policies. The policy instrument that we study is the probability of migration which, for a given country size, is equivalent to a migration quota. Even though countries employ both screening and quotas as migration policy instruments, in this chapter we follow the received literature and study the latter. As pointed out in section 1, quotas are practiced often, and hence it is pertinent to assume them.[8] We focus on the interaction between the two countries, thereby extending the recent literature which, policy-wise, looks only at the sending country. This is a first step and we leave the elaboration of the case of several sending and receiving countries to future research.

Undoubtedly, implementing a restrictive migration regime is costly. We make the assumption that the costs depend on the probability of migration: the smaller the probability, that is the tighter the policy, the larger the financial outlay required to implement it. Enforcing a closed-economy regime entails the highest cost. In terms of migration controls and policy cost, unhindered movement is cost free.

Denote by $C^j(m)$ the cost of migration controls, which is assumed to be country-specific so as to allow for differences in the technologies of control between the sending country and the receiving country. We assume that $C^j(0) \equiv \widehat{C}^j > 0$; $C^j(1) = 0$; $0 < C^j(m) < \widehat{C}^j$ for $0 < m < 1$; $\frac{\partial C^j(m)}{\partial m} < 0$; $\frac{\partial^2 C^j(m)}{\partial m^2} > 0$; and that $\lim_{m \to 1} \frac{\partial C^j(m)}{\partial m} = 0$. The resources required to implement the desired migration policy are secured through the levying of a lump-sum tax on all the native members of a country's population. The assumption of a lump-sum tax implies that the decision to acquire human capital is not affected by the tax-based financing of the migration policy.[9] When country j enforces the migration quota, it pays the control costs which, in per capita terms, are $c^j(m) = \frac{C^j(m)}{N^j}$.

3.1 The policy-formation power rests with the sending country

We first consider the case where the sending country has the exclusive policy-setting power, such that the receiving country does not play any policy-formation role at all. This analysis resembles the case studied by Stark and Wang (2002), with the difference that here, a cost component is present and there is limited transferability of human capital. Following Stark and Wang (2002), the optimal migration probability is found by maximizing the difference between the level of welfare in an open-economy setting and the level of welfare in a closed-economy setting for the representative individual who does not end up migrating,[10] given that the representative migrant, who ends up subjecting his human capital to the $\beta^{mR}(> \beta^{S})$ productivity parameter, is clearly better off than the identical – in terms of the human capital endowment and the cost of forming human capital – individual who stays behind.

With $\Psi(\widetilde{\vartheta}^{S*})$ and $\Psi(\vartheta^{S*})$ indicating the levels of welfare of a non-migrating individual in the open-economy setting and in the closed-economy setting, respectively, the objective function is:

$$\begin{aligned} G^{nmS}(m) &= \Psi(\widetilde{\vartheta}^{S*}) - \Psi(\vartheta^{S*}) - c^{S}(m) \\ &= \beta^{S}\ln(\widetilde{\vartheta}^{S*}+1) + \eta\ln(\widetilde{\overline{\vartheta}}^{S*}+1) - k\widetilde{\vartheta}^{S*} \\ &\quad - \left[\beta^{S}\ln(\vartheta^{S*}+1) + \eta\ln(\overline{\vartheta}^{S*}+1) - k\vartheta^{S*}\right] - c^{S}(m) \end{aligned} \qquad (9.7)$$

where the superscript *nm* indicates that the welfare calculus is performed for a non-migrating individual.

Since

$$\frac{\partial G^{nmS}(m)}{\partial m} = \frac{\partial \widetilde{\vartheta}^{S*}}{\partial m}\left[\frac{\beta^{S}}{\widetilde{\vartheta}^{S*}+1} - k + \frac{\eta}{\widetilde{\overline{\vartheta}}^{S*}+1}\right] - \frac{\partial c^{S}(m)}{\partial m}$$

and noting, from (9.6), that

$$k = \frac{m(\beta^{mR}-\beta^{S})+\beta^{S}}{\widetilde{\vartheta}^{S*}+1}$$

and that

$$\frac{\partial \widetilde{\vartheta}^{S*}}{\partial m} = \frac{\beta^{mR}-\beta^{S}}{k}$$

the first order condition for an interior maximum is

$$\frac{\beta^{mR}-\beta^{S}}{k}\left[\frac{\eta}{\widetilde{\overline{\vartheta}}^{S*}+1} - \frac{m(\beta^{mR}-\beta^{S})}{\widetilde{\vartheta}^{S*}+1}\right] - \frac{\partial c^{S}(m)}{\partial m} = 0 \qquad (9.8)$$

Equation (9.8) implicitly defines the optimal migration probability for the sending country, m_C^{S*}.[11]

The following Proposition summarizes the implications of incorporating the cost of migration control.

Proposition 1 If implementing a tight migration policy is cost free, that is if $C^j(m) = 0 \,\forall\, m$, then the optimal migration policy for the sending country is $m^{S*} = \frac{\eta}{\beta^{mR} - \beta^S}$, cf. Stark and Wang (2002). When the implementation of a restrictive migration policy is costly, then the optimal policy for the sending country is $m_C^{S*} > m^{S*}$.

Proof The first part of Proposition 1 follows from the assumption of a homogeneous workforce, that is, $\tilde{\tilde{\vartheta}}^{S*} = \tilde{\vartheta}^{S*}$, which implies that for the bracketed term in equation (9.8) to be equal to zero, we must have that $\eta = m(\beta^{mR} - \beta^S)$. The assumption that $\beta^{mR} > \beta^S + \eta$ guarantees that $m^{S*} < 1$.

When the implementation of a restrictive migration policy is costly, we can easily see from (9.8) that for $m = m^{S*}$, the bracketed term is equal to zero while the term $-\frac{\partial c^S(m)}{\partial m}$ is positive. Hence (9.8) cannot hold, that is, m cannot be equal to m^{S*}. Since $-\frac{\partial c^S(m)}{\partial m}$ is positive, the bracketed term must be negative. For the bracketed term to be negative, we need $\frac{\eta}{\tilde{\tilde{\vartheta}}^{S*} + 1} < \frac{m(\beta^{mR} - \beta^S)}{\tilde{\vartheta}^{S*} + 1}$. This yields a higher optimal migration probability, that is, $m_C^{S*} > m^{S*}$. Notice that, as $\lim_{m \to 1} \frac{\partial C^j(m)}{\partial m} = 0$, the maximization problems without and with costs coincide as m approaches 1 and the assumption $\beta^{mR} > \beta^S + \eta$ ensures that also $m_C^{S*} < 1$. ■

The intuition underlying this result is straightforward. If migration controls are costly, the cost component becomes lower as m becomes larger. It is therefore beneficial to select a migration policy that is less tight.

3.2 The policy-formation power rests with the receiving country

We next consider the case in which the receiving country has the exclusive policy-setting power. The receiving country chooses the migration probability m that maximizes the welfare gain of the native members of its population in a world in which migration is a distinct possibility, bearing in mind that controlling migration is costly. We maintain that since the receiving country cares only about the welfare of its native citizens, the welfare of the migrants is not incorporated in its measure of welfare. As in the case of the sending country, for normalization purposes the welfare gain is measured in comparison to the welfare of the native members of the population in a 'migration-less' world. To this end, the level of human capital of the incoming migrants and how that level adjusts to the possibility of migration, cf. equation (9.6), are obviously important. Denoting by $\Psi(\tilde{\vartheta}^{R*})$ and by $\Psi(\vartheta^{R*})$ the welfare functions of the representative native individual in the receiving country with and without migration, respectively, the objective function for country R is:

$$\begin{aligned} G^R(m) &= \Psi(\widetilde{\vartheta}^{R*}) - \Psi(\vartheta^{R*}) - c^R(m) \\ &= \left[\beta^R \ln(\widetilde{\vartheta}^{R*}+1) + \eta \ln(\widetilde{\overline{\vartheta}}^{R*}+1) - k\widetilde{\vartheta}^{R*}\right] \\ &\quad - \left[\beta^R \ln(\vartheta^{R*}+1) + \eta \ln(\overline{\vartheta}^{R*}+1) - k\vartheta^{R*}\right] - c^R(m) \end{aligned} \tag{9.9}$$

Recalling (see the first paragraph of section 2.2) that the individually-optimal level of human capital in the receiving country is not affected by the opening up of the country, that is, $\widetilde{\vartheta}^{R*} = \vartheta^{R*}$, equation (9.9) reduces to:

$$G^R(m) = \eta \ln(\widetilde{\overline{\vartheta}}^{R*}+1) - \eta \ln(\overline{\vartheta}^{R*}+1) - c^R(m) \tag{9.10}$$

where the average level of human capital in the receiving country with migration, $\widetilde{\overline{\vartheta}}^{R*}$, is:

$$\widetilde{\overline{\vartheta}}^{R*} = \frac{\overline{\vartheta}^{R*} N^R + \widetilde{\overline{\vartheta}}^{S*} m N^S}{N^R + mN^S} \tag{9.11}$$

Differentiating equation (9.10) with respect to m, we obtain:

$$\frac{\partial G^R(m)}{\partial m} = \frac{\eta}{\widetilde{\overline{\vartheta}}^{R*}+1} \frac{\partial \widetilde{\overline{\vartheta}}^{R*}}{\partial m} - \frac{\partial c^R(m)}{\partial m} \tag{9.12}$$

where, using (9.6) and (9.11), $\frac{\partial \widetilde{\overline{\vartheta}}^{R*}}{\partial m}$ is given by:

$$\begin{aligned} \frac{\partial \widetilde{\overline{\vartheta}}^{R*}}{\partial m} &= \frac{-(\overline{\vartheta}^{R*} - \widetilde{\overline{\vartheta}}^{S*}) N^S N^R + mN^S \frac{\partial \widetilde{\overline{\vartheta}}^{S*}}{\partial m}(N^R + mN^S)}{(N^R + mN^S)^2} \\ &= \frac{-\left[\frac{\beta^R - \beta^S}{k} - \frac{m(\beta^{mR} - \beta^S)}{k}\right] N^S N^R + mN^S \frac{\beta^{mR} - \beta^S}{k}(N^R + mN^S)}{(N^R + mN^S)^2} \end{aligned} \tag{9.13}$$

Opening up to migration has two opposite effects on the receiving country: a negative average human capital diluting effect, and a positive inducement effect. To see this formally, we refer to the far right-hand side of (9.13). A higher m leads to a larger number of migrants (as can be gleaned from the first term in the numerator). The average level of human capital of these migrants is below the level of human capital formed by workers in the receiving country. Yet a higher probability of migration increases the optimal level of human capital that workers in the sending country choose to acquire and migrate with (the inducement effect, captured by the second term in the numerator); this effect is positive.

Had enforcing a tight migration policy been cost free (and with no concern for the welfare of the workers in the sending country), the receiving country would have chosen to close its borders completely, $m^{R*}=0$. Indeed, for $m=0$, we have that $\frac{\partial \bar{\vartheta}^{R*}}{\partial m}<0$, implying, quite obviously, that any positive level of migration lowers the average level of human capital in R. In the presence of control costs, any $m \in [0, 1]$ can be a solution to the above maximization problem depending on the exogenous parameterization of the cost function and on the degree of transferability of human capital between the two countries. We consider the two corner solutions 0 and 1 uninteresting, unrealistic and hence irrelevant. To guarantee the existence of an interior solution we therefore introduce further restrictions on the cost function such that $\frac{\partial G^R(m_C^{R*})}{\partial m}=0$, and $\frac{\partial^2 G^R(m_C^{R*})}{\partial m^2}<0$ for at least a quota $m_C^{R*} \in (0, 1)$. Then, m_C^{R*} represents a global maximum if $G^R(m_C^{R*})>G^R(1)$ and $G^R(m_C^{R*})>G^R(0)$: the first inequality requires limited transferability of human capital; the second inequality requires a sufficiently high $\widehat{C}^R$.[12]

3.3 Welfare assessment

Consider first a setting where the sending country alone determines the migration policy.

Corollary 1 When the policy-making power rests with the sending country, its choice imposes a welfare loss on the receiving country in comparison with a closed-economy setting.

Proof The proof follows straightforwardly from the ensuing decline in the average level of human capital in the receiving country. ■

When the receiving country chooses the migration policy, could a migration probability, m_C^{R*}, confer a welfare gain upon the sending country even if it differs from that which the sending country would have set had it been the (only) country choosing the migration regime? For any m_C^{R*}, the migrants themselves are certainly better off. The question is whether the non-migrants in the sending country could benefit as well in comparison with the closed-economy setting, that is, whether $G^{nmS}_{c^S=0}(m^*)>0$, where the subscript $c^j=0$ indicates that country j is not bearing any cost. To this end, we state the following:

Proposition 2 As long as $m^*<\widehat{m}^S$, with $\widehat{m}^S$ defined such that $G^{nmS}_{c^S=0}(\widehat{m}^S)=0$ and $\left.\frac{\partial G^{nmS}_{c^S=0}}{\partial m}\right|_{m=\widehat{m}^S}<0$, the sending country reaps a welfare gain.

Proof The proof of Proposition 2 is akin to the proof of Proposition 2 in Stark and Wang (2002), and thus is omitted here. ■

The straightforward implication is that when $m_C^{R*}<\widehat{m}^S$, the sending country experiences a welfare improvement even when the receiving country wields sole migration control power. The intuition is that when migration controls are costly, the *R* country may optimally allow a modicum of migration, which is conferring a welfare gain upon *S*.

Note that increasing $\beta^{mR} - \beta^S$ affects $G^{nmS}_{c^S=0}(m)$ in such a way that the limit migration probability for a welfare improvement, $\widehat{m}^S$, decreases. The larger the difference, the more limited the scope for a welfare gain, as the interval $[0, \widehat{m}^S]$ shrinks. Notice that $\beta^{mR} - \beta^S$ depends both on the different degree of development of the two countries and on the transferability of skills. Given the level of development of the sending country, the probability range that will confer a welfare gain upon it is the more restrictive the more developed the receiving country, and/or the higher the transferability.

This is a good point to revisit our assumption of constant marginal products, cf. equation (9.1). In the presence of a homogeneous workforce, as assumed in this chapter, consider a more general production function where wages are flexible and endogenously determined. In the standard case, migration affects private returns in both countries: they increase in the sending country, and decrease in the receiving country. The rise in wages in the sending country will increase the benefits to the workers who are left behind, whilst the fall in wages in the receiving country will add to the cost of receiving migrants. In this respect, the assumption of constant private returns is a conservative one. At the same time, a helpful property of the constant private returns assumption, which is quite valuable for the questions addressed in this chapter, is that it provides a setting where migration controls can be used as a 'pure' policy instrument to restrict migration, since in and by itself migration is not restricted by decreasing marginal returns to human capital at destination.

4 Policy-making power rests with both the sending and receiving country

We now consider the case where both countries have a say in the determination of the migration policy and hence the probability of migration. We model the interaction between the sending and the receiving country as a non-cooperative two-stage (Stackelberg) game in which the receiving country is the first mover: it sets its optimal migration policy anticipating the sending country's best reply.[13] It stands to reason that if either of the two countries chooses a migration probability m^j, the probability space of the other is $[0, m^j]$: in a two-country world, emigration and immigration flows must be equal, and once one country chooses a probability level m^j, the other country cannot choose a less restrictive (that is, higher) probability. We assume that the country that prefers the smaller migration probability will incur the cost $c^j(m)$ of implementing the policy.

4.1 Equilibrium

We here determine the equilibrium of the game, establish whether the sending country or the receiving country ends up controlling migration, and analyze the ensuing welfare repercussions.

Proposition 3 The equilibrium migration probability, m^*, of the two-stage game is:

$$m^* = \begin{cases} m_C^{R*} & \text{if } G^R(m_C^{R*}) > G^R_{c^R=0}(m_C^{S*}) \text{ and } m_C^{R*} \in (0, m_C^{S*}) \\ m_C^{S*} & \text{otherwise} \end{cases}$$

With m^*, there is a welfare gain for the sending country as compared to the closed-economy setting, and the receiving country minimizes its welfare loss.

Proof See Appendix.

Proposition 3 establishes that any of the two countries can be the equilibrium setter. Welfare gains for the sending country are maintained, and in some instances maximized, even if the receiving country has some policy-formation power and a first-mover advantage.

In the alternative sequence in which the sending country moves first, the sending country can take advantage of the possibility of limiting the policy space of the receiving country and therefore stands to reap a welfare gain *a fortiori*. This result is independent of the two-stage structure of the game. In fact, it can be shown quite easily that also in a one-shot game where the sending country and the receiving country move simultaneously, welfare gains for the sending country always obtain.

In Figure 9.1, we illustrate one of the cases encompassed by Proposition 3.[14] Namely, we consider a configuration in which $m_C^{R*} < m_C^{S*}$ and $G^R(m_C^{R*}) > G^R_{c^R=0}(m_C^{S*})$: in this case, it is easy to see that the receiving country can reduce the loss it incurs by setting a more restrictive migration policy than that which is optimal for the sending country, even though it has to bear the cost of the controls.

Figure 9.2 illustrates the case where $m_C^{R*} < m_C^{S*}$ and $G^R(m_C^{R*}) \leq G^R_{c^R=0}(m_C^{S*})$: in this case, the receiving country cannot reduce its loss by choosing a more restrictive migration policy and m_C^{S*} emerges as the equilibrium.

Clearly, if the setting of a restrictive migration regime were cost free, the equilibrium migration policy in this two-stage non-cooperative game where the receiving country moves first would be $m^* = 0$; there would be no migration in equilibrium which, in turn, implies that there would be no opportunities for welfare gains for the sending country.

4.2 Side-payments

In the preceding section we considered a non-cooperative environment and we characterized the equilibrium migration policy, m^*, which is implemented

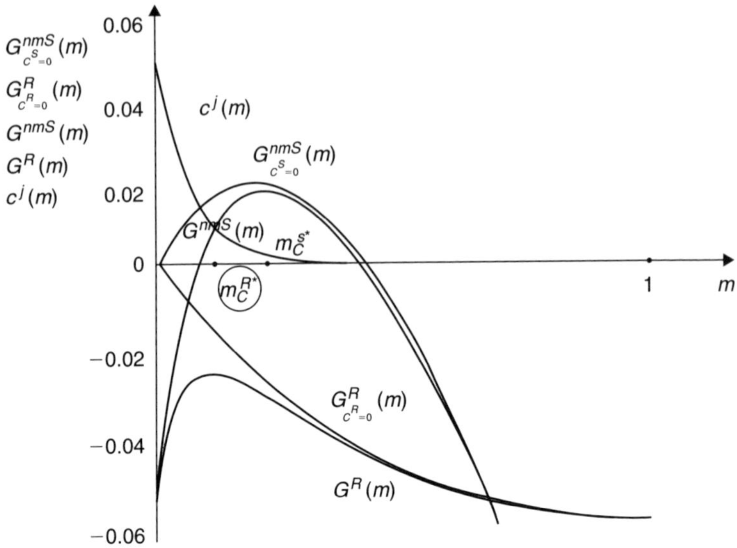

Figure 9.1 Case $m_C^{R*} < m_C^{S*}$ and $G^R(m_C^{R*}) > G^R_{c^R=0}(m_C^{S*})$

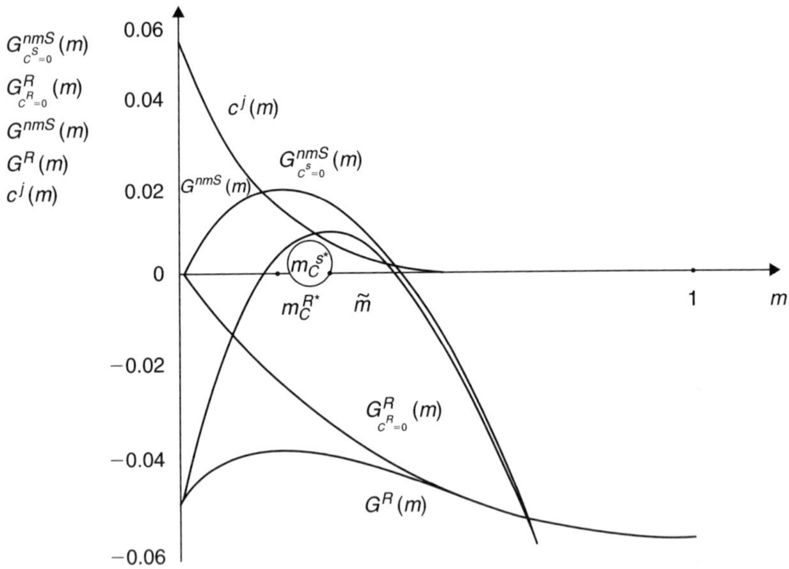

Figure 9.2 Case $m_C^{R*} < m_C^{S*}$ and $G^R(m_C^{R*}) \leq G^R_{c^R=0}(m_C^{S*})$

by the country that consequently incurs the associated cost. With the solution m^* as a starting point, we now seek to explore the possibility that the country that does not set the migration probability can influence the equilibrium policy in a way that increases its welfare by resorting to the device of side-payments. We consider a specific type of transfer between the countries – support for the controls, for example funds for border enforcement. We identify conditions in which side-payments of this type arise as a natural welfare-improving mechanism.

Let the parameter $\alpha \in [0, 1]$ capture the degree of cost-sharing in controlling migration. In the presence of a cross-country 'subsidization', the actual per capita control cost for country j, $c^j_\alpha(m)$, when country j sets the equilibrium migration policy, is:

$$c^j_\alpha(m) = (1-\alpha)c^j(m) \tag{9.14}$$

When $\alpha = 0$, country j does not receive any side-payment, $c^j_\alpha(m) = c^j(m)$, and we are back to the case of $m^* = m^{j*}_C$. For $\alpha > 0$, the country which implements its preferred migration policy incurs only a fraction $(1-\alpha)c^j(m)$ of the control cost, while the remaining fraction $\alpha c^j(m)\frac{N^j}{N^i}$ is borne by country i. The term $\alpha c^j(m)\frac{N^j}{N^i}$ therefore denotes the per capita side-payment from country i to country j. When solving for the optimal migration probability from the perspective of country j, an increase in α is analytically equivalent to a proportional reduction in per capita costs, $c^j(m)$. For example, if the sending country is determining the migration probability, the relevant control cost is $c^S(m)$. In per capita terms, a fraction $(1-\alpha)c^S(m)$ of this cost is borne by the sending country, the remaining $\alpha c^S(m)\frac{N^S}{N^R}$ is paid by the receiving country in per capita terms if side-payments are operative. Starting from the case of no transfers, an increase in side-payments between the countries is represented by a variation in α.

Denoting by m^{j*}_α the optimal migration policy chosen by country j when a transfer takes place, we state the following Proposition.

Proposition 4 Consider the case where $m^* = m^{S*}_C$. An increase in α is Pareto improving if $\left.\frac{\partial G^R_{c^R=0}(m)}{\partial m}\frac{\partial m^{S*}_\alpha}{\partial \alpha}\right|_{m=m^{S*}_C} > c^S(m^{S*}_C)\frac{N^S}{N^R}$. The receiving country will therefore pay the sending country to decrease the equilibrium migration probability.

Proof See Appendix.

Proposition 4 states that if the sending country fixes the migration probability at $m^* = m^{S*}_C$ and if, when it does so, it incurs all the control costs, that is, if $\alpha = 0$, then a positive transfer to it from the receiving country, which reduces $c^S(m)$ to some $c^S_\alpha(m)$, can be Pareto improving. The sending country is willing to trade off a more restrictive migration probability for a control cost subsidy. Note that if N^R is large, side-payments are more likely to increase welfare throughout.

Our analysis serves to show that the receiving country can induce the sending country to reduce migration: it is in the interest of the receiving country to support the sending country's control activities when the benefit to it is larger than the cost that it has to bear.

We now consider the case where $m^* = m_C^{R*}$, that is, where without side-payments the equilibrium migration probability is the probability which minimizes the welfare loss of the receiving country. We ask whether in such a situation the sending country can resort to side-payments in order to tilt the equilibrium migration probability in its favour. It is easy to work out why this will not be possible: there is no scope for side-payments, in terms of the sharing of the migration-control costs, from the sending country to the receiving country. This follows from the fact that when $m^* = m_C^{R*}$ and $\alpha = 0$, an increase in α, that is, a transfer from the sending country to the receiving country, will induce the latter to decrease its optimal migration probability even further, since $\frac{\partial m_\alpha^{R*}}{\partial \alpha} < 0$. (Recall that if the receiving country were to receive a delightfully large transfer, it would choose $m^* = 0$). Given that a lower migration probability makes the sending country worse off, there is no point in it incurring the transfer.

5 Conclusions

We have expanded the analysis of Stark and Wang (2002) to a setting in which the receiving country plays an active role in the determination of migration policy, yet implementing a migration policy involves a cost. We have shown that even in such a setting, the sending country can still benefit from the response of its workers' human capital acquisition decisions to the prospect of migration. For the sending country alone to decide its migration policy (probability) is a sufficient condition for it to reap a welfare gain but, as we have shown, it is not a necessary condition. A welfare gain can be obtained by the sending country in more realistic models in which the receiving country has the sole power to set migration policy or the migration probability is set non-cooperatively in a game in which both countries have a say in the choice of migration policy. The result in the non-cooperative game holds independently of which country ends up setting the equilibrium probability of migration.

We have also shown that side-payments can arise as a welfare-improving mechanism. This analytical finding can serve as a rationale for bilateral agreements on migration. We note, however, that side-payments are an option only when the receiving country cannot implement its (constrained) preferred policy. If it could, it would be reluctant to deviate from it in a way that merely benefits the sending country, assuming that the receiving country pursues only its self-interest.

The migration policy instrument to which we have alluded in this chapter is a migration probability (quota) in the setting of a homogeneous workforce. This configuration does not lend itself to the study of the case in which the home country loses its most skilled workers to migration. This requires analysis of screening policies in a heterogenous workers framework in which the home country and the receiving country interact on policy selection and implementation. We develop and analyze such a framework in a companion chapter in this volume (Stark, Casarico, and Uebelmesser, 2008).

6 Appendix

Proof of Proposition 3

The receiving country moves first and decides whether to set a migration policy or to leave the decision to the sending country. In the latter case, the sending country will clearly choose its optimal migration policy m_C^{S*}. In the first case, the best reply of the sending country is to accept the policy m proposed by the receiving country if $m \in [0, \tilde{m}]$ with $\tilde{m}$ such that $G^{nmS}_{c^S=0}(\tilde{m}) = G^{nmS}(m_C^{S*})$ and $\left.\frac{\partial G^{nmS}_{c^S=0}(m)}{\partial m}\right|_{m=\tilde{m}} < 0$ (Figure 9.2 illustrates $\tilde{m}$), and to set m_C^{S*} if the receiving country proposes $m \in (\tilde{m}, 1]$. To understand this claim, note that the sending country cannot choose a less restrictive migration policy to the right of $\tilde{m}$, since $\tilde{m}$ limits the space of choice for the sending country, and that $G^{nmS}_{c^S=0}(m) > G^{nmS}(m)$ for any m. Anticipating the said reactions by the sending country, the receiving country's optimal policy depends on the position of m_C^{R*}, and on the welfare level associated with m_C^{R*}. We have to distinguish between two cases: $m_C^{R*} < m_C^{S*}$, and $m_C^{R*} \geq m_C^{S*}$.

When $m_C^{R*} < m_C^{S*}$, the equilibrium migration policy m^* can either be m_C^{R*} or m_C^{S*}, depending on $G^R(m_C^{R*})$ being higher or lower than $G^R_{c^R=0}(m_C^{S*})$. When $G^R(m_C^{R*}) > G^R_{c^R=0}(m_C^{S*})$, the receiving country chooses m_C^{R*}, which the sending country accepts since $m_C^{R*} < \tilde{m}$. When $G^R(m_C^{R*}) \leq G^R_{c^R=0}(m_C^{S*})$, the best strategy for the receiving country is to leave the migration policy decision to the sending country, which will then set m_C^{S*}. Figures 9.1 and 9.2 serve to illustrate.

When $m_C^{R*} \geq m_C^{S*}$, the equilibrium migration policy is always m_C^{S*}. To see this, notice that m_C^{R*} is always on the decreasing portion of $G^R_{c^R=0}(m)$. This follows from the first order conditions for an internal maximum (9.12) and from observing that $-\frac{\partial c^R}{\partial m} > 0$. Knowing this, assume that $G^R(m_C^{R*}) > G^R_{c^R=0}(m_C^{S*})$ so that m_C^{R*} is the equilibrium migration policy. The last inequality trivially implies $G^R_{c^R=0}(m_C^{R*}) > G^R_{c^R=0}(m_C^{S*})$ which contradicts that $m_C^{R*} \geq m_C^{S*}$ and that m_C^{R*} is in the decreasing portion of the $G^R_{c^R=0}(m)$ curve. Therefore, given that $G^R(m_C^{R*}) \leq G^R_{c^R=0}(m_C^{S*})$ always for $m_C^{R*} \geq m_C^{S*}$, the receiving country will let the sending country set its optimal migration policy m_C^{S*}; see Figure 9A.1.

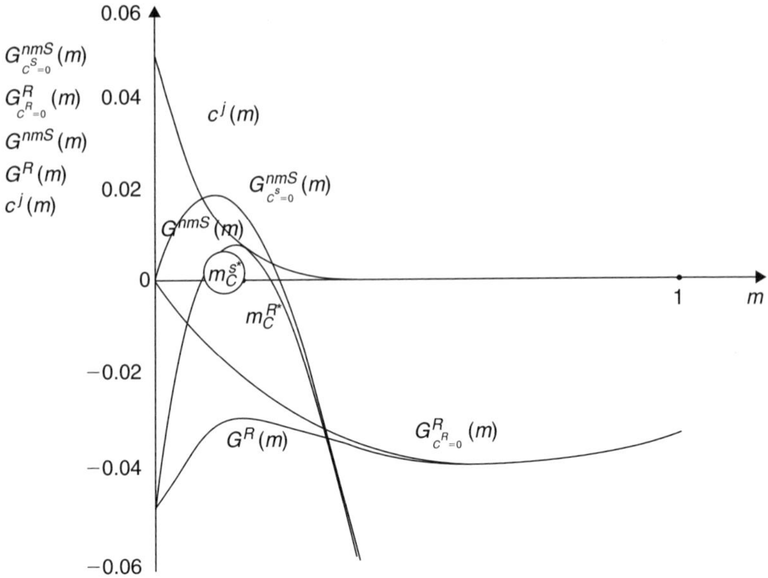

Figure 9A.1 Case $m_C^{R*} \geq m_C^{S*}$

Graphical representation

For the purpose of graphical representation we make the following parameter assumptions: $\beta^S = 1$, $\beta^R = 4$, $\eta = 0.2$, $k = 0.4$, $N^S = N^R = 1$. The cost function is specified as

$$c^j(m) = \frac{(m-1)^a}{N^j} \widehat{C}^j$$

where $\widehat{C}^j = 0.05$. Varying the speed at which costs decrease as measured by a and the degree of transferability of skills, as captured by β^{mR}, we obtain the three different cases represented in Figures 9.1, 9.2 and 9A.1. Namely, the curves in Figure 9.1 are drawn for $\beta^{mR} = 2$ and for $a = 14$. In Figure 9.2 $a = 6$ is set, holding $\beta^{mR} = 2$. For the curves in Figure 9A.1, $a = 10$ and $\beta^{mR} = 2.8$ are assumed.

In all the Figures, the chosen parameters guarantee that m_C^{R*} is a global maximum.

Proof of Proposition 4

Control costs $c_\alpha^S(m) < c^S(m)$ lead to a smaller optimal migration quota, $\frac{\partial m_\alpha^{S*}}{\partial \alpha} < 0$, as can be inferred from (9.14) in conjunction with Proposition 1. Graphically, starting at $\alpha = 0$, a transfer from the receiving country to the sending country moves the $G^{nmS}(m)$ curve towards $G^{nmS}_{c^S=0}(m)$ – call it $G_\alpha^{nmS}(m)$ – with $G^{nmS}(m) \leq G_\alpha^{nmS}(m) \leq G^{nmS}_{c^S=0}(m)$ for every $m \in (0, 1)$. The new maximum for the sending country is upward and to the left of the maximum of the $G^{nmS}(m)$ curve, with lower migration and no welfare loss. For the receiving country, two opposite effects are at work: the reduction of migration makes the receiving country better off, $\left.\frac{\partial G^R_{c^R=0}(m)}{\partial m}\frac{\partial m^{S*}_{\alpha}}{\partial \alpha}\right|_{m=m^{S*}_C} > 0$ as $\left.\frac{\partial G^R_{c^R=0}(m)}{\partial m}\right|_{m=m^{S*}_C} < 0$. At the same time, however, natives experience an increase in per capita costs due to the transfer: this is given by $\left[c^S(m^{S*}_C) + \alpha\frac{\partial c^S(m)}{\partial m}\frac{\partial m^{S*}_{\alpha}}{\partial \alpha}\right]\frac{N^S}{N^R}$ which reduces to $c^S(m^{S*}_C)\frac{N^S}{N^R}$ at $\alpha = 0$. The receiving country is therefore better off if the increase in per capita welfare exceeds the cost, that is, if

$$\left.\frac{\partial G^R_{c^R=0}(m)}{\partial m}\frac{\partial m^{S*}_{\alpha}}{\partial \alpha}\right|_{m=m^{S*}_C} > c^S(m^{S*}_C)\frac{N^S}{N^R}. \qquad \blacksquare$$

Notes

1. See Moretti (2005) for a recent succinct review of the existing evidence on geographical – and intertemporal – spillover effects in human capital.
2. Any world-wide human capital externality would proportionally affect the social returns in both the sending and the receiving country, leaving the relative social returns unchanged.
3. The second-order condition for a maximum, $\frac{-\beta^j}{(\vartheta^j+1)^2} < 0$, holds.
4. The socially optimal investment in human capital in the closed economy is $\widehat{\vartheta}^{j*} = \frac{\beta^j+\eta}{k} - 1$, as established in Stark and Wang (2002). That work identifies the conditions under which, from a social point of view, too little human capital formation takes place in the economy, and studies the link between the actual and the socially optimal formation of human capital in the presence of the possibility of migration. Stark and Wang (2002) identify conditions under which the per capita output and level of welfare of all workers are higher with migration than in its absence, and they show that a restrictive migration policy which is controlled by the sending country can enhance welfare and nudge the economy toward the social optimum.
5. Introducing a lump-sum cost of mobility will not affect the individual's human capital formation decision. If the cost depends on the level of education, this will affect the individual's decision about his education. The results of this section will be reinforced if we assume that migration is cheaper the higher the level of human capital.
6. The second-order condition for a maximum, $-\frac{m(\beta^{mR}-\beta^S)+\beta^S}{(\widetilde{\vartheta}^S+1)^2} < 0$, holds.
7. To see this, note that $m(\beta^{mR} - \beta^S) + \beta^S = m\beta^{mR} + (1-m)\beta^S < \beta^{mR} \leq \beta^R$. For a hypothetical $m = 1$, $\widetilde{\vartheta}^{S*} = \vartheta^{R*}$ if and only if $\beta^{mR} = \beta^R$.
8. For a study in which the focus is on an optimal selective migration policy implemented by the receiving country in the presence of informational asymmetries see Stark, Casarico, and Uebelmesser (2008) in this volume.
9. To simplify the notation, we do not include the lump-sum tax in the individuals' maximization problem.
10. Notice that if, instead of having as objective function the difference between a measure of welfare in the open economy and a measure of welfare in the closed economy, we use as objective function a measure of welfare in the open economy, the optimality conditions identified below will remain unchanged. Taking the

difference is a convenient normalization for the graphical representation of the results which will follow, as it allows us to compare the welfare gains or losses brought about by the open migration policy, as opposed to a closed economy.

11. For a sufficiently large N^S, $c^S(m_C^{S*})$ will be small enough to yield $G^{nmS}(m_C^{S*}) > 0$. The second order condition for a maximum is guaranteed by the convexity of the cost function.
12. The numerical illustration that we use for graphical representation shows that there are instances where an interior global maximum obtains. In an earlier version of the chapter we assumed perfect portability which yielded $m_C^{R*} = 1$ as the optimal solution where the receiving country wields sole migration control power. Notice that the assumption regarding the transferability of human capital does not influence the results of section 4 where policy-setting power rests with both the sending and the receiving country.
13. We relegate the discussion of the structure of the game, in particular the implications of having different assumptions for the sequence of the players' moves and of the possibility of adopting a simultaneous set-up, as opposed to a two-stage set-up, until after the presentation, and the proof, of the equilibrium (that is, until after Proposition 3).
14. In the Appendix we specify the parameterization used for the graphical representation.

References

Bhagwati, J., and Wilson, J.D. (1989) *Income Taxation and International Mobility* (Cambridge, MA: MIT Press).

Boeri, T., and Bruecker, H. (2005) 'Why are Europeans so Tough on Migrants?', *Economic Policy* 20, 630–703.

Fan, C.S., and Stark, O. (2007) 'International Migration and "Educated Unemployment"', *Journal of Development Economics* 83, 76–87.

Moretti, E. (2005) 'Social Returns to Human Capital', *NBER Reporter*, Spring 2005, pp. 13–15.

Mountford, A. (1997) 'Can a Brain Drain be Good for Growth in the Source Economy?', *Journal of Development Economics* 53, 287–303.

Patinkin, D. (1968) 'A "Nationalist" Model', in W. Adams (ed.), *The Brain Drain* (New York: Macmillan).

Stark, O., Casarico, A., and Uebelmesser, S. (2008) 'An Optimal Selective Migration Policy in the Absence of Symmetric Information and in the Presence of Skill Formation Incentives', in this volume.

Stark, O. and Fan, C.S. (2007) 'Losses and Gains to Developing Countries from the Migration of Educated Workers: An Overview of Recent Research, and New Reflections', *World Economics* 8, 259–69.

Stark, O. and Fan, C.S. (2008) 'The Brain Drain, "Educated Unemployment", Human Capital Formation, and Economic Betterment', in this volume.

Stark, O., Helmenstein, C. and Prskawetz, A. (1997) 'A Brain Gain with a Brain Drain', *Economics Letters* 55, 227–34.

Stark, O., Helmenstein, C. and Prskawetz, A. (1998) 'Human Capital Depletion, Human Capital Formation, and Migration: A Blessing or a "Curse"?', *Economics Letters* 60, 363–7.

Stark, O., and Wang, Y. (2002) 'Inducing Human Capital Formation: Migration as a Substitute for Subsidies', *Journal of Public Economics* 86, 29–46.

Part 3

Public Utility Reform

10
Redesigning Public Utilities: the Key Role of Micro-institutions

Claude Ménard

1 Introduction

The movement towards reforming public utilities that developed during the 1980s has largely contributed to placing institutions high on the agenda of economists. Indeed, difficulties encountered in implementing successful change in the provision of essential goods and services revealed the importance and influence of the institutional background. Although most of the initial attention of reformers focused on the most profitable sectors among network industries, namely: telecoms, electricity, and gas, the importance of water and sewerage and the need to find ways to provide them to large segments of the population that do not have access to safe water around the world was increasingly acknowledged.

In what follows, I focus on water, although sewerage is its essential complement. Indeed, among public goods, water is the most universal since it meets a fundamental need of human beings, making it inescapable. There is no substitute for water, while everybody can (almost) survive without telephones or electricity! Another aspect that makes water particularly significant when it comes to the analysis of the impact of the institutional environment on its provision is that this is a sector that has not been challenged and/or reshaped by technological change, contrary to telecommunications or the electricity industry, so that we do not have to disentangle the complex interactions between organizational and institutional change on the one hand, and technological transformation on the other hand.

Once technological change is put aside as non-significant, we still have to identify the relevant dimensions of the institutional environment in order to understand the characteristics of, and limits to reforming urban water systems. Most analyses of institutional factors, whether in the water sector or other public utilities, have so far focused on the nature and role of regulators in the reforming process. In what follows, I submit that notwithstanding the importance of this component, regulators are one and only one (and often a minor one) of the institutions framing the reform of public utilities. Several other institutional mechanisms should be taken into consideration, which mostly operate at the micro level: I call these devices '*micro-institutions*'. Two of their distinctive characteristics are that (i) they are distinct from, although embedded in, their general institutional environment; (ii) they are often not specific to one sector but cover several utilities.

My analysis of these micro-institutions is informed by a new institutional perspective, which means paying particular attention to the interaction of different devices, including regulators, which determine the modes of organization chosen, the transaction costs involved and, therefore, the comparative performance of the arrangements implemented. Although the limited space available prevents one from providing details, the references refer to a set of studies in which I have been involved (or which are partially overlapping with those in which I have been involved), on the reform of urban water systems in developing countries (Savendoff and Spiller, 1999; Shirley, 2002; Ménard, Clarke and Zuluaga, 2002; Guasch, Laffont and Straub, 2005; Guasch, 2005) as well as in developed ones, mostly in France (Ménard and Saussier, 2002; Ménard et al., 2004).

The chapter is organized as follows. Section 2 briefly summarizes the theoretical background of the discussion that underlies my analysis, contrasting the standard approach with a new institutional perspective. Section 3 discusses the limited role of regulators and regulation when dealing with decentralized public utilities that have characteristics of a natural monopoly. Section 4 develops the idea that in order to understand and eventually succeed in reforming public utilities of that type, we must go beyond the role of regulators: micro-institutions need to be implemented and/or reformed. The conclusion emphasizes the long way we still have to go in that direction.

2 From a standard approach to an institutional perspective

Reform of public utilities is almost always initiated when they face major problems: endogenous forces clearly prevail over exogenous ones (such as political change). A short reminder of these problems helps to understand the solutions proposed by the standard approach developed in the 1980s and to point out some limits that the new institutional approach allows one to identify and potentially to overcome.

2.1 Basic infrastructure services, natural monopolies, and reforms

The provision of essential services, particularly water, usually calls for reform because it is plagued with increasing problems. The major symptoms, often interdependent so that difficulties get amplified, are the following:

1 Low performance that makes the provision of water particularly expensive, due to excess labour, low productivity, and a high rate of unaccounted for water.

2 Prices that do not cover long-run costs, often because political opportunism interferes with the needs of the operator, whether it is public or private, so that under-investment and/or financial bottlenecks develop.
3 Provision of services that are highly politicized, with government interference taking many different forms, from price control to intervention in the daily management of the utility (for example, by imposing constraints on the management of human resources) to cross-subsidies favouring the wealthier (that is, through high connection changes and/or pricing that introduces severe distortion for example when it is based on fixed rates rather than on water consumption).
4 Significant fractions of the population may not have access to the service, or have only intermittent access (as when water is delivered for only a few hours per day), or have access to the service at outrageous cost (as when households depend on the delivery of water by trucks through private suppliers).
5 Available water is polluted because of inadequate or even non existing sewerage systems, exposing the poor who cannot count on alternative supply of water to epidemics etc.

These problems, which water supply largely shares with other mismanaged public utilities, are amplified by the specific aspects of water, particularly:

(a) Large economies of density and/or economies of scale in water systems translating into rapidly declining average costs, which provide strong incentives towards integration, making water systems among the closest to the essence of natural monopolies.
(b) The high level of sunk costs in water systems, representing over 80 per cent of total costs, compared to about 30 per cent for gas and less than 60 per cent for electricity (Savendoff and Spiller, 1999, p. 5), with fixed assets that have almost no alternative uses, so that it involves high risks for potential private investors.
(c) Related to the above, far less revenue is needed to cover current expenditure than with other public utilities, so that operators tend to continue their activities as long as these revenues cover their variable costs. This provides incentives for public authorities to underprice the service, generating under-investment.
(d) The broad range of users, who strictly overlap all citizens in the case of water, make the provision and pricing of water highly sensitive from a political point of view.

All in all, the combination of these problems makes the reform of water particularly difficult which may explain the slow pace of reform in that sector, notwithstanding the urgency of doing so, particularly in developing countries.

2.2 The core of the standard approach developed in the 1980s

Confronted by these problems, mainstream economists developed a set of reforms that can be summarized in five different components. First, they recommended privatization, viewed as a way to 'depoliticize' public utilities while simultaneously taking advantage of the presumed superior efficiency of private firms and unbundling economic efficiency from social goals. Second, they emphasized the possibility and advantages of disentangling the competitive segments from natural monopoly segments in order to introduce 'competition in the market' for the former, 'competition for the market' in the latter. Third, they carefully explored alternative mechanisms for allocating competitive segments (for example, different modalities of auctions) in order to find the optimal one. Fourth, they designed regulatory reforms for controlling the vertically integrated natural monopoly and for monitoring the relationship between the competitive segment and the natural monopoly segment. Fifth, they defined characteristics of an optimal regulator that would be efficient and credible in implementing these reforms.

The underlying logic of this approach was that if optimal characteristics could be identified along the five dimensions identified above, a model would be available that would fit all reforms. This is the 'one-size-fits-all' principle that was predominant, implicitly or explicitly, in the late 1980s and the early 1990s. This model was part of what became known as 'The Washington Consensus'.

2.3 A new institutional perspective

However, the failure of many reforms became obvious in numerous cases in the second half of the 1990s, particularly in the water sector and particularly in developing countries and showed how the 'one-size-fits-all' approach could severely hamper the expected performance from reform (World Development Report, 2001). One important dimension to explain these failures, which became high on the agenda of many economists and policy-makers, was the neglect of institutional endowments when designing and implementing reform. Comparative studies showed that similar reforms implemented in different institutional environments could produce radically different, even opposite results (Ménard and Shirley, 2002, ch. 1). This observation permitted aspects of the work of the new institutionalists – notably, Ronald Coase, Douglass North and Oliver Williamson – to be taken into consideration.

Important lessons can be learned from a diverse series of studies by these new institutionalists; from Coase (1974) on the regulation of maritime traffic through lighthouses to Williamson (1985, ch. 13) on the franchise bidding for cable television rights or Joskow (1991) on the reform of electricity, Levy and Spiller (1994) on telecommunications and Shirley (2002) on urban water systems. What these studies and others showed was that the efficient restructuring of public utilities needed finely-tuned reform far removed from the 'one-size-fits-all' approach. Specifically, reform needed to take into account:

i. The specificity of investment required, and the related risks of opportunistic behaviour and delaying 'hold-up' strategies by involved parties: the nature of assets are crucial when deciding on the mode of organization (and the characteristics of proposed contracts), with a wide variety of alternative solutions;
ii. The industrial endowments within which reform is embedded, as these endowments determine the feasibility of reform: existing institutions, and conditions delineating the possibility of adjusting these institutions, and have a direct impact on the characteristics – and success or failure – of reform. Not all institutional change can be implemented.

In that respect, the main message from new institutional economics is that any projected reform should consider the transaction costs involved in the design and implementation of the new arrangement, without assuming the absolute superiority of one form over another: the success or failure of reform is primarily a governance issue.

Table 10.1 shows the three linked areas that motivate the need for reform, the constraints on reform imposed by the institutional environment and the anticipated outcome after implementation. These are essential to the examination of potential reform or evaluation of ongoing experiments.

Table 10.1 The determinants of reform

Motivations for Reform	*Constraints on Design*	*Determinants of Outcome*
Sector crisis	Information available	Incentives
Macro crisis	Credibility of parties	Commitment
Political change	Relative power of winners and losers	Micro-institutions

3 The role of regulators and their limits with respect to decentralized public utilities

Let us now turn to the more specific institutions involved in reforming public utilities with particular attention to decentralized ones, that is, public utilities that deliver services essentially on a local or regional basis (water is the main case in point here, but sewerage and urban public transportation are other relevant examples). Again I would like to contrast, to the point of oversimplifying, the standard approach that has prevailed since the late 1980s to some lessons we can learn from an institutional perspective (Estache and Martimort, 2001).

3.1 The standard approach

The standard approach to the reform of decentralized public utilities does not differ from the recommendation for global ones (such as railroads, electricity or telecommunications). Besides the general propositions identified in section 2.2, with its special emphasis on unbundling previous 'natural' monopolies' and the privatization of all activities in the competitive segment, the main problem in that approach, when it comes to regulating the segment remaining in the non-competitive segment and its relationship with the competitive segments, relates to the nature of regulators at the decentralized level, for example, the municipality level. However, the attention remained focused on what should be implemented at the higher level in the search for optimal regulation and regulatory laws, and emphasis has tended to be placed on the experience gained in the 1980s and 1990s: namely expertise, independence, accountability, credibility and some flexibility. This should be allied to the search for an optimal contract, which must above all minimize information asymmetry and rein in as much as possible the discretionary power of the regulator, thus reducing if not eliminating opportunities for political intervention.

However, the problems already encountered by sector regulators operating at the aggregate level of an industry become even more acute when it comes to regulating decentralized public utilities that necessarily must adapt to local or regional circumstances (such as the geology, demography, and other factors that mould water, sewerage or urban transportation systems). Among the most significant problems are the following:

(a) Does it make sense to have a single-sector regulator at the local or regional level? If not, what would be the relevant domain for a multi-sector regulator? Should it be the traditional public works department (then we are far away from the intended purposes of reforms according to the standard approach)?
(b) How can a local or regional regulator overcome information asymmetry if one considers the difficulties this issue already raises at a global level at where greater competence exists?
(c) What device could guarantee forms of control avoiding capture, to which local authorities are particularly exposed?
(d) Considering that contracts with high incentives provide large rents, how can an optimal contract be designed that limits the risky reactions against these rents among political constituencies?

All of these questions suggest that regulators at a decentralized level confront amplified versions of the more general problems identified in regulatory issues. They also all point at the significance of the institutional environment within which decentralized public utilities are embedded (Estache and Martimort, 2001).

3.2 An institutional perspective

Indeed, reforming decentralized public utilities faces severe institutional constraints. The leading idea pushed forward in a new institutional perspective is that the selected regulatory devices should minimize transaction costs among parties to the arrangement. This induces two consequences that involve problems that are unlikely at the regulatory level to be solved alone. The consequences are that: (1) regulation is a governance issue, which depends largely on institutional endowments; (2) ex post implementation of contracts is most of the time more important than their design ex ante (Goldberg, 1976; Levy and Spiller, 1994).

When it comes to reforming the water sector, these consequences involve both general and specific problems. The main general problems, that is, problems that exceed the sector under review, are the following. First, institutional endowments are imperfect and/or limited, which imposes tight constraints. Indeed, the limited scale at which local authorities operate necessarily restricts the regulatory tools available (for example, they may have constraints regarding the duration of contacts that are imposed by laws defined at national level). Second, even big cities rely on limited human assets, particularly in developing countries, so that installing a regulator with the characteristics identified above is not obvious at all. Third, local or regional regulators are usually subject to multiple layers of regulation, which not only limits their capacity to monitor operators and/or contracts, but may generate institutional conflict.

Besides these difficulties that all decentralized public utilities share, there are other problems affecting the water sector.

(a) Incompleteness of contracts is particularly noticeable in this sector because of the combination of unusually high specificity of investments with the significant level of uncertainty due to changes in population density and the limited planning of cities' development (an issue most acute in developing countries). As a result, renegotiation at short intervals is the rule (Guasch, Laffont and Straub, 2005; Guasch, 2005). These renegotiations are usually plagued by political interference as voters and users overlap so closely.
(b) Because of its centrality for human beings, water pricing is highly sensitive from a political point of view. More generally, it frequently involves subsidies and redistribution issues. This trend is clearly amplified in developing countries, because of poor tax systems, so that redistribution cannot be monitored through taxation.

(c) Incentives for governments to hold up operators (even public ones) once specific investments have been made, is particularly strong, again even more so in developing countries. Credible commitments from local public authorities become a major challenge, which may be amplified by the diversity of levels of policy-makers involved (for example, provincial and central governments on top of local ones).

Characteristics and limits of institutions operating at the local or regional level then become a major issue.

4 The key role of 'micro-institutions'

I do not pretend that a new institutional approach provides an adequate answer to all of these problems. However, research has highlighted major components involved in the success or failure of reforms of decentralized public utilities, besides the role of regulators.

4.1 Administrative procedures and the major role of local authorities

I have already emphasized the role of local authorities in monitoring decentralized public utilities. As a result, two aspects should be of particular concern for policy-makers.

First, there is the problem of the allocation of regulatory rights and, more generally, of monitoring capabilities between the different levels of government with respect to decentralized public utilities. Full centralization of regulation and /or of administrative supervision as in unified political systems has the advantage of lower transaction costs since agreements do not have to be negotiated and implemented among a large number of parties. However, it confronts the risks associated with the 'one-size-fits-all' approach, since the temptation is powerful for the central authority to impose a single model. The other polar case, full decentralization, has the advantage of allowing the introduction of diversity, therefore of comparison and, ultimately, of some form of benchmarking, thus favouring regulatory mechanisms closer to markets. However, it involves higher transaction costs (for example, operators have to tailor different contracts for different municipalities, and local authorities must consider non-standard contracts as well), higher risks of conflict between the different departments, and the multiplication of potential sources of political interference.

Second, the administrative burden on local authorities of designing and monitoring a reform increases the key role of conflict resolution systems. New institutional economists have established a reputation in emphasizing the significance of ex post conditions in developing reform (and, more generally, organizational change), because of the risk of hold-ups and capture resulting from the opportunistic behaviour of the parties (Williamson, 1985, ch.13). One important question is the level at which conflict resolution should be monitored: at the local, regional, or central level of government? Another crucial aspect is the trade-off between agreements that involve the full commitment of the parties (that is, through very detailed and almost complete contracts), which not only severely restricts arbitrary decisions in dispute resolution, but also involves costly contractual processes and embeds potentially harmful rigidities in the agreement. Furthermore, flexible arrangements that lower initial transaction costs but create much more room for administrative discretionary power, render dispute resolution quite opaque.

4.2 Human assets in monitoring decentralized public utilities

One major aspect in reforming local or regional public utilities is that it requires heavy investment in human capital.

Indeed, one important advantage of public utilities operated at a decentralized level is that it can provide some 'benchmarking', notwithstanding the necessary adjustments for taking into account local variations (for example, in the physical environment, in the density and/or distribution of population). However, in order to make a comparative approach possible for policy-makers as well as for users, adequate information must be made available. As we know from the past experience of reforming public utilities, the information revelation principle is not that easy to implement through contracts. In that respect, one major difficulty when it comes to decentralized utilities is the availability of adequate human capital for collecting and diffusing information. Most of the time, there is limited capability at local level: *ex ante*, for designing and allocating contracts through procedures that are often very complex and by far exceeds the competence of local authorities, putting them at risk of being in an asymmetric position when negotiating with large operators; and *ex post*, when it comes to the necessity for local authorities to collect and process information in order to monitor adequately operators, and to pass that information to users.

Although the problem of limited staff resources and skill is particularly severe in developing countries, it exists and creates significant problems in developed countries as well – particularly for small and medium-sized cities. In that respect, the French experience of 'Basin Agencies', that is, agencies structured along the main pools of water resources (in this case, main rivers) and in charge of coordinating the actions of municipalities regarding not only the provision of water, but also the coordination of usage (between drinkable water, industrial use, agricultural needs) is one that could inspire policy-makers abroad. Indeed, it has the advantage of pooling human resources over a relatively wide area and handling the different uses of water.

4.3 The role of judicial review

There has been an increasing emphasis in the 1990s, in the economic literature on reform of public utilities, on the key role of an independent judiciary that can review agreements and arbitrate on conflicts between parties as well as dealing with consumers' complaints. The existence of an adequate legal system is now conventionally introduced as central to successful reform.

Although I do not deny the importance and significance of an adequate legal system, I would argue that the role of the judiciary in the recent literature on reform tends to be overstated. This is so for at least three reasons: (a) Going to law usually signals a major conflict, that both sides of the contractual arrangement, public authorities and operators (private, but also public when the latter has some autonomy, as with public corporations) want to avoid because it might challenge the continuity of the relationship which is crucial. This is particularly so where highly specific investment is concerned which may represent most of the cost of the investment, as in water systems. (b) Going to law involves high transaction costs. As we all know, there is no such a thing as free lawyers! Judicial procedures are costly, for both parties, but particularly for local authorities when they are dealing with large operators who may be able to spread their legal fees over several contracts with different authorities. Therefore, most renegotiation and most conflicts are resolved out of court. Only a small percentage of conflicts are resolved in court. It does not mean that the judiciary is unimportant; but, that its role is one of dissuasion in last resort against opportunism. (c) Last, one cannot ignore the fact that most countries have poor legal competence available. Judges and lawyers competent in commercial affairs are a scarce resource, which is costly to develop (Hadfield, 2005). Costs are particularly significant when conflict involves the intervention of exogenous judiciary systems, such as international courts.

Considering the high and frequent rate of renegotiation of contracts, particularly with respect to local or regional public utilities (Guasch, 2005), one interesting solution to explore further might be the building of regional micro-institutions charged with helping to solve disputes through arbitration procedures, with arbitrators covering different categories of public utilities (such as urban water, sewerage, and public transportation) and able to operate in one or more regions, so as to avoid depending solely on the human assets of specific local authorities. This would reduce the cost of arbitration procedures, reduce the role of the judiciary, and also potentially limit the risk of capture. These micro-arbitration institutions could take over at regional level the role that public commissions played regarding national utilities (telecoms, electricity) in the Anglo-American tradition.

4.4 Political responsibilities

A leading motivation for reforming public utilities has been the reduction, if not the total elimination, of political interference. Indeed, numerous public utilities operating as government departments have been plagued, by overstaffing, underpricing, underinvestment and obscure cross-subsidies often favouring those with lobbying skills. Privatization was considered the main tool for putting an end to these problems. As it happened, and as is

well-documented through several case studies (Shirley ed., 2002) as well as statistical data (Guasch, 2005), changing the allocation of property rights is at best only part of the solution. Indeed, risks of capture and of corruption, or even of distortion because of the very nature of public utilities, cannot be ignored.

4.4.1 *Can political interference be avoided?*

I would argue that political interference is almost inevitable in most decentralized public utilities, particularly with water systems. This is for several reasons. First, there are the unique characteristics of water systems already mentioned, namely the high level of sunk costs and the specificity of investment involved, making them as close as possible to what has been traditionally identified as natural monopolies. Second, there is the total overlapping, at least in democratic and even in authoritarian regimes between users and voters, which makes the provision of water and its pricing highly sensitive from a political point of view. Third, and partially related to the factors above, there are strong incentives for politicians to monitor public utilities, particularly water systems, as tools of redistribution, either as compensation for poorly developed tax systems that cannot do the job or because it is an easy way to get support from their political constituencies.

The conventional wisdom is that these trends should be balanced by a combination of privatization and of checks and balances through regulatory authorities and judiciary control. However, I have already emphasized how costly and disruptive the latter can be and how high the risks of capture are for the former. Moreover, as also argued in previous subsections, regulatory control at the local or even regional level is often almost impossible because of the lack of adequate human capital, a problem that does not only differentiate developed from developing countries, but also small cities from big ones. Therefore, political interference can hardly be avoided.

4.4.2 *Is there legitimacy for political interference?*

One might go even further and argue that there is legitimacy to some political monitoring of public utilities, particularly of water and sewerage systems, at least in a democratic regime. Water and sewerage systems share many properties of a natural monopoly, with one extra characteristic: they are absolutely essential to human survival, in the short term for water, in the long run for sewerage. In that respect, water and sewerage differ from other public utilities. In a democratic society, it is the duty of elected politicians with a minimum of concern for the wellbeing of the population they represent to guarantee these services. Otherwise, what would be the role of a democratic regime? Some political control is therefore not only unavoidable, but legitimate: the provision of water cannot be delegated to regulators or technocrats without any political control.

This probably explains why all developed countries have had their water and sewerage systems developed by public departments under political control or by private operators tightly supervised by public authorities (as in the concession system). And it is noticeable that public–private participation became fashionable in recent decades less because of the observable failure of water and sewerage systems in developed countries than because of financial constraints faced by developing countries. In that perspective, the central question may not be: 'to privatize or not to privatize', but rather: what institutions can be designed at the local or regional level that can attract private participation while avoiding micro-management and/or corruption, without denying the active role of public authorities?

5 Conclusion

There is a long way to go in order to answer that question. However, there are some lessons we have already learned from experience and also from insights that an institutional perspective provides.

First, 'one-size-does-not-fit-all'! In designing and implementing reforms of public utilities, institutional endowments must be at the top of the agenda. Moreover, not only should we take into account the global institutional environment, but it is also necessary to dig deeper and understand the characteristics and properties of institutions at both local and regional levels. Reforming decentralized public utilities requires considering and/or reforming the micro-institutions operating at the level of these utilities.

Second, as emphasized early on by Joskow (1991, p. 281), '...the [free market] cannot always replicate efficiently internal organization and complex contractual arrangements'. Therefore, trade-offs between public and private or mixed arrangements and trade-offs among different modes of organizations deserve serious analysis taking into account the institutional capabilities available for implementing more or less complex solutions and the transaction costs involved in these solutions.

Third, certain main goals should be kept in mind and remain at the core of all reform. (a) Water and sewerage services must be provided to all citizens: there are no substitutes, and no way to escape the necessity of these services for human survival. This makes these services particularly sensitive from a political viewpoint, and political responsibility cannot be eliminated from the picture. (b) In order to meet these needs, reforms must provide incentives to invest, and this is true whether the delivery of the service is under public or private responsibility. It means that resources should cover long-run average costs in order for these universal services to be sustainable. (c) Political intervention, through the monitoring of the system, cross-subsidies, regulation of quality and prices, and so on, being almost unavoidable, institutions should be designed, not only at the national level, but also at the local or regional level primarily to guarantee transparency of any interference, so that, in the last resort, voters can arbitrate.

Hence, four priorities (and questions) should be at the top of the agenda of researchers and policy-makers. (i) What decentralized institutions can be built that are feasible, with decision rights at local or regional levels leaving room for transparency? (ii) What institutional endowments are really central for decentralized public utilities, which require demystifying the role of the judiciary? (iii) What human assets are crucial in order to make the monitoring of decentralized public utilities efficient without purely transferring discretionary power from politicians to technocrats (or so-called 'experts')? (iv) What incentives, monetary and organizational, can be implemented besides political motivations for making local regulators and/or supervisors accountable for their decisions?

One way to deal with these questions may be to capitalize the past experience of developed countries, particularly with respect to the development of water and sewerage systems in the nineteenth and early twentieth centuries. Economists tend to neglect historical lessons. However, this is clearly a case in which *memory could help*!

References

Coase, R.H. (1974) 'The Lighthouse in Economics', *Journal of Law and Economics*, vol. 17 pp. 357–76.

Estache, A. and D. Martimort (2001) 'Transaction Costs, Politics, Regulatory Institutions and Regulatory Outcomes', in L. Manzetti (ed.), *Regulatory Policy in Latin America: Post-Privatization Realities* (Miami: North-South Press Center of the University of Miami), pp. 49–82.

Goldberg, V. (1976) 'Regulated and Administered Contracts', *Bell Journal of Economics*, vol. 7, pp. 527–43.

Guasch, J. L. (2005) *Granting and Renegotiating Infrastructure Concessions: Doing it Right* (Washington, DC: The World Bank).

Guasch, J.L., J.J. Laffont and S. Straub (2005) 'Infrastructure Concessions in Latin America: Government-led Renegotiations', *Policy Research Working Paper Series*, no. 3749, The World Bank.

Hadfield, G. K. (2005) 'The Many Legal Institutions that Support Contractual Commitments', in C. Ménard and M. Shirley (eds), *Handbook of New Institutional Economics* (Berlin, Boston and Dordrecht: Springer).

Joskow, P. (1991) 'The Role of Transaction Cost Economics in Antitrust and Public Utility Regulatory Policies', *Journal of Law, Economics and Organization*, vol. 7, pp. 253–83.

Joskow, P. (1999) 'Regulatory Priorities for Reforming Infrastructure Sectors in Developing Countries', *Annual World Bank Conference on Development Economics 1998* (Washington, DC: The World Bank, April), pp. 191–223.

Laffont, J.J. and J. Tirole (1993) *A Theory of Incentives in Procurement and Regulation* (Cambridge and London: MIT Press).

Levy, B. and P. Spiller (1994) 'The Institutional Foundations of Regulatory Commitment', *Journal of Law, Economics and Organization*, vol. 9, pp. 201–46.

Ménard, C., G. Clarke and A. M. Zuluaga (2002) 'Measuring the Welfare Effects of Reform: Urban Water Supply in Guinea', *World Development*, vol. 30, no. 9, pp. 1517–37.
Ménard, C. and S. Saussier (2002) 'Contractual Choice and Performance', in E. Brousseau and J.M. Glachant (eds), *The Economics of Contracts: Theory and Applications* (Cambridge: Cambridge University Press).
Ménard, C. and M. Shirley (2002) 'Cities Awash: A Synthesis of Country Cases', in M. Shirley (ed.) *Thirsting for Efficiency: The Economics and Politics of Urban Water System Reform* (Amsterdam: Pergamon-Elsevier-World Bank) ch. 1, pp. 1–42.
Ménard, C., S. Saussier, C. Staropoli and F. Huet (2004) 'Mode de gestion et efficacité de la distribution d'eau en France'. Report to the French Ministry of Environment, June.
Savendoff, W. and P. Spiller (eds) (1999) *Spilled Water* (Washington: Inter-American Development Bank).
Shirley, M. (ed.) (2002) *Thirsting for Efficiency: The Economics and Politics of Urban Water System Reform* (Amsterdam: Pergamon-Elsevier-World Bank).
Williamson, O. E. (1985) *The Economic Institutions of Capitalism* (New York: The Free Press-Macmillan).
World Development Report 2002 (2001) *Building Institutions for Markets* (Oxford: Oxford University Press).

11

Does Regulation and Institutional Design Matter for Infrastructure Sector Performance?

*Luis A. Andrés, José Luis Guasch and Stephane Straub**

1 Introduction

During the 1990s, as part of structural reform in infrastructure industries more than US$750 billion was invested in 2,500 private infrastructure projects in developing economies. Nearly half went to the Latin American region, mainly through the divestiture of public assets in telecommunications and electricity sectors and transport concessions. Six countries – Argentina, Brazil, Chile, Colombia, Mexico and Peru – absorbed more than 90 per cent of private investment. Overall, the region was the most important beneficiary of the huge flow of private investments for infrastructure worldwide with private investment finance peaking at around US$130 billion in 1997. Since then, investors' appetites have waned, public support for privatization has decreased, and the role of public investment in the provision of infrastructure services has gained momentum again.[1] While the increase of public investment is welcomed, given the magnitude of infrastructure needs in the region – roughly 4 to 6 per cent of gross domestic product (GDP) per year to catch up or keep up with countries that once trailed it, such as China and Korea – and the fiscal limitations of the public sector, private sector financing for infrastructure will always be important in Latin America.

Whereas in Latin American countries, state-owned enterprises continue to account for more than 10 per cent of gross domestic product, 20 per cent of investment, and about 5 per cent of formal employment (Kikeri, 1999); however, the infrastructure sector has changed dramatically. Specifically, while at the beginning of the 1990s only 3 per cent, 3 per cent and almost 0 per cent of the subscribers of fixed telecommunications, electricity and water distribution, respectively, were in private hands, by 2003 these ratios were 86 per cent, 60 per cent and 11 per cent. Furthermore, the setting of a regulatory

* Findings, interpretation and conclusions expressed herein do not necessarily reflect the views of the Board of Executive Directors of the World Bank or the governments they represent.

framework has accompanied the increase of private sector participation in infrastructure.

There is strong evidence supporting the generally positive economic results of these policies. Examples include Boardman and Vining (1989) and Megginson, Nash, and van Randenborgh (1994) (see Megginson and Netter, 2001, and Chong and Lopez-de-Silanes, 2003, for more recent reviews). Yet, public perceptions of the outcome are less positive. Chong and Lopez-de-Silanes (2003) have, among others, summarized and addressed the most frequent cited criticisms.

In the case of Latin American countries (LACs) and for the infrastructure sector, apart from case studies, there is little empirical literature analysing the impact determinants. Most of it has focused on all sectors and on the performance of financial indicators (see Megginson, Nash, and van Randenborgh, 1994). Recently Andres, Guasch, Haven and Foster (2008) have evaluated the impact of private-sector participation on output, efficiency, labour productivity, quality, coverage and prices, using a large cross-country data set for Latin America. The impact of competition has been analysed in Andres, Guasch, Haven and Foster (2008), the issue of renegotiation of concessions in Guasch (2006), Guasch, Laffont and Straub (2003 and 2004), and finally the profitability of private infrastructure firms in Sirtaine, Pinglo, Guasch, and Foster (2005).

However, little work that has focused on the determinants of sectors' performance and most particularly on the impact of regulation on those outcomes. Even though the theory suggests that regulation matters, there is a shortage of empirical work analysing this issue. Some exceptions are Wallsten (2001), Jamasb (2005), Cubbin and Stern (2005) and Stern and Cubbin (2004).

The objective of this chapter is to add to that scarce literature, testing the impact of regulation from three different angles: (a) on the alignment of costs with tariffs – firms and profitability, (b) on reducing/deterring opportunistic renegotiation, and (c) its effects on productivity, quality of service, coverage and prices. This is discussed in Sections 2, 3 and 4 respectively.

For this, we used an extensive data set of about 1000 concessions granted in Latin America from the late 1980s to the early 2000s, compiled by Guasch (2003).

2 Testing the impact of regulation on aligning costs with tariffs and firms' profitability

Unlike normal competitive business sectors, the profitability of concessions is not simply a reflection of market conditions and managerial competence, but is to a considerable extent determined – or at least circumscribed – by regulatory decisions. Infrastructure companies operate mostly under a monopoly regime and are thus subject to regulation of tariffs. Thus, the observed profitability of these concessions should in part reflect the quality of the regulatory framework and the regulators' performance.

2.1 Theoretical framework

Regulation aims to protect consumers from abuse of monopoly power and investors from opportunistic behaviour by the government, given the politically sensitive nature of infrastructure tariffs and the large sunk costs characteristic of the companies' investments. As a result, regulatory decisions have a substantial impact on the profitability of companies. Ideally, the regulator's objective should be to maintain alignment between a company's rate of return and the cost of its capital. This is because a rate of return in excess of the cost of capital inappropriately penalizes consumers, while a rate of return that is below the cost of capital inappropriately discourages further investment. The closeness of that alignment will depend, among other things, on the quality of regulation.

In theory, the closeness with which the rate of return tracks the cost of capital will also depend on the chosen regulatory regime. Under rate of return regulation, the regulator has the possibility of making frequent price adjustments to realign the company's rate of return with its cost of capital. Under price cap regulation, on the other hand, the regulator sets tariffs so that expected returns match the cost of capital *ex ante*, but allows these returns to diverge *ex post* during the periods between regulatory reviews. However, in practice, in Latin America, the distinction between 'price cap' and 'rate of return' system of regulation is somewhat blurred due to frequent renegotiation of infrastructure contracts (Guasch, 2004; Guasch and Spiller, 1999; Gomez-Ibanez, 2003)[2], and to the fact that review methodologies sometimes take into account historic divergence between the rate of return and the cost of capital in adjusting future prices, which goes against the forward looking principles of 'price cap' regulation. Thus, the practice in the region would best be described as a hybrid regime.

Therefore, instead of focusing on the dichotomy between price cap and rate of return regulation, we develop a measure of the overall quality of the regulator that oversees each of the companies in the sample. We therefore empirically evaluate the impact of the quality of regulation on the profitability of firms. The hypothesis is that the better the quality of regulation, the closer the correspondence between the firm's rate of return and the firm's cost of capital.

2.2 Measuring regulatory quality

In order to test this hypothesis a quantitative measure of regulatory quality is needed. Good regulation is defined by clear, stable and predictable rules, a purely professional and technical interpretation of the law and contract, ability to withstand influences and pressures from the stakeholders, such as government and operators, and the establishment of a predictable and adequate allocation of resources. Based on this definition, the index developed here considers three key dimensions of regulatory quality: legal solidity, financial strength, and decision-making autonomy. The construction of each of these indices and associated scoring method are detailed in Table 11.1 below.

Legal solidity refers to the stability, and more space predictability, of the regulatory regime. The strongest legal foundation is obtained when the regulatory framework is embedded into law, as opposed to a weaker legal instrument – that is easier to change (such as a decree or a contract if the judiciary is not reliable).

Financial strength refers to the resources given to the regulatory agency to undertake its functions. This dimension has two aspects. The first aspect is financial independence, which is achieved when a regulatory entity has its own source of revenue (for example, via a sectoral surcharge) and does not depend on the government budget. The second aspect is financial strength, which is a function of the size of the agency's budget.

Decision-making autonomy measures the likelihood that regulatory decisions are based on technical as opposed to political criteria. This dimension has three aspects. The first aspect is independence of appointment, which measures the extent to which the appointment process avoids a purely political appointee without adequate technical knowledge of the sector. The second aspect is duration of appointment, which indicates whether a regulator can be reappointed and hence might be less likely to act independently and issue professionally and technically based decisions. The third aspect is collegiality of decisions, which measures the relative difficulty of regulatory

Table 11.1 Regulatory quality index: components and construction

	Weight	*Scoring*
Legal solidity	0.33	1 if regulatory framework established by law, 0 otherwise.
Financial capacity	0.34	Sum of scores on factors detailed below.
• Financial independence	0.17	• 1 if funded from regulatory levy, 0 if funded from public budget
• Financial strength	0.17	• Regulatory budget as % sectoral GDP normalized on [0,1] scale
Decision-making autonomy	0.33	Sum of scores on factors detailed below.
• Independence of appointment	0.11	• 0 if appointed directly by Executive, 1 if screening by legislature
• Duration of appointment	0.11	• 1 for a single fixed term, 0 for indefinite appointment
• Collegiality of decisions	0.11	• 1 if headed by regulatory commission, 0 if by individual regulator

Note: Scores between 0 and 1 are given for intermediate cases.

capture, thought to be lower when multiple regulators act jointly within a board structure.

While each of these elements is individually relevant, it is also of interest to aggregate them into a single quality index that gives equal weight to each of the three dimensions that have been identified. For the sample of companies covered in this study, the average score on this index of overall regulatory quality is 0.51 against a potential maximum of 1.0, suggesting that the quality of regulation is not very high overall. However, there is significant variation in quality of regulation across countries and sectors, with scores ranging widely between 0.12 and 0.85. The highest average score is obtained on legal solidity, 0.65, as against decision-making autonomy, 0.56, and financial strength, 0.34. Pair-wise correlations between each of the regulatory quality measures are typically low at around 0.20, and in no case greater than 0.57. In some cases, pair-wise correlations had a negative value, suggesting that high regulatory quality along one dimension is correlated with low regulatory quality along another dimension. This result illustrates that few countries consistently apply all the design principles needed to ensure good quality regulation.

The indices of regulatory quality were used to try to explain differences in the divergence between rate of return and cost of capital across the different companies in the sample. This was done by regressing the difference between the project internal rate of return and the weighted average cost of capital (IRR-WACC) against the set of explanatory variables. The hypothesis is that the better the quality of regulation, as measured by the index, the smaller the differential should be, suggesting that the regulatory quality sub-indexes would enter the regression with negative signs.

Two separate measures of the IRR-WACC differential were considered. The first measure is the simple IRR-WACC differential. This captures the quality of regulation purely from a short-term consumer's perspective, since the smaller the IRR-WACC differential (including negative values), the lower the resulting tariffs for consumers. However, this constitutes a myopic view since a negative IRR-WACC undermines investment incentives and therefore ultimately penalizes consumers through declining service quality, decelerating service expansion, and potential flight of investors. Therefore, the absolute IRR-WACC differential is taken as a second relevant measure. According to this indicator, what matters is minimizing the distance between IRR and WACC, with positive and negative differentials regarded as equally reflective of poor regulatory decisions.

2.3 Simple differential (myopic consumer protection)

The results for the first set of regressions are reported in Table 11.2, using each of the four measures of IRR-WACC differential.[3] Despite small sample sizes, three out of the four models show that the regulatory quality variables are

Table 11.2 Summary of regression results

Dependent variable	*Simple differential 1*	*Simple differential 2*	*Simple differential 3*	*Simple differential 4*
Financial independence	−0.340	−0.174	−0.151	−0.135
Financial strength	−0.372	−0.332**	−0.355**	−0.370**
Legal solidity	−0.026	0.077	0.070	0.080
Independence of appointment	−0.109	−0.068	−0.101	−0.109
Duration of appointment	−0.125	−0.011	−0.038	−0.030
Collegiality of decisions	0.455**	0.256**	0.271**	0.267**
Constant	−0.341	−0.047	−0.022	0.002
P-value	0.156	0.072*	0.052**	0.045**
Adjusted R-squared	0.124	0.208	0.237	0.248
No. of observations	32	30	30	30

Notes: Regressions based on 30 observations; *, **, *** indicate significance at 10%, 5%, and 1% level respectively.

significant in overall terms, and are on their own capable of explaining 20–25 per cent of the IRR-WACC differential. Moreover, some of the regulatory quality variables are also individually significant. Thus, the financial strength variable is significant at the 5 per cent level in most of the regressions with the expected negative sign, indicating that regulators with larger budgets tend to have greater success in minimizing the IRR-WACC differential. In addition, the collegiality of decision variable is also significant at the 5 per cent level, but takes a positive sign. This suggests that, arguably contrary to expectations, regulatory entities headed by a single superintendent do a better job at reducing the IRR-WACC differential than do broader based regulatory commissions.[4]

2.4 Absolute differential (protecting both consumers and investors)

The results of the second set of regressions are reported in Table 11.3. Given that taking the absolute value of the IRR-WACC differential reduces the spread across observations in an already small sample, a log-linear specification is used to ensure that there is adequate variation for the purposes of the regression. Overall, this second set of regressions did not perform as well as the first. Nevertheless, two of the models show overall significance at the 5–10 per cent level and are able to explain around 20 per cent of the variation in the IRR-WACC differential. As before, the financial strength variable proves to be significant in some specifications, though not always with the expected sign. On the other hand, the collegiality of decisions is no longer statistically significant. The lower level of significance and explanatory power associated with this second set of regressions may simply reflect the fact that regulatory efforts are more strongly motivated by short-term

Table 11.3 Summary of regression results

Dependent variable	*Absolute differential 1*	*Absolute differential 2*	*Absolute differential 3*	*Absolute differential 4*
Financial independence	1.071	−0.653	−0.001	0.071
Financial strength	2.619**	−2.478	−2.488**	−2.140**
Legal solidity	−0.697	0.928	0.412	0.844**
Independence of appointment	1.147	0.974	0.577	−0.050
Duration of appointment	−0.478	1.412	1.053	0.767
Collegiality of decisions	−1.771	−0.810	−0.456	−0.243
Constant	−1.104	−2.618**	−2.365**	−2.487**
P-value	0.094*	0.273	0.125	0.049**
R-squared	0.171	0.069	0.156	0.242
No. of observations	32	30	30	30

Notes: Regressions based on 30 observations; *, **, *** indicate significance at 10%, 5%, and 1% level respectively.

considerations of keeping prices as low as possible for current consumers, than by-long term considerations of keeping returns as close as possible to hurdle rates for investors.

The conclusion of this analysis is that regulation matters in aligning the cost of capital and rate of return, as variations in quality across regulatory regimes are significant and material in determining the size of the IRR-WACC differential. However, regulatory efforts seem to be more closely associated with minimizing the simple IRR-WACC differential (and thereby keeping tariffs as low as possible for current consumers), than with minimizing the absolute IRR-WACC differential (and thereby keeping profitability well aligned with hurdle rates of return). Another striking feature of the results is that regulatory quality variables seem to have overall significance, more than individual significance, in determining IRR-WACC differentials. This is in fact consistent with the fact that performance along different dimensions of regulatory quality is not highly correlated, and that the benefits of high regulatory quality along one dimension can be completely offset by low regulatory quality along another dimension. Thus, for regulation to be effective, one needs the whole package of regulatory characteristics. If some of the key ingredients are missing, the effectiveness of regulation is highly diminished.

2.5 Summary

We have analysed the differences between returns and cost of capital and shown that the variation of net returns across concessions can be partially explained by the quality of regulation. We have shown that the better the quality of regulation the closer the alignment between financial returns and costs of capital as is desirable. Quality of regulation is found to be a significant determinant of the divergence between the overall profitability of the concession and its corresponding hurdle rate, explaining around 20 per cent of the variation. Thus we have shown that regulation does indeed matter. However, regulatory efforts seem to be more closely associated with keeping tariffs as low as possible for current consumers, than keeping profitability well aligned with hurdle rates of return.

The policy implications are clear. Significant efforts are needed to improve the quality of regulation.

3 Testing the impact of regulation on reducing/deterring opportunistic renegotiation

3.1 Concession contracts in Latin America

In Latin America, the majority of privatization cases took the form of concession contracts. This was mostly to avoid political, legal and constitutional impediments to the outright sale of state assets to private operators that were often foreign firms. A concession contract grants a private firm or consortium the right to operate a given infrastructure in exchange for the revenues generated by users' payments, and lasts for a limited period of time (in general between 15 and 30 years), after which the underlying assets are reformed to the state.

However, concession contracts have suffered from a number of problems, the most serious of which has been renegotiation. Considering an exhaustive sample of more than 1,000 concessions in Latin America and the Caribbean during the period 1985–2000 (excluding telecommunications where most projects were real privatizations with transfer of assets), 41 per cent of all projects in the three remaining sectors were renegotiated at some point. In water and transport, renegotiations have affected 74 per cent and 55 per cent of the projects respectively, and have occurred 1.6 years and 3.1 years on average after the award (Guasch, 2004).

These renegotiations have had a negative impact on users, including the need for additional risk premium *ex ante* (Guasch and Spiller, 1999), and *ex post* service disruption, non-compliance with expansion targets and excessive prices due to cost pass-through charged to customers, among others. For example, the Mexican toll road programme, which consisted of 52 highways built in the early 1990s, was finally bailed out by the government in 1997. The estimated cost was between 1 and 1.7 per cent of GDP (Guasch, Laffont and Straub, 2005). It is really important to understand the reasons for these failures and in particular the role of regulation in determining these outcomes. This section aims to explore these issues.

3.2 Renegotiations of concession contracts and their determinants

Renegotiation may be of two types: initiated by operators (Guasch, Laffont and Straub, 2003) at the initiative of local or national government (Guasch, Laffont and Straub, 2005) or instituted by the government.

Table 11.4 Renegotiation by type of initiator 1989–2000

	1989	*1990*	*1991*	*1992*	*1993*	*1994*	*1995*	*1996*	*1997*	*1998*	*1999*	*2000*	*Total*
All countries													
Outstanding concessions	10	38	38	50	78	103	123	132	156	187	187	165	na
Number of renegotiations	0	13	3	9	12	14	23	15	15	11	27	20	162
Firm-led renegotiations	0	12	2	2	0	1	3	3	11	4	1	14	53
Govt-led renegotiations	0	0	0	0	10	13	19	11	3	7	25	6	94
Joint-led renegotiations	0	1	1	7	2	0	1	1	1	0	1	0	15

Source: Guasch, Laffont and Straub (2005).

Firm-led renegotiations might be related to economic shocks following a devaluation or a recession, or might be opportunistic, when a firm that was previously awarded a concession seeks a bilateral negotiation with the government or the regulatory agency to strike a better deal than the one that was initially agreed upon. This may significantly reduce the benefit of the competitive pressure introduced by the *ex ante* auction procedure, first simply because the agreed parameters (tariffs, transfers) are modified and second because firms that anticipate this may be tempted to strategically undercut rivals at the bidding stage.

Government-led renegotiations may sometimes be of a Pareto improving nature (related to unforeseen contingencies), but most of them are opportunistic, where politicians during or after an election campaign renege on previous contracts to please their constituencies. Recent cancellations of water concessions includes that of 2005 in Bolivia and the ongoing renegotiations of most concessions in Argentina after the 2001 crisis, when the government refused any significant adjustment of the rates converted to devalued pesos despite contract clauses that contemplated indexation to the US$ and US inflation.

A look at the data in Table 11.4 shows that regional volatility seems to play an important role in the timing of these renegotiations. For example, a number of them occurred around the hyperinflation at the end of the 1980s in Argentina, during and after the Tequila crisis in 1995 in Mexico and at the time of the Real devaluation in 1999 in Brazil. It is therefore interesting to find out if economic shocks were the only determinants of renegotiations, or if there were other flaws, in contract or regulatory framework design, that were pivotal in explaining the high incidence of renegotiation.

The Guasch, Laffont and Straub (2003 and 2005) results are based on a sample comprising 307 projects in the water and transport sectors, in five countries (Argentina, Brazil, Chile, Colombia and Mexico), over 12 years, with a total of 1,287 observations (see Guasch, 2004). For each contract, there is information on the general characteristics of the projects (sector, year of award, duration), on the award process, the investment and financing conditions, the institutional and regulatory context and the type of price regulation in place (price capping versus rate of return), and other contract clauses (arbitration, income guarantees, take-over clauses). These are completed by macroeconomic data (growth rate, exchange rate evolution), dummies for national and local elections and a full set of institutional indicators (corruption, quality of the bureaucracy, rule of law).

The initial estimations are based on a random effect probit, which is a linearized version of the equations giving the probabilities of firm-led and government-led renegotiations in the respective theoretical models:

$$y_{int} = I[y^*_{int} = x_i\alpha_1 + \alpha_2 z_{int} + E_{nt}\alpha_3 + e_{int} < 0],$$

For concession i, in country n, at time t, y_{int} is the binary variable indicating whether there was a renegotiation by the firm (respected by the government), x is a vector of time-invariant characteristics of the contract, z is the time elapsed since the award, and E is a vector of the environmental characteristics, including economic shocks, elections and quality of institutions.

Alternatively, Guasch, Laffont and Straub (2003) present a competing risk duration model, which allows for both types of renegotiations hazard simultaneously. The specific model used follows Han and Hausman's (1990) semi-parametric competing risk model, with a non-parametric baseline hazard consisting of a set of dummy variables for each period. This model is estimated using a bivariate probit with the complete set of period dummies.

One major econometric issue is the fact that most contract clauses, such as the type of price regulation or specific guarantees included, must be considered to be endogenous. Indeed, we expect the contracting parties to choose them according to their observable and unobservable characteristics and to those of the projects. For example, the type of tariff regulation chosen is likely to be affected by the potential efficiency of the concessionaire (more efficient firms would prefer price capping regulation, which is more risky but makes them residual claimant for their cost savings) and also by the fact that riskier projects would call for lower-powered (rate of return) regulation. Similarly, most types of guarantee have in general been included to convince private agents to take on more risky concessions, as in the case of toll-road programmes for which demand proves difficult to predict accurately. The challenge is thus to control for this *ex ante* self-selection effect in order to assess correctly the *ex post* specific incentive effect of the variables under study.

To tackle this, we implement in the two models mentioned above a two-stage instrumental variable procedure using as instrument a number of exogenous characteristics of the environment such as institutional quality,

Table 11.5 Sign of main variables affecting the occurrence of both types of renegotiations

	Firm-led renegotiation	*Government-led renegotiation*
Existence of a regulator prior to the award	–	–
Price capping regulation	+	+
Duration since award	+	+
Investment requirements	–	+
Exclusive private financing	+	–
Quality of bureaucracy	–	–
Control of Corruption	–	+
National elections	+	+
Growth	–	–
Minimum income guarantee clause	+	+

Source: Guasch, Laffont and Straub (2003; 2005).

Table 11.6 Estimates of the determinants of renegotiations

	Firm-led renegotiations	*Government-led renegotiations*
Existence of regulatory body	–1.09*** (0.22)	–1.40*** (0.34)
Price capping	0.68* (0.38)	–0.46* (0.40)
Investment requirements	0.96** (0.40)	–0.70*** (0.24)
Private financing	0.35 (0.28)	–1.23*** (0.24)
Bureaucratic quality	–0.35** (0.15)	–0.57*** (0.16)
Elections -1	0.31 (0.20)	0.21 (0.19)
Growth -1	–0.06*** (0.02)	–0.05** (0.03)
Growth -2	–0.14*** (0.02)	–0.08**(0.03)
Transport dummy	0.53 (0.36)	–0.38 (0.36)
Log likelihood	–251.1	na
Number of observations		1132

Source: Guasch, Laffont and Straub (2003, 2005). Significance at the 1%, 5% and 10% level is noted by ***,**,* respectively.

sectors of activity and the existence of a regulator. For the variables found to be endogenous according to the Rivers and Vuong (1988) test, we take the predicted values from the first stage estimations, insert them in the second stage model and adjust the standard errors with a bootstrapping procedure. Unsurprisingly, the variables for which exogeneity is rejected are price capping regulation, the investment and financing variables, and clauses such as minimum income guarantee and existence of an arbitration body.

The results from both models are strongly consistent. Table 11.5 summarizes the sign of the main variables found to have a significant impact on both types of renegotiations. It shows that contract characteristics, political and economic variables, and regulation all matter in explaining the frequency of renegotiations.

3.3 Regulation and renegotiation

First, the existence of a regulator at the time the concession contract is signed appears to be crucial in avoiding failures during the early life of concession projects. This aspect has the strongest marginal effect of all variables found to be statistically significant. Comparing three specific contracts from the initial sample, and using the probabilities predicted by the empirical model, Guasch, Laffont and Straub (2003) show that had a regulator been in place at the time of awarding the contract, the respective probabilities of renegotiation in the last year of existence of the contract would have been reduced from 29.7 per cent, 9.9 per cent and 3.1 per cent, to 5.3 per cent, 0.3 per cent and 0.2 per cent respectively.

Depending on the type of renegotiation that is considered, at least two complementary lines of explanation are relevant here. On the one hand, regulators seem to allow for better contracts from the start, which reduces the necessity of later adjustments for unforeseen contingencies (this is particularly relevant for firm-led renegotiations). In the Latin American context, characterized by frequent, and difficult to predict, economic shocks and by the imperfect enforcement of contracts, drafting complete contracts is bound to fail. Moreover, long and complex contracts are often inefficient, because they lack transparency and lend themselves to contradictory interpretations and therefore opportunistic revision claims. As a consequence, most contracts are short concession-specific documents that rely on complementary rules contained in the relevant jurisprudence. This approach makes previous regulatory experience in dealing with the design of concessions contracts pivotal in limiting the occurrence of later renegotiations.

On the other hand, regulators are even more effective in weak governance environments and appear to constitute a barrier to opportunistic behaviour by governments (Guasch, Laffont and Straub, 2005). This conclusion is supported by several significant interactions showing, for example, that the previous existence of a regulator has a stronger marginal effect in a context characterized by more corruption, or that a good quality bureaucracy is more effective in limiting the incidence of renegotiations after elections. Finally, Guasch, Laffont and Straub (2005) also show that the fact that the regulator does not belong to a ministry significantly reduces the probability of government-led renegotiation. In that regard, these firm-level results confirm the results of some cross-country studies that demonstrate the importance of experienced and independent regulators in the telecommunication and electricity sectors (Wallsten, 2001; Cubbin and Stern, 2005).

Second, the choice of price regulation, between a price capping and a rate of return scheme, is of utmost importance. Besides well-known concerns with price capping regulation, in particular regarding the impact on quality and the implied risk transfer from consumers to the firm, is discussed in Guasch, Laffont and Straub (2003, 2005) show that the main consequence of choosing a price capping regulatory scheme is the increased probability of renegotiation. Looking again at the marginal effect shows, for example, that had the three sample contracts been under a rate-of-return scheme, the respective probabilities of firm-led renegotiation in the last year of existence of the contract would have been reduced from 29.7 per cent, 9.9 per cent and 3.1 per cent, to 13.8 per cent, 3.3 per cent and 0.8 per cent respectively.

Given that in the sample under study, over 70 per cent of concessions are regulated by price capping, this is clearly a major concern. Moreover, price capping schemes increase the riskiness of projects, which is reflected in an increase of the cost of capital, and implies that firms end up facing higher interest. In contexts where institutions are weak, inexperienced and often unable to resist political pressures, the consequence is that most regulated firms (or the government and interest groups related to the firms) appropriate the gains when the conjuncture is favourable, but are able to transfer the losses to consumers during bad times.

As a consequence, there is a growing pragmatic tendency to advocate the abandonment of price capping regulation, considered a synonym for the higher risk of renegotiation and higher cost of capital, and to advocate a return to a hybrid type of regulation, including some elements of rate of return (see for example Estache, Guasch and Trujillo, 2003). Such a move would imply the recognition that a shift to a hybrid regulatory scheme is imposed *de facto* by *ex post* renegotiations, which carry high associated social costs, because they tend to endogenize the regulatory review lags. In this situation, it could prove less costly to adapt regulatory rules from the start by adopting lower-powered price regulation schemes.

3.4 Summary

In summary, two related dimensions of regulation matter when it comes to avoiding disruptive renegotiations. The first is the regulatory environment, including the very existence of a regulator from the start, but also its independence from potential political pressure. The second is the type of price regulation itself. It should be noted that these two aspects can hardly be separated. Indeed, price capping regulation has often been the salient choice of governments lacking previous experience with regulation, because it appeared to be less informationally demanding. The absence of a regulator when initiating transfers of infrastructure to the private sector and the choice of price cap therefore often went in tandem. The results mentioned above show that a better strategic approach would be for governments to consider a sequence including first the development of a correctly endowed and reasonably independent regulatory agency, which would subsequently be in charge of the definition of the contract and the appropriate price regulation.

4 Testing the impact of regulation on its effects on productivity, quality of service, coverage and prices

4.1 Overview

This section uses the framework developed in Andres, Guasch, Haven and Foster (2008). As already described, their analysis splits the data into three periods: 'pre-privatization', transition, and post-privatization, where the transitional period commences after the concession announcement and lasts until one year after the concession award. The motivation for this segmentation is that some of the more important changes start simultaneously with the privatization announcement and lasts one year after the change in ownership. In addition, some of these indicators are driven by firm-specific time trends and not privatization itself; therefore, the authors also control for this effect. Their main results are summarized as follows:

(i) After controlling for a positive firm-specific time trend, data for service coverage suggests that privatization has an upward impact on telecommunications, but no effect on electricity, water or sanitation;
(ii) Indicators for technical losses are positively affected by privatization. While most of the improvement in electricity during the transition period, occur in the case of telecommunications, water, and sanitation occur later on;
(iii) Prices also significantly increased for the sectors during and after the transition except in telecommunications, as the average cost of installation of a residential line decreased in every period (the monthly charge for residential service, however, increased substantially);
(iv) Labour productivity significantly changed in all three sectors, mainly during the transition period, and fundamentally caused an important reduction in labour redundancy: in the electricity and water and sanitation sectors, employment decreased on average 10 per cent per year during the transition period; and
(v) The outcomes' results are significantly heterogeneous across firms.

The current analysis is based on the last conclusion that shows the heterogeneity across firms. Our proposal attempts to improve the understanding of the determinants for this heterogeneity across utilities. The hypothesis is that procedural and regulatory differences might explain some of these variances.

We focus on four basic regulatory characteristics: (1) budget autonomy; (2) the legal autonomy of the regulatory body; (3) tariff regulation (price capping, rate of return, among others); and (4) duration of the regulatory board. Additionally, we will control for some additional features such as the award process (direct selection versus auction process), the award criteria (highest price; lower tariff or investment plan), and the nationality of the concessionaire. The premise is that these divergences may significantly affect the incentives involved in the managerial decision process, which, in turn, affects firm performance on efficiency, quality, and price.

4.2 Procedure

Ideally, to assess the impact of privatization, the performance of utilities under private operation should be evaluated against comparable publicly operated firms from similar environments, assuming these firms are the contra-factual of the privatized ones. In most cases, it is hard to identify an analogous firm; hence, most of the literature compares the evolution of selected indicators before and after the change in ownership.

Most of the literature employs two different strategies to estimate the effect of privatization. First, since Megginson, Nash, and van Randenborgh (1994), there have been several studies using means and medians of the periods before and after the event of privatization, together with testing on the significance of the change. Some research considers different samples of SOEs among countries and evaluates indicators. Another branch of literature assumes these policies to be treatments and follows the literature of programme evaluation (see Heckman and Robb, 1985) by proposing a dummy for those periods where the SOE was privately owned, and checks its significance, as well as other interactions with characteristics specific to each paper (for example, Boardman and Vining, 1989).

In this section we propose to modify Andres, Guasch, Haven and Foster (2008). We introduce interactions between the privatization dummies and the characteristics described previously. More specifically, we define a dummy for the transition and another for the after-transition period:

$$\ln(y_{ijt}) = \delta^T DUMMY\_TRAN_{ijt} + \delta^P DUMMY\_POST_{ijt} + \sum_{ij} \phi_{ij} D_{ij} + \nu_{ijt} \quad (11.1)$$

where

$$DUMMY\_TRAN_{ijt} \begin{cases} 1 & \text{if } -2 \leq s_{ijt} \leq +1 \\ 0 & \text{otherwise} \end{cases}$$

and

$$DUMMY\_POST_{ijt} \begin{cases} 1 & \text{if } s_{ijt} \geq 2 \\ 0 & \text{otherwise} \end{cases}$$

where y_{ijt} are the variables of interest (outputs, inputs, labour productivity, efficiency, quality, coverage and prices). The main coefficients in this model are the dummies $DUMMY\_TRAN_{ijt}$ and $DUMMY\_POST_{ijt}$ that are equal to one, if the firm *i* of country *j* were in a transitional or port-transitional year at time *t*. Given the fact that there are several variables not observable to the econometrician, fixed effects are included to capture the characteristics of the firm, such as management, initial conditions, size, density of the network, as well as other aspects, which we assume to be constant for each firm across time. Additionally, s_{ijt} is a time trend with a value equal to zero for the privatization award year. Thus, the first dummy identifies the average change in the dependent variable during the transition with respect to the average level prior to those years. The second dummy identifies the average change of the dependent variable after the transition with respect to the first period. Therefore, δ^T and δ^P capture the effect on the outcome of interest, during the transition and after that, given by the change in ownership.

A second version of equation (11.1) will also be estimated here with the introduction of a firm-specific time trend:

$$\ln(y_{ijt}) = \delta^T DUMMY\_TRAN_{ijt} + \delta^P DUMMY\_POST_{ijt} + \sum_{ij} \phi_{ij} D_{ij} + \sum_{ij} \theta_{ij} t_{ij} + \nu_{ijt} \tag{11.2}$$

Equation (11.2) will use the same dependent variables as well as the dummies used in the static model. However, the fourth coefficient captures the time trend of the variable of interest. Several factors, for example the initial conditions, may affect this. Hence, it is important to control for the firm's specific value.

To identify the different characterization effects of the privatization process as well as the regulation, we test the variables with the two main dummies. More precisely:

$$\ln(y_{ijt}) = \delta^T DUM\_TRAN_{ijt}{}^{*} X_{ijt} + \delta^P DUM\_POST_{ijt} * X_{ijt} + \sum_{ij} \phi_{ij} D_{ij} + \nu_{ijt} \tag{11.3}$$

$$\ln(y_{ijt}) = \delta^T DUM\_TRAN_{ijt}{}^{*} X_{ijt} + \delta^P DUM\_POST_{ijt} * X_{ijt} + \sum_{ij} \phi_{ij} D_{ij} + \sum_{ij} \theta_{ij} t_{ij} + \nu_{ijt} \tag{11.4}$$

Now δ^T, which was used as a scalar number in our previous specifications, becomes a vector with the coefficients for each characteristic of the vector X_{ijt} that is of the form $(1, x^1_{ijt}, \ldots, x^N_{ijt})$ with N as the total number of characteristics evaluated. The first coefficient of the vector δ^T will became the average effect of change in ownership during the transitional period on a given indicator for a firm without the characteristics evaluated in the other elements of the vector X_{ijt}. Equivalently, the vector δ^P contains the coefficients for the different characteristics of vector X_{ijt}, but for the post-transitional years.

Since we are using a semi-logarithmic functional form of these models for each of the indicators, when interpreting the coefficient estimates of the dummy, it should be remembered that the percentage impact in each indicator is given by $e^{\delta} - 1$.

Correcting for potential nonspherical errors requires a more adequate approach, such as the Generalized least square (GLS); however, this estimation requires the knowledge of the unconditional variance matrix of ν_{ijt}, Ω, up to scale. Hence, we must be able to write $\Omega = \sigma^2 C$, where C is a known $G \times G$ positive definite matrix. As this matrix is unknown, we will follow a Feasible GLS (FGLS) approach that replaces the unidentified matrix Ω with a consistent estimator.

4.3 Data

For our research we use an official dataset provided by public and private sectors, as well as one built by the World Bank. First, by using the official data reported by the firms to their investors and statistical reports of the regulator agencies of each country, we build an unbalanced panel dataset of key indicators on outputs, inputs, labour productivity, efficiency, quality, coverage, and prices. Furthermore, we requested information from each of the companies and international organizations including the International Telecommunication Union (ITU), the Latin American Organization of Energy (OLADE), as well as information provided by each regulatory office. We make a particular effort in reconstructing the company data with several public sources and with data from the firms provided by different governmental offices. We were also particularly cautious about the consistency and comparability of the data across time and countries (see Andres, Guasch, Haven and Foster, 2008). Second, the novel dataset built by the World Bank describes the characteristics of nearly 1,000 infrastructure projects awarded in Latin American and Caribbean countries from 1989 to 2002, in the sectors of telecommunications, energy, transportation and water. (see Guasch, 2003).

The analysis focuses on several indicators of outcomes, inputs, labour productivity, efficiency, quality, coverage and prices. Some of these variables are used by other authors with other samples, such as Ros (1999), who employs equivalent indicators for *coverage*, *labour productivity*, *quality* and *prices* for the telecommunications sector. Ramamurti (1996) uses analogous indicators in *output*, *coverage*, and *labour productivity* for the four Latin American telecommunications firms of his study. Saal and Parker (2001) use similar indicators for *output*, *employment*, *quality*, and *prices* for water and sewerage companies in England and Wales.

Table 11.7 shows the summary statistics of these variables in each sector.

The countries analysed include: Argentina, Bolivia, Brazil, Chile, Colombia, El Salvador, Guatemala, Guyana, Jamaica, Mexico, Nicaragua, Panama, Peru, Trinidad and Tobago, and Venezuela. The sample consists of unbalanced panel data that includes 181 firms and 1,885 firm-year observations. Each of the sample firms contain at least one year of pre-privatization data,

Table 11.7 Summary statistics

Variable	*No.*	*Mean*	*Median*	*SD*	*Min*	*Max*
Electricity Distribution						
Number of subscribers	98	497,776	225,230	681,698	2,700	3,884,579
Output [thousand of KWHs]	100	2,850	789.5	5,282	13.8	34,300
Number of employees	87	1,421	625	2,115	18	13,642
Subscribers per employee	84	558.81	506.67	244.20	210.45	1,523.27
Output per employee	84	2,343.48	2,116.46	1,298.60	663.86	7,323.09
Distributional losses [%]	90	15.3	13.6	6.6	2.0	33.9
Duration of interruptions per subscriber	65	25.26	20.36	21.01	1.75	100.00
Frequency of interruptions per subscriber	67	22.63	16.03	21.24	1.07	100.00
Subscribers per 100 HHs (%)	86	74.6	81.3	20.7	7.0	100.0
Av. price per KWH (US$)	92	88.70	85.34	35.43	7.47	323.61
Fixed Telecommunications						
Number of subscribers	16	2,423,040	824,594	3,150,005	28,048	9,642,200
Output (million of minutes)	13	20,500	6,200	28,800	774	83,100
Number of employees	16	12,268	9,732	12,097	966	47,949
Subscribers per employee	16	209.30	109.27	241.96	33.81	736.65
Output per employee	13	1,627.35	844.29	1,790.44	257.10	6,419.45
% of digital lines	16	67.0	70.3	26.4	14.6	100.0
% of completed calls	12	67.0	64.8	20.4	20.0	98.8
Subscribers per 100 inhabitants	16	9.84	8.40	5.83	2.96	22.01
Price of 3-minute call [US$]	14	0.13	0.07	0.25	0.01	0.99
Monthly charge for a resid. sv. [US$]	15	6.16	6.01	4.52	0.36	19.97
Price for the installation of a line [US$]	15	343.75	309.51	339.35	1.20	1,102.26
Water and Sewerage						
Total subscribers for water	48	147,119	78,864	223,803	1,894	1,282,074
Total subscribers for sewerage	43	107,286	42,991	173,795	435	799,994
Water production	47	91,400	28,900	2,110	145.6	13,700,000
Number of employees	42	528	258	997	9	6,346
Water subscribers per employee	42	312.23	283.10	153.56	43.34	772.36
Water production per employee (%)	33	39.1	37.3	12.7	15.3	62.8
Continuity (hours per day)	21	19.40	22.97	6.57	–	24.00
Potability (%)	29	88.5	98.9	26.1	0.0	100.0
Water subscribers per 100 HHs	44	74.83	88.29	34.30	0.01	100.00
Sewerage subscribers per 100 HHs	34	64.61	71.99	27.83	0.30	97.70
Av. price for water [US$/m^3]	27	0.48	0.44	0.16	0.17	0.84
Av. price for sewerage [US$/m^3]	12	0.40	0.39	0.22	0.07	0.97

Note: each observation is the average for the available information for 5 years before the change in ownership and 5 years after.
Source: authors' calculations

while 150 of the 181 firms provide information for at least the previous three years.

We matched our previous dataset with the novel dataset built by the World Bank that describes the characteristics of nearly 1,000 infrastructure projects awarded in Latin American and Caribbean countries from 1989 to 2002, in the sectors of telecommunications, energy, transportation and water (see Guasch, 2004). This dataset contains information with respect to the privatization process: the number of bidders who participated, the contract process,[5] the award critera,[6] and the type of concession.[7] With respect to the regulatory framework, we know how the legal framework would be set up,[8] the regulation of tariffs,[9] if there were a possibility of contractual renegotiation, and (if this were the case) who would initiate it.[10]

The data also contain additional contractual clauses, such as, if it considered a termination clause, about the arbitration process, claim solving institution, obligation to provide universal service, duration of the contract, contract renewal, government's guarantees, if the government granted subsidies, frequency of tariff review, and how the exchange and commercial risk were borne. If the contract was renegotiated, we know when this was, the reason given for it, and the outcome.

Some characteristics of the regulators' regime include: an index of its autonomy, its budget source, the duration of the regulatory board member mandate, as well as the year of the regulatory board's inceptions. Among these variables we selected those with enough variation across firms to allow us to better identify the effect of the differences in each outcome. Hence, Table 11.7 indicates the variables that we were able to use in this analysis, while Table 11.8 shows the summary statistics of the characteristics across the sectors.

Table 11.8 Description of the characteristics used in the analysis

Variable	*Description*
Regulatory Board	
AUTON_YES	Dummy with value 1 if the Regulatory Board was fully autonomous.
AUTON_PART	Dummy with value 1 if the Regulatory Board was partially autonomous.
DURATION	Dummy with value 1 if the duration of the Regulatory Board was 5 or more years (CHECK)
Tariff Regulation	
TARIFF_RR	Dummy with value 1 if the tariffs were regulated according to the Rate of Return
TARIFF_PC	Dummy with value 1 if the tariffs were regulated according to Price Cap.

Table 11.9 Summary statistics of the characteristics used in the analysis

Variable	*Fixed telecommunications*		*Electricity distribution*		*Water and sanitation*	
	No. of firms	*Mean (%)*	*No. of firms*	*Mean (%)*	*No. of firms*	*Mean (%)*
Regulatory Board						
AUTON_YES	11	36.4	84	39.3	33	0.0
AUTON_PART	11	9.1	84	38.1	33	27.3
DURATION	4	75.0	56	41.1	9	100.0
Tariff Regulation						
TARIFF_RR	8	25.0	106	20.8	38	23.7
TARIFF_PC	8	62.5	106	91.5	38	89.5

4.4 Main results

Tables 11.10, 11.11 and 11.12 present the results. There are four different specifications for each indicator. As may be intuitive, there are some indicators that follow the firm-specific time trend. This is the case for output, labour productivity, and coverage indicators; therefore, for these variables we include firm-specific time trends.

The results in this chapter suggest that most of these characteristics significantly affect the outcomes of each of the indicators; however, while some characteristics have a positive effect on certain indicators, the same characteristics may have a negative outcome in other instances. If the target is the expansion of the network, the strategy will focus on certain characteristics; however, if the target is an efficiency increase, other sets of characteristics may be analysed. We also found that in these same cases, not all the sectors react evenly to an identical set of characteristics.

The remainder of this section describes the more robust results across the different specifications.

4.4.1 Number of connections

Table 11.10 indicates that in those concessions with a partially autonomous regulatory board, we observe a reduction of between 3.1 per cent and 7.2 per cent below the firm-specific time trend. Later changes are not significantly different from the transition, nor are they unusual as compared to concessions with total autonomy. The duration of the regulatory boards seems to have no significant effect on the number of connections.

The two main award criteria include the highest price as well as the best investment plan. Reductions between 1.1 per cent and 2.6 per cent are observed during the transition; this is below the firm-specific time trend when the concession were awarded to the highest bidder. Any following changes result in no significant difference during the transitional period.

In identifying the effects of tariff regulation on network expansion, we analyse the effects of the rate of return and price capping regulation on the number of connections. We found that those firms regulated by the rate of return method, resulted in a increased number of connections between 2.4 per cent and 6.1 per cent above the firm-specific time trends during the transition. We also observed additional increases after the transition. No significant results were evidenced in the reduction of regulation levels through price cappings.

We split the sample by sector to identify particular effects that differ from those described above.[11] We found that autonomy had positive effects on telecommunications.

4.4.2 Output

During the transition period, partial autonomy reduces the output flow of measures between 6.1 per cent and 8.6 per cent, which are below the firm-specific time trend. Any following changes are not significantly different from the transition. Total autonomy results in negative outcomes; however, the size of the effects are smaller than the partial autonomy coefficients. Further, during the transition, the duration of the Regulatory Board, firms regulated by board with longer duration resulted with a reduction between 10.2 per cent and 12.3 per cent, which is below the firm-specific time trend. When exploring the sectoral specifications, we observe that in the case of electricity, the total autonomy had higher decreases than partial autonomy; whereas, for water distribution, firms under price capping regulation experience level decrease.

4.4.3 Number of employees

We observe that during transitional periods partial autonomy of the regulatory board results in a reduction of employees between 10 per cent and 48 per cent below the pre-transition levels. Increases in the number of employees subsequent to that are not always significant. Total autonomy experiences greater falls than partial autonomy. These changes total between 27 per cent and 54 per cent, while later changes did not result in significantly different levels from transition levels.

Regulatory Boards show significant positive changes in transitional levels, but as more controls are added, the coefficients become highly negative. Firms regulating tariffs by using a rate of return system, present higher reductions in the number of employees than those regulating under price cap tariffs. For periods under a price capping system, we observe some reductions during the transition period; however, after controlling for other factors, these changes were not significant.

Table 11.10 Regression analysis – output, number of employees and labour productivity

	(ln) connections				*(ln) flow units*			
	(1)	*(2)*	*(3)*	*(4)*	*(5)*	*(6)*	*(7)*	*(8)*
dum_priv_tr	0.024**	0.014***	0.024	0.020*	0.180***	0.078***	0.216***	0.099***
	(0.011)	(0.005)	(0.015)	(0.012)	(0.039)	(0.017)	(0.054)	(0.036)
dum_priv_post	0.040***	0.014***	0.029	0.004	−0.060	0.019	−0.040	0.003
	(0.015)	(0.005)	(0.018)	(0.008)	(0.053)	(0.017)	(0.061)	(0.032)
tr_bid	−0.070***	−0.060***	–	–	−0.012	−0.016	–	–
	(0.023)	(0.012)			(0.038)	(0.026)		
pt_bid	0.006	−0.009	–	–	0.010	−0.010	–	–
	(0.022)	(0.007)			(0.037)	(0.022)		
tr_auton_part	−0.039	−0.031***	−0.072***	−0.035***	−0.076**	−0.070***	−0.086***	−0.061***
	(0.027)	(0.010)	(0.020)	(0.012)	(0.038)	(0.023)	(0.032)	(0.023)
pt_auton_part	−0.013	−0.001	0.001	−0.005	−0.029	−0.001	−0.036	0.000
	(0.022)	(0.007)	(0.013)	(0.008)	(0.033)	(0.018)	(0.029)	(0.019)
tr_auton_yes	0.035	0.030**	−0.010	0.009	−0.090**	−0.004	−0.087	−0.054**
	(0.024)	(0.012)	(0.015)	(0.011)	(0.040)	(0.021)	(0.055)	(0.027)
pt_auton_yes	−0.030	0.010	−0.010	0.005	0.013	−0.045**	−0.038	−0.046*
	(0.026)	(0.008)	(0.019)	(0.009)	(0.056)	(0.019)	(0.062)	(0.027)
tr_rb_dur	−0.009	–	−0.004	–	−0.102***	–	−0.123**	–
	(0.010)		(0.011)		(0.035)		(0.049)	
pt_rb_dur	−0.028**	–	−0.021	–	0.071	–	0.039	–
	(0.014)		(0.016)		(0.050)		(0.058)	
tr_nation_f	0.012	0.017**	−0.018*	−0.010	−0.046*	−0.045**	−0.029	−0.115***
	(0.008)	(0.007)	(0.010)	(0.008)	(0.026)	(0.019)	(0.051)	(0.033)
pt_nation_f	−0.006	−0.007	0.003	−0.003	−0.041*	−0.026	−0.054	−0.016
	(0.008)	(0.006)	(0.011)	(0.008)	(0.025)	(0.016)	(0.037)	(0.033)
tr_nation_b	–	–	−0.016	−0.022**	–	–	−0.015	−0.038
			(0.011)	(0.010)			(0.043)	(0.033)
pt_nation_b	–	–	0.004	0.008	–	–	0.019	0.018
			(0.011)	(0.008)			(0.038)	(0.031)
tr_award_prc	–	–	−0.011	−0.026**	–	–	−0.034	0.044
			(0.017)	(0.012)			(0.056)	(0.032)
pt_award_prc	–	–	−0.010	−0.000	–	–	0.038	−0.010
			(0.013)	(0.008)			(0.038)	(0.025)
tr_tar_rret	0.061***	0.055***	0.034*	0.024**	0.045	0.036	0.028	0.028
	(0.024)	(0.014)	(0.018)	(0.011)	(0.081)	(0.026)	(0.078)	(0.032)
pt_tar_rret	0.014	0.020**	0.024	0.019*	0.027	0.018	0.018	0.006
	(0.023)	(0.010)	(0.017)	(0.010)	(0.088)	(0.022)	(0.084)	(0.026)
Constant	11.448***	10.119***	12.652***	10.080***	12.592***	19.851***	13.552***	16.211***
	(0.029)	(0.014)	(0.022)	(0.013)	(0.088)	(0.039)	(0.058)	(0.026)
Firm FE	Yes	Yes	Yes	Yes	Yes	Yes	Yes	Yes
Firm specific trend	Yes	Yes	Yes	Yes	Yes	Yes	Yes	Yes
Observations	450	715	428	693	430	639	408	617
Log-likelihood	1136.9	1675.0	1079.9	1606.5	644.5	997.9	586.8	948.2
Number of firms	45	74	43	72	44	68	42	66

Note: Standard errors in parentheses.
*significant at 10%; **significant at 5%; ***significant at 1%
Source: authors' calculations

(ln) number of employees				*(ln) connection per employee*			
(9)	*(10)*	*(11)*	*(12)*	*(13)*	*(14)*	*(15)*	*(16)*
0.394***	0.067**	0.450***	0.162**	−0.243**	−0.047	−0.194*	0.141**
(0.105)	(0.034)	(0.113)	(0.074)	(0.101)	(0.041)	(0.112)	(0.066)
−0.046	−0.178***	−0.148	−0.070*	−0.019	0.131***	0.069	0.018
(0.090)	(0.031)	(0.097)	(0.039)	(0.099)	(0.040)	(0.112)	(0.040)
−0.222***	−0.196***	–	–	−0.081	−0.025	–	–
(0.073)	(0.056)			(0.080)	(0.053)		
−0.182***	−0.095**	–	–	0.117	−0.064	–	–
(0.067)	(0.044)			(0.080)	(0.047)		
−0.449***	−0.100**	−0.651***	−0.137***	0.066	0.194***	−0.018	0.041
(0.132)	(0.050)	(0.119)	(0.053)	(0.225)	(0.054)	(0.219)	(0.061)
0.154*	0.085**	0.034	0.063	−0.301***	−0.162***	−0.284**	−0.072*
(0.085)	(0.038)	(0.068)	(0.039)	(0.111)	(0.042)	(0.111)	(0.041)
−0.596***	−0.315***	−0.769***	−0.532***	0.345***	0.082*	0.471***	0.202***
(0.110)	(0.055)	(0.148)	(0.083)	(0.109)	(0.045)	(0.151)	(0.071)
−0.041	−0.058	−0.104	0.097	−0.167	−0.050	−0.127	−0.320***
(0.094)	(0.044)	(0.129)	(0.073)	(0.107)	(0.040)	(0.129)	(0.065)
−0.365***	–	−0.295***	–	0.236**	–	0.268***	–
(0.098)		(0.106)		(0.093)		(0.101)	
−0.150*	–	−0.143	–	0.109	–	0.155	–
(0.083)		(0.091)		(0.091)		(0.096)	
0.005	−0.122**	−0.317***	−0.375***	−0.011	0.036	0.038	−0.005
(0.066)	(0.053)	(0.108)	(0.086)	(0.053)	(0.044)	(0.116)	(0.067)
−0.004	0.047	−0.071	−0.061	0.072	−0.026	0.017	−0.079*
(0.057)	(0.041)	(0.091)	(0.055)	(0.054)	(0.037)	(0.095)	(0.046)
–	–	−0.151*	−0.139**	–	–	−0.111	−0.209***
		(0.082)	(0.071)			(0.083)	(0.063)
–	–	0.040	−0.147***	–	–	−0.099	0.040
		(0.071)	(0.042)			(0.079)	(0.044)
–	–	−0.023	0.002	–	–	−0.176	−0.176**
		(0.121)	(0.084)			(0.133)	(0.075)
–	–	−0.064	−0.294***	–	–	0.047	0.305***
		(0.110)	(0.072)			(0.111)	(0.060)
−0.920***	−0.027	−0.923***	−0.051	–	–	–	–
(0.131)	(0.061)	(0.131)	(0.066)				
0.309**	−0.028	0.354***	−0.087*	–	–	–	–
(0.122)	(0.051)	(0.124)	(0.046)				
7.040***	6.618***	7.342***	6.220***	6.987***	5.329***	4.686***	4.558***
(0.257)	(0.239)	(0.111)	(0.130)	(0.152)	(0.100)	(0.232)	(0.083)
Yes	Yes	Yes	Yes	Yes	Yes	Yes	Yes
No	No	No	No	Yes	Yes	Yes	Yes
357	586	335	564	350	610	328	588
127.2	156.4	131.7	185.1	365.7	542.7	328.5	528.6
37	63	35	61	37	**66**	35	64

Table 11.11 Regression analysis – labour productivity, distributional losses, quality and coverage

	(In)flow units per employee				*(In)distributional losses*			
	(17)	*(18)*	*(19)*	*(20)*	*(21)*	*(22)*	*(23)*	*(24)*
dum_priv_tr	−0.024	−0.000	0.009	0.054	−0.234***	−0.069**	−0.218**	−0.080
	(0.133)	(0.052)	(0.143)	(0.083)	(0.055)	(0.032)	(0.087)	(0.052)
dum_priv_post	0.056	0.157***	0.159	−0.018	0.488***	−0.071**	0.488***	0.080***
	(0.118)	(0.052)	(0.132)	(0.040)	(0.088)	(0.029)	(0.090)	(0.015)
tr_bid	0.007	−0.044	–	–	−0.016	−0.076	–	–
	(0.098)	(0.064)			(0.113)	(0.050)		
pt_bid	0.112	−0.140**	–	–	−0.367***	−0.102**	–	–
	(0.097)	(0.058)			(0.116)	(0.040)		
tr_auton_part	−0.106	0.176***	−0.141	−0.027	0.015	0.059	−0.058	0.010
	(0.198)	(0.057)	(0.191)	(0.070)	(0.108)	(0.049)	(0.054)	(0.040)
pt_auton_part	−0.500***	−0.197***	−0.542***	−0.162***	0.295**	−0.142***	0.053	−0.106***
	(0.123)	(0.048)	(0.135)	(0.052)	(0.115)	(0.038)	(0.060)	(0.036)
tr_auton_yes	0.194	0.142***	0.381**	0.433***	0.256**	0.152***	0.160***	0.084*
	(0.140)	(0.049)	(0.191)	(0.095)	(0.106)	(0.042)	(0.056)	(0.044)
pt_auton_yes	−0.253**	−0.103**	−0.145	−0.210***	−0.250*	−0.042	−0.470***	−0.253***
	(0.124)	(0.042)	(0.151)	(0.073)	(0.135)	(0.032)	(0.104)	(0.048)
tr_rb_dur	0.074	–	0.068	–	0.145***	–	0.110*	–
	(0.122)		(0.133)		(0.043)		(0.057)	
Pt_rb_dur	0.055	–	0.124	–	−0.567***	–	−0.483***	–
	(0.106)		(0.114)		(0.082)		(0.083)	
tr_nation_f	−0.155**	−0.003	0.007	0.133	−0.063	0.018	−0.032	−0.007
	(0.068)	(0.049)	(0.143)	(0.095)	(0.042)	(0.032)	(0.066)	(0.047)
pt_nation_f	−0.037	0.019	−0.065	0.025	0.049	−0.036	−0.127**	−0.328***
	(0.066)	(0.041)	(0.113)	(0.053)	(0.042)	(0.031)	(0.062)	(0.028)
tr_nation_b	–	–	−0.022	−0.074	–	–	−0.021	−0.043
			(0.102)	(0.078)			(0.069)	(0.048)
pt_nation_b	–	–	−0.092	0.088*	–	–	−0.165***	−0.234***
			(0.098)	(0.045)			(0.062)	(0.024)
tr_award_prc	–	–	−0.185	−0.318***	–	–	0.062	0.008
			(0.163)	(0.090)			(0.087)	(0.048)
pt_award_prc	–	–	−0.073	0.088	–	–	−0.034	0.139***
			(0.133)	(0.070)			(0.090)	(0.044)
tr_tar_rret	–	–	–	–	–	–	–	–
pt_tar_rret	–	–	–	–	–	–	–	–
Constant	8.531***	4.256***	8.520***	13.130***	−1.957***	−2.027***	−1.821***	−2.782***
	(0.179)	(0.104)	(0.190)	(0.126)	(0.375)	(0.400)	(0.134)	(0.200)
Firm FE	Yes	Yes	Yes	Yes	Yes	Yes	Yes	Yes
Firm specific trend	Yes	Yes	Yes	Yes	No	No	No	No
Observations	335	552	313	530	353	604	331	582
Log-likelihood	297.1	464.3	267.4	447.5	241.5	331.2	232.9	358.6
Number of firms	36	62	34	60	39	68	37	66

Note: Standard errors in parentheses.
* significant at 10%; ** significant at 5%; *** significant at 1%.

(In)quality index				*(In) coverage*			
(25)	*(26)*	*(27)*	*(28)*	*(29)*	*(30)*	*(31)*	*(32)*
−1.078***	−0.018	0.266	−0.159**	0.037**	0.019	0.015	0.033***
(0.214)	(0.019)	(2,469.903)	(0.065)	(0.016)	(0.013)	(0.020)	(0.012)
0.004	0.017	0.213**	0.069*	0.031*	0.008	0.029	0.001
(0.041)	(0.016)	(0.089)	(0.036)	(0.018)	(0.012)	(0.021)	(0.008)
0.040	0.231***	–	–	−0.028	−0.031**	–	–
(0.123)	(0.073)			(0.018)	(0.014)		
0.664***	0.206***	–	–	0.010	0.002	–	–
(0.114)	(0.040)			(0.018)	(0.012)		
	−0.275**	−0.500	−0.197**	−0.017	−0.012	−0.022*	−0.023**
	(0.110)	(2,469.903)	(0.098)	(0.016)	(0.010)	(0.013)	(0.011)
−0.704***	−0.155***	−0.249**	−0.077*	0.008	0.000	0.010	−0.005
(0.113)	(0.053)	(0.114)	(0.045)	(0.016)	(0.009)	(0.013)	(0.009)
1.087***	−0.014	0.063	−1.358***	−0.027*	−0.008	−0.036***	−0.028***
(0.246)	(0.068)	(2,469.903)	(0.228)	(0.014)	(0.006)	(0.008)	(0.007)
−0.583***	−0.081**	−0.150	0.007	−0.019	0.013**	−0.002	−0.003
(0.113)	(0.033)	(0.115)	(0.095)	(0.017)	(0.006)	(0.017)	(0.008)
1.060***		−0.469		−0.026**		−0.009	
(0.213)	–	(2,469.903)	–	(0.011)	–	(0.011)	–
0.013	–	−0.000	–	−0.028**	–	−0.020	–
(0.038)		(0.063)		(0.013)		(0.015)	
−0.086	−0.265***	−0.063	0.014	0.009	0.006	−0.034***	−0.035***
(0.071)	(0.067)	(0.068)	(0.063)	(0.009)	(0.007)	(0.012)	(0.008)
−0.030	−0.102***	−0.021	0.028	−0.000	−0.002	0.020*	−0.004
(0.041)	(0.028)	(0.042)	(0.033)	(0.009)	(0.006)	(0.012)	(0.008)
–	–	–	–	–	–	−0.022*	−0.036***
						(0.012)	(0.011)
–	–	–	–	–	–	0.011	0.008
						(0.012)	(0.009)
–	–	0.258**	0.266***	–	–	0.023	−0.001
		(0.116)	(0.054)			(0.018)	(0.011)
–	–	0.022	0.132***	–	–	−0.018	0.017**
		(0.071)	(0.033)			(0.017)	(0.008)
–	–	−0.293**	1.559***	–	–	–	–
		(0.121)	(0.234)				
–	–	0.014	−0.034	–	–	–	–
		(0.081)	(0.092)				
−1.251***	−0.819***	0.047	−0.918***	1.374***	−0.008	4.140***	1.385***
(0.214)	(0.239)	(2,469.903)	(0.233)	(0.036)	(0.018)	(0.032)	(0.036)
Yes	Yes	Yes	Yes	Yes	Yes	Yes	Yes
No	No	No	No	Yes	Yes	Yes	Yes
219	346	219	346	444	688	422	666
200.6	204.0	114.5	208.4	1172.0	1695.0	1131.5	1634.2
26	43	26	43	50	77	48	75

Table 11.12 Regression analysis – prices US$

	(ln) average prices US$				*(ln) average prices in real currency*			
	(33)	*(34)*	*(35)*	*(36)*	*(37)*	*(38)*	*(39)*	*(40)*
dum_priv_tr	0.213***	0.140***	0.389**	0.565***	0.165***	0.111***	0.300***	0.250***
	(0.035)	(0.021)	(0.152)	(0.098)	(0.029)	(0.019)	(0.083)	(0.048)
dum_priv_post	−0.189***	0.104***	−0.235***	−0.111*	0.198***	0.130***	0.259***	0.169***
	(0.032)	(0.019)	(0.056)	(0.059)	(0.025)	(0.017)	(0.036)	(0.033)
tr_bid	1.086***	0.191***	–	–	0.511***	0.144***	–	–
	(0.046)	(0.065)			(0.086)	(0.055)		
pt_bid	−0.340***	−0.060**	–	–	−0.210***	−0.120***	–	–
	(0.038)	(0.029)			(0.038)	(0.026)		
tr_auton_part	−0.601***	−0.738***	−0.224	−0.723***		−0.456***	2.009***	−0.338***
	(0.066)	(0.079)	(0.195)	(0.081)		(0.069)	(0.129)	(0.063)
pt_auton_part	0.316***	−0.108***	0.239***	−0.023	0.266***	−0.108***	0.183**	−0.223***
	(0.072)	(0.039)	(0.070)	(0.046)	(0.083)	(0.037)	(0.079)	(0.043)
tr_auton_yes	−1.142***	−0.301***	−0.137	−0.153**	−0.382***	−0.079	0.193***	−0.010
	(0.049)	(0.072)	(0.090)	(0.063)	(0.081)	(0.056)	(0.053)	(0.038)
pt_auton_yes	0.243***	−0.161***	−0.090**	−0.253***	0.133***	0.098***	0.019	0.063**
	(0.036)	(0.030)	(0.041)	(0.037)	(0.043)	(0.025)	(0.031)	(0.029)
tr_rb_dur	−0.083**	–	0.019	–	−0.096***	–	−0.182***	–
	(0.034)		(0.105)		(0.028)		(0.066)	
pt_rb_dur	0.306***	–	0.126***	–	−0.112***	–	−0.175***	–
	(0.029)		(0.027)		(0.022)		(0.023)	
tr_nation_f	−0.007	0.073**	−0.112	−0.182*	−0.108***	−0.059**	−0.020	−0.189***
	(0.035)	(0.036)	(0.117)	(0.093)	(0.026)	(0.025)	(0.052)	(0.038)
pt_nation_f	0.227***	0.024	0.156**	0.085	0.070***	0.046**	0.070**	0.021
	(0.030)	(0.027)	(0.064)	(0.061)	(0.025)	(0.021)	(0.031)	(0.030)
tr_nation_b	–	–	−0.255**	−0.403***	–	–	–	–
			(0.109)	(0.096)				
pt_nation_b	–	–	0.176***	0.197***	–	–	–	–
			(0.058)	(0.057)				
tr_award_prc	–	–	−0.060	−0.184**	–	–	−0.052	−0.157***
			(0.198)	(0.078)			(0.043)	(0.043)
pt_award_prc	–	–	0.034	0.094**	–	–	−0.010	−0.076***
			(0.047)	(0.038)			(0.027)	(0.029)
tr_tar_rret	–	–	–	–	–	–	−0.188*	0.061
							(0.113)	(0.052)
pt_tar_rret	–	–	–	–	–	–	−0.126***	−0.060*
							(0.040)	(0.033)
Constant	3.839***	−1.227***	4.435***	−1.183***	4.193***	6.614***	4.593***	6.715***
	(0.027)	(0.093)	(0.095)	(0.088)	(0.033)	(0.085)	(0.056)	(0.082)
Firm FE	Yes	Yes	Yes	Yes	Yes	Yes	Yes	Yes
Firm Specific trend	No	No	No	No	No	No	No	No
Observations	372	550	350	528	370	548	348	526
Log-likelihood	316.7	281.2	288.7	280.6	381.3	400.5	373.5	388.7
Number of firms	44	65	42	63	44	65	42	63

Note: Standard errors in parentheses.
* significant at 10%; ** significant at 5%; *** significant at 1%.

4.4.4 Labour productivity

Most differences in characteristics seem not to affect indicators related to labour productivity. Among those with similar differences is the autonomy of the board. Those firms with a regulator exercising partial autonomy reported mixed effects during the transitional phase. Total autonomy shows significant change during the transition which measured between 9 per cent and 60 per cent above the firm-specific time trend. After transitioning, partial autonomy presents significant reductions in labour productivity after the time trend correction. In addition, evidence of deceleration in the improvements of labour productivity is also present.

The duration of the regulatory board is another characteristic that seems to affect labour productivity. Longer-lasting board concessions resulted in significant improvements above the trend of between 27 per cent and 31 per cent in their connection-per-employee ratio during the transition; however, no significant changes are later observed with respect to the transition itself. These results are the consequence of the higher reduction in the number of employees for firms regulated by a regulatory board holding higher tenure.

Finally, when tariffs are regulated using a price-capping system, we find evidence of reduction of levels during the transition; however, when regulated by rate of return system, we find a significant increase in productivity above the time trend.

4.4.5 Distributional losses

There is an absence of significant transitional effects on regulatory boards consisting of partial autonomy. The results are a bit mixed, but in general we noted a reduction in distributional losses. However, distributional when the board possesses total autonomy, we find significant increased losses during the transitional period, ranging between 8 per cent and 22 per cent, followed by important reductions on losses. The total effects result in higher reductions than those cases with partial autonomy. These results suggest that there are increases in losses during the transition, when the regulatory board had longer duration, which were then followed by important reductions of around 27 per cent with respect to the level before the transition.

We further explore the differential effects across sectors and find that electrical companies with fares regulated by a rate of return reduced their losses by 4 per cent during the transition and by an additional 33 per cent after that.

4.4.6 Quality

We also observe how different characteristics affected changes in quality. Total autonomy yielded mixed results, increasing quality during the transition and after that, whereas partial autonomy has negative effects on quality during the transition period of between 15 per cent and 24 per cent. An additional reduction in these indicators is observed after the transition.

Some evidence of quality improvement was present when the board had longer duration; however, the results are mixed. When tariffs are regulated by a rate of return, firms significantly improved on quality during the transition; however, under a price capping system there were reductions in quality during the transition and no significant change thereafter.

4.4.7 *Coverage*

With respect to the autonomy of the regulatory board, we noted that partial autonomy yielded a reduction of 2 per cent below the firm-specific time trend present during the transition. However, other changes were not significantly different in the transition period or concessions with total autonomy.

Regulatory boards of longer duration seem to have negative effects on increased coverage after controlling for trends.

4.4.8 *Average prices*

Table 11.11 indicates that concessions regulated by a board with partial autonomy, in general, show higher reductions on average prices than firms regulated with a total autonomous agency. Agencies with longer board duration seem to have higher reductions in average prices during the transition, although after this period, prices in dollars increase significantly while those in real terms decreased. Finally, we establish that when tariff regulations are adjusted by rate of return mechanisms, average prices show some reductions.

4.5 Conclusions and policy recommendations

From after this short overview of infrastructure reform in Latin America during the 1990s, two main results emerge. First, privatization generated important improvements, but beyond the transition period these benefits were not always transferred to consumers. Second, significant heterogeneity within and between sectors may be explained by the intrinsic characteristics of the reform process, the privatization mechanism, the level of regulatory development and the concession design.

(i) Generally autonomous regulatory bodies seem to be correlated with a higher reduction in the number of employees, while older (longer duration) institutions produce lower price increases;
(ii) When pricing is regulated according to the rate of return, companies have higher network expansion than in the case of price-capping regulation. Consistently, those firms under price-cap have higher reductions of their labour force, but lower increases in labour productivity. Additionally, the latter firms present less improvement in both distributional losses and quality, while also showing higher price increases than those under the rate-of-return regulation.

These results suggest one main policy implication: change in ownerships has significant effects in term of improving efficiency and quality. However, regulatory quality is an important determinants in these outcomes.

Additionally, for the existing private utilities, there is a need to complete the reforms, particularly the so-called 'second generation regulatory reforms'. Without these reforms – that include the completion of the regulatory framework, avoiding excessive contract renegotiations, and increasing competition when feasible – post-privatization improvements are limited and probably unsustainable, whereas private financing will be difficult to attract. Obviously, the importance of competition, regulation, and contract design is closely related to technological characteristics within an industry. For example, the reduction in the telecommunications costs and substitution by means other than fixed telephony, which increases the role of competition, with regulation is a tool to avoid abuse of dominance and is relatively less relevant for contract design. In water and sanitation, remaining natural monopolies make the move towards market competition a more difficult task. This implies relying to a higher degree on well-designed concession contracts with regulation as a tool to guarantee the appropriate contract management. In either case, regulation is a key instrument, especially if one needs to reduce regulatory risks and attract private investments to support the Latin American needs in infrastructure.

5 Final remarks

Having tested the impact of the regulation of private infrastructure operators on sector performance, from three separate angles, we have reached the following conclusions:

- Quality of regulation is a significant determinant of the divergence between the overall profitability of the concession and its corresponding hurdle rate, explaining around 20 per cent of the variation. However, regulatory effort seems to be more closely associated with keeping tariffs as low as possible for current consumers, rather than with keeping profitability well aligned with hurdle rates of return.
- Price capping led a significant increase of the probability of renegotiation
- Existence of a regulator at the signing of contract reduces renegotiations:
  - The regulators filter and dissuade opportunistic private operator-led renegotiation;
  - In the case of government-led renegotiation, the regulator acts as barrier against political opportunism; and
  - The impact of the regulator is stronger in weak governance environments.

- Differences in private sector participation in infrastructure outcomes are explained to some extent by differences in the design and quality of the regulatory design.
- Finally, regulation is crucial.

Notes

1. In Brazil, for example, disatisfaction with privatization increased from 40 to 60 per cent of the population during 1998–2004 while in smaller countries, such as Guatemala and Panama, this index reached more than 80 per cent of the population. Even in Chile, commonly seen as the champion of structural reform, dissatisfaction is predominant (see Latinobarómetro surveys for 1998 and 2004). Indeed, public authorities and multilateral institutions, such as the IMF and the World Bank, once sponsors of privatization, are now discussing ways of increasing public investment in infrastructure without jeopardizing sound fiscal management. The policy-making pendulum is, then, back to public investment as either if infrastructure reforms and privatization had never been implemented or, even worse, as if reforms were fully completed, all lessons had been taken, and adjustments had been made.
2. Guasch (2004) shows that the incidence of renegotiation is about 42 per cent of all concessions and about 55 per cent and 75 per cent for concessions in the transport and water sectors. The incidence is even higher for concessions regulated under a price-cap regime. Even more striking is how fast renegotiations take place. The time interval between the granting of concessions and renegotiation is about 2.1 years, while for water concessions it is even quicker, about 1.6 years.
3. Simple differential 1 excludes terminal value; simple differential 2 includes terminal value; simple differential 3 includes terminal value and adjustment for management fee; simple differential 4 includes terminal value and adjustments for management fee and transfer pricing.
4. One weakness of regulatory commissions, perhaps captured here in these estimates, is the higher political intervention, since often each relevant political party gets to designate its own commissioner.
5. Bid, direct adjudication, invitation, petition or request.
6. Highest cannon, highest price, tariff, lowest government subsidy, investment plan, shorter duration of the concession or multiple criteria.
7. Operation, BOT, BOO, privatization, etc.
8. Law, decree, contract or license.
9. Revenue capping, price capping, rate of return or no regulation.
10. The government, the concessionaire, both or nobody.
11. These tables are available upon request.

References

Andres, L., J. L. Guasch, T. Haven and V. Foster (2006) *The Impact of Private Sector Participation in Infrastructure: Higher Shadows and the Road Ahead* (Washington, DC: The World Bank).

Angrist, J. (1991) 'Instrumental Variables Estimation of Average Treatment Effects in Econometrics and Epidemiology', National Bureau of Economic Research, technical working paper no. 115.

Boardman, A. and A. R. Vining (1989) 'Ownership and Performance in Competitive Environments: A Comparison of the Performance of Private, Mixed, and State-Owned Enterprises', *Journal of Law Economics*, vol. 32, pp. 1–33.

Chong, A. and F. López-de-Silanes (2003) 'The Truth about Privatization in Latin America', Inter-American Development Bank, Latin American Research Network, Research Network working paper no. R-486, October.

Cubbin, J. and J. Stern (2005) 'Regulatory Effectiveness: The Impact of Regulation and Regulatory Governance Arrangements on Electricity Industry Outcomes', World Bank Policy Research Working Paper no. 3536, Washington DC.

Estache A., L. Guasch, and L. Trujillo (2003) 'Price Caps, Efficiency Payoffs, and Infrastructure Contract Renegotiation in Latin America', World Bank Policy Research Working Paper no. 3129, Washington DC.

Gomez-Ibanez, J. A. (2003) *Regulatory Infrastructure: Monopoly, Contracts and Discretion* (Cambridge MA: Harvard University Press).

Guasch, J. L. (2004) *Granting and Renegotiating Infrastructure Concessions – Doing it Right* (Washington, DC: The World Bank).

Guasch, J.L., J.J. Laffont, and S. Straub (2003) 'Renegotiation of Concession Contracts in Latin America', World Bank Policy Research Working Paper no. 3011, Washington DC.

Guasch, J.L., J.J. Laffont, and S. Straub (2005) 'Concessions of Infrastructure in Latin America: Government-led Renegotiations', World Bank Policy Research Working Paper no. 3749, Washington DC.

Guasch, J.L. and P. Spiller (1999) 'Managing the Regulatory Process: Design, Concepts, Issues, and the Latin America and Caribbean Story', World Bank Latin American and Caribbean Studies, The World Bank.

Han, A.K. and J. Hausman, (1990) 'Flexible Parametric Estimation of Duration and Competing Risk Models', *Journal of Applied Econometrics*, vol. 5, pp. 1–28.

Heckman, J. and R. Robb (1985) 'Alternative Methods of Evaluating the Impact of Interventions', in J. Heckman and B. Singer (eds), *Longitudinal Analysis of Labor Market Data* (New York: Cambridge University Press), pp. 156–245.

Jamasb, T., R. Mota, D. Newberry, and M. Pollitt (2005) 'Electricity Reform in Developing Countries: A Survey of Empirical Evidence on Determinants and Performance', World Bank Policy Research Working Paper no. 3549.

Kikeri, S. (1999) 'Privatization and Labor: What Happens to Workers When Governments Divest?' World Bank technical paper no. 396. Washington, DC.

Megginson, W., R. Nash, and M. van Randenborgh (1994) 'The Financial and Operating Performance of Newly Privatized Firms: An International Empirical Analysis', *Journal of Finance*, vol. 49, pp. 403–52.

Megginson, W. and J. Netter (2001) 'From State to Market: A Survey of Empirical Studies on Privatization', *Journal of Economic Literature*, vol. 39, pp. 321–89.

Rivers, D. and Q. Vuong (1988) 'Limited Information Estimators and Exogeneity Tests for Simultaneous Probit Models', *Journal of Econometrics*, vol. 39, pp. 347–66.

Sirtaine, S., M. E. Pinglo, J. L. Guasch, and V. Foster (2005) 'How Profitable Are Private Infrastructure Concessions in Latin America? Empirical Evidence and Regulatory Implications', *The Quarterly Review of Economics and Finance*, vol. 45, pp. 380–402.

Stern, J. and Cubbin, J.S. (2004) 'Regulatory Effectiveness: The Impact of Regulation and Regulatory Governance Arrangements on Electricity Outcomes – A Review Paper', World Bank Policy Research Working Paper no. 3535.

Wallsten, S. (2001) 'An Econometric Analysis of Telecom Competition, Privatization, and Regulation in Africa and Latin America', *The Journal of Industrial Economics*, vol. 49, no. 1, pp. 1–19.

12

Institutional Evolution and Energy Reform in the UK

*Richard Green**

1 Introduction

Over the last twenty-five years, the UK's energy utilities of electricity and gas have been completely transformed. Publicly-owned monopolies have been replaced by competing private companies. In gas, the formerly integrated vertical stages have been separated, and the nature of vertical integration in the electricity industry has also changed. New regulators are responsible for overseeing key parts of the industry, and new markets have been created.

The transformation was not planned as such from the start. The first attempt to create competition did not include any institutions to support competition, and was an utter failure. The first privatization, of the gas industry, was accompanied by the creation of a new regulator, but this regulator was not given enough powers to ensure the development of competition. It was a decade later that the gas incumbent decided to split itself on vertical lines. The structure chosen for the electricity privatizations in England and Wales took the lessons from the gas industry into account, with vertical separation, a regulator with more powers, and a centralized wholesale market operating from the start. Even in this case, however, the way in which the regulator used its powers evolved over time, and the government eventually decided to replace the original wholesale market with a completely new design.

These institutional features – vertical structures, regulators, and wholesale markets – are the subject of this chapter. 'Institutional design' is the phrase most often used to describe the way in which governments or other agencies have attempted to transform the way in which an industry operates. In this case, however, the industries have moved so far from the institutions created at privatization that the phrase places too much weight on the initial changes, compared to what came later. 'Institutional re-design' would focus

* Support from the Leverhulme Trust, through the award of a Philip Leverhulme Prize, is gratefully acknowledged. I would like to thank Claude Ménard for helpful comments.

attention on the subsequent changes. Many of those changes were gradual, however, and made by regulators or companies without direct stimulus from the government. 'Institutional evolution' is a phrase that tries to capture this, without losing the ideas of design and re-design.

The chapter will use three case studies to draw out some general themes. The issue of an industry's vertical structure is discussed with reference to the gas industry, which moved from an integrated monopoly to a structure which now has less vertical integration than the electricity industry. The evolution of regulation is discussed with reference to the electricity industry and ways in which price controls on network charges are set. Wholesale markets and their rules are also discussed in the context of the electricity industry. Before moving on to these case studies, however, the chapter starts with some background on the industries' characteristics, structures under public ownership, and privatizations. There is only space for a brief overview here, and there is more information in Vickers and Yarrow (1988), Armstrong, Cowan and Vickers (1994) and Newbery (1999).

2 Background

Both electricity and gas are network utilities – for practical purposes, they have to be delivered to consumers through a network of wires or pipes. These networks are natural monopolies – it would be prohibitively expensive to build two separate networks to supply the same group of consumers. Furthermore, it is essential to coordinate the flows over those networks to ensure that they continue to operate within safe limits. In the gas industry, the ability to change the pressure within the pipeline system allows a lot of leeway on an hour-to-hour timescale, but inflows and outflows must match from day to day if supplies are not to be interrupted. If supplies are disrupted, the task of restarting them must be undertaken very carefully – explosions can be the result of allowing air into the system. Compared to gas, electricity is perhaps safer, and certainly harder to control. A power failure (as opposed to the failure of devices that rely on electricity) will not directly cause casualties, although the power surges that often cause the failure can be dangerous. The problem with electricity, however, is that flows have to be managed from second to second, but cannot be directly controlled. Electricity follows Kirchhoff's laws to flow over a network in inverse proportion to the resistance (or rather impedance) on each route, and the flows will immediately redistribute themselves if the failure of one component changes the routes available. The timescales are too short for human intervention, and so every important piece of equipment has circuit-breakers to protect itself automatically in the event of a power surge, while system operators must ensure that the network is always in a state that would allow its continued safe operation, even if any one component were suddenly to fail.

For many years, it was accepted that the need to coordinate flows over the networks, coupled with the natural monopoly nature of those networks, meant that the entire industries were natural monopolies – it would not be possible to have competing companies within any one area. This did not necessarily mean that there was only one company in the industry – larger companies responsible for transmission at high voltages or high pressures sometimes sold to smaller distribution companies which dealt with final consumers. Gas companies rarely produced all of their gas themselves, even where they were close to gas fields, but bought from gas producers. Electricity companies were more likely to combine both generation and transmission, but could also buy power from neighbouring companies or from industrial self-generators with a surplus. Final consumers, however, did not have a choice of where to buy their energy, and there was indeed no word for the activity of selling energy to consumers, as distinct from distributing it to them. It was only during the debates over deregulation that the phrases 'energy supply' (in the UK) or 'retail wheeling' (and later just 'retailing') (in the US) came into use.

In the UK, the gas and electricity industries had been in nationalized public ownership since 1948 and 1947 respectively. By 1980, the Central Electricity Generating Board (CEGB) was responsible for generation and transmission in England and Wales, selling power under a bulk supply tariff to 12 Area Electricity Boards, which sold it on to final consumers. In Scotland, there were two vertically integrated Electricity Boards, for the north and south of the country. In Northern Ireland, the industry was once again vertically integrated. Most of the country's power came from coal, with about one-fifth from nuclear power stations. Nuclear power had proved a high-cost technology under British conditions (and station designs), while the industry bought almost all of its coal from the nationalized coal industry, again at well above the price of coal on the (then rather thin) international markets. The British Gas Corporation was an integrated body buying gas from producers in the North Sea[1] (and producing some gas itself), and then transmitting and distributing it to end users. Before the discovery of North Sea gas, the industry was essentially federal, with 12 Area Gas Boards producing and distributing coal gas. The Corporation had been formed in 1972, taking over the Area Gas Boards in order to build a national transmission system and convert the country to natural gas, an engineering task which was regarded as a great success.

During the 1960s and 1970s, an increasingly explicit system for controlling the nationalized industries was developed. The industries were public corporations run by boards appointed to, but only indirectly accountable to, ministers. They were exhorted to use marginal cost pricing and to earn a target rate of return on their assets, requirements that can be consistent if the target return is suitably chosen. In the early 1970s, however, these principles were subordinated to the need to fight inflation, and the industries were required to keep prices down, despite the effect on their returns. This policy was reversed a few years later, and external financing limits on the amount that the industries could borrow (or had to return to the Treasury) became the chief factor in their control. The external financing limits were supplemented by new rate of return targets after 1978, but the focus of government attention on the nationalized industries was soon to turn from controlling the existing monopolies, to reforming their structures.

The first stage in the UK's energy reforms came with the Energy Act 1981, intended to expose the industries to competitive forces. The Area Electricity Boards were required to buy power from independent generators, at the Boards' avoided cost, which was effectively the price given by the CEGB's bulk supply tariff. The following year, the CEGB changed the bulk supply tariff, introducing a fixed component for each Area Board, and reducing the unit charges for electricity supplied to the Boards. This immediately reduced the Boards' avoided cost by around 10 per cent, cutting the prices that they could offer to independent generators, without affecting the overall revenue received by the CEGB. The first attempt to create competition without appropriate supporting institutions (such as constraints on the CEGB's behaviour) was thus a failure.

3 Privatization

The word 'privatization' does not appear in the 1979 Conservative election manifesto, although there were plans to sell shares in some of the companies owned by the state. These gathered momentum in the early 1980s, while the problem of British Telecommunications (BT) rose up the government's agenda. BT needed to invest heavily in upgrading its network, but the thrust of macroeconomic policy was to keep state spending low. Under the government's accounting conventions, BT's investment would count as government spending, and it proved impossible to change this unless BT was sold to the private sector. Selling BT would of course also fit in with the government's general desire to shrink the size of the state and encourage private enterprise and ownership.

The government accordingly started the legal process of changing BT from a public corporation to a limited company that could be owned by institutions and individuals. Most of the previously privatized companies had been sold mainly to institutions, but BT was believed to be too large for the institutions to absorb, and so it was decided to market the company to individual investors as well. This was a delicate task, since financial services laws meant that only authorized advisers could suggest that it would be a good idea to buy shares in a particular company, and the government's advertising campaign concentrated on explaining what shares were, and telling people that BT shares would soon be on sale. In the event, the campaign was very successful, the share issue was heavily over-subscribed, and the shares rose by

86 per cent on their first day of trading in December 1984, a pattern that was to be repeated in many subsequent privatizations.

Those financial gains made privatization popular with many people, and so the government continued down the path it had set, privatizing almost all of the nationalized industries over the next 12 years. Privatization was not universally popular, however, and the main opposition, the Labour Party, had a policy of renationalization without compensation in the mid-1980s. This had an important impact on the regulatory structures set up to constrain BT's behaviour (Levy and Spiller, 1996).

BT's right to operate, and the terms on which it could do so, were enshrined in a licence, a contract that the courts would be expected to uphold. In general, contracts can only be changed by mutual agreement, but it was recognized that a company and its regulator might well be unable to agree. An arbitrator was therefore needed, and the Telecommunications Act 1984 gave this duty to the Monopolies and Mergers Commission (MMC). The MMC, now the Competition Commission, had been in existence since 1948, with a large number of part-time members, and a full-time chairman and staff. When a merger, or a possible case of market abuse, was referred to it, a group of MMC members would investigate and rule on whether the matter might be expected to operate against the public interest. The public interest was a broad concept, including matters such as employment and the UK's trade balance as well as prices to consumers, but one that was generally accepted. The MMC had a good reputation for competences and impartiality, making it suitable to act in the potentially controversial role of arbitrator.

While the MMC would be the arbitrator, the government decided that a new institution would be needed to act as BT's regulator. This institution was also modelled on part of the UK's competition policy apparatus, the Office of Fair Trading (OFT). The OFT was responsible for the first-stage investigation of mergers and monopolies, among other duties, and was staffed by civil servants, with a single head, the Director General of Fair Trading. Decisions to recommend a merger for investigation by the MMC,[2] for example, were the legal responsibility of the DGFT alone, although he was advised by his staff.

The Telecommunications Act therefore created the post of Director General of Telecommunications, and the Office of Telecommunications to support him. The first Director General, Sir Bryan Carsberg, an academic accountant, was advised that it would be a part-time job, although it rapidly became apparent that it required his full-time attention. The regulator had powers over several areas of BT's activity, including the terms on which it had to offer connections to its network to its single rival, Mercury. Mercury had been licensed as a competitor to BT in 1982, and was developing a network, but could only effectively compete if it had fair access to the larger company's network. BT's licence allowed Mercury to ask the regulator to intervene if the companies failed to agree terms, but the wording was perhaps too vague.

When the negotiations between the companies did break down, the regulator had to resort to court action to enforce his power to impose terms on BT.

The regulator's most significant power, however, was to be over the level of BT's prices. Before the privatization, the civil servants involved had been unable to agree on the way in which prices should be controlled, fearing that adopting rate-of-return regulation, as practised in the US, would give BT few incentives for efficiency. Professor Stephen Littlechild was asked to decide between two alternative schemes, and came up with a third (Littlechild, 1983). In his view, regulation would be a temporary feature of the market, until competition became effective, and so should focus on the matter of most concern to consumers, the prices that they had to pay. He recommended that the average price of a basket of services should be indexed to the retail price index (RPI), but required to fall by a specified amount each year, reflecting the scope for technical progress. With no figure in mind, he used the algebraic X for this reduction, and his formula became known as 'RPI – X'. The key to preserving the company's incentives to keep costs down was that this formula removes the link between its costs and its prices, while the RPI term compensates the company for general inflation. Professor Littlechild warned that the scheme would lose much of its attractiveness if it proved necessary to reset the control at some future date, as this would inevitably have to restore the link between prices and costs. BT's licence was written so that the price control would lapse in 1989, five years after privatization, unless the regulator and company agreed an extension, or the MMC concluded that not extending the control would be against the public interest.

This regulatory structure was repeated for the other utility privatizations, but with variations. Some of these may have been because BT's privatization was led by the Department of Trade and Industry, the sale of the water industry by the Department of the Environment, and the energy privatizations by the Department of Energy, each using its own team of draftsmen. Some were due to different circumstances – the water regulator had (and has) a much weaker duty towards promoting competition than the other regulators, reflecting the limited scope for competition in that industry. The passage of time was also important – later acts gave the regulators more power to demand information, after the initial regulators found the companies uncooperative. Other differences have no simple explanation – there was an independent Gas Consumers' Council, responsible for representing consumers and dealing with complaints, while electricity consumers were represented through fourteen regional committees appointed by the regulator and staffed by his office.

The industrial structures chosen for the two energy privatizations were very different, however. The decision to privatize British Gas (BG) was taken soon after the BT sale, and the timetable for the sale was relatively short, with the sale achieved in December 1986. The company was to be privatized intact, reflecting this timetable and the company's political influence. The Gas Act

1986 allowed competition to supply gas to any customer with an annual demand of more than 25,000 therms, and required BG to offer terms to any that wished to use its network to supply those 'contract' consumers, and to publish information on the tariffs that it would charge for this. Prices to small consumers were regulated by the Director General of Gas Supply, based at Ofgas, but he had no power to intervene in the market for large consumers, presumably because it was expected to be competitive.

By the time that the electricity privatization was planned, British Gas had already been referred to the MMC for its behaviour in the contract market, and it was (even more) obvious that competition would not be established without supporting institutions. The CEGB was divided into three generation companies and a transmission company. This National Grid Company (NGC) was not allowed to generate or trade power, except from the pumped storage stations that contributed to system operations. While it was ultimately owned by the 12 Area Electricity Boards, renamed Regional Electricity Companies (RECs), a holding company structure insulated it from pressure from these owners. The transmission system operator had so much scope to discriminate between different users of the grid that it was vitally important to ensure that it had no incentive to do so.

Competition was to be allowed in both generation and supply. The creation of three generation companies was intended to produce competition, although a larger number would have been more effective from this point of view. Generation was immediately opened to new entry, while supply was opened in three stages between 1990 and 1998. The tariffs for using the transmission and distribution systems were regulated by the Director General of Electricity Supply and his staff at Offer. This regulation controlled their average level, while their structure also had to be agreed with the regulator. The RECs were required to keep separate accounts for distribution and supply, and to use their own published distribution tariffs when setting prices to final customers, with a ban on cross-subsidy or discrimination.

There were strict limits on vertical integration by both the RECs (moving into generation) and the major generators (selling to large customers). This meant that most customers would have to be supplied via wholesale trading. A new wholesale market, the Electricity Pool of England and Wales, was created. The Pooling and Settlement Agreement set out the market rules (with most of the functions performed by various subsidiaries of NGC) and the procedure for changing those rules. To ensure that minority interests could be protected, changes were made difficult, with a need for super-majorities and the right of appeal to the regulator. Financial Contracts for Differences were superimposed on Pool trading to hedge the impact of variable spot prices on companies' costs and revenues, and other contracts passed the cost of expensive British coal to captive small consumers. The complex new structure took effect at midnight on 31 March 1990, the industry's Vesting Day.

4 The structure of the gas industry

As already mentioned, British Gas was privatized in 1986 with minimal changes to its structure. It had a monopoly to supply gas to small consumers, and an effective monopoly in supplying gas to larger consumers, even though this contract market had notionally been opened to competition. The company had signed individual, confidential, contracts with its larger customers, and tailored their terms to the customers' circumstances. Customers that had installed equipment to burn an alternative fuel obtained the lowest prices. Customers that were believed (by BG) to be able to install such equipment relatively easily had to pay more, but less than customers with no possibility of using an alternative fuel. This approach to pricing came close to the textbook model of first-degree price discrimination – BG was effectively trying to charge every customer its reservation price. This would be an efficient way of recovering a fixed revenue requirement with the minimum distortions, but BG was using the approach to maximize its profits, which is less desirable.

Competition was meant to protect these customers, but competitors would have to use BG's system. BG had published two examples of what it would charge rival suppliers, but as these differed along three important dimensions (distance, pressure, and volume) it was impossible to infer anything about a more general policy. A competitive supplier would have to reveal which customer it was attempting to target, and while BG's pipeline operation was calculating a price for using the network, its supply division would have an opportunity to renegotiate the customer's contract. Entry on those terms would be all but impossible, and no rival company tried. In 1987, less than a year after privatization, BG was referred to the MMC. The reference was made by the Director General of Fair Trading, because the gas regulator had no jurisdiction over the contract market.

When the MMC reported (MMC, 1988), it was clear that significant changes would be needed to create effective competition. BG was required to publish both a schedule of charges for using its network, and a schedule of prices for supplying gas to end users. The company had to give up its confidential contracts, although the MMC suggested that prices could vary with the amount of gas that a user took. BG was also required to buy no more than 90 per cent of the gas from new fields in the North Sea – potential suppliers had been concerned that they would be unable to obtain gas from producers that would not want to annoy the company that would inevitably remain their biggest customer in the UK for the foreseeable future. A rule forcing BG not to buy all of the gas available ensured that some would be left for new competitors.

In the event, other suppliers bought more than 10 per cent of the gas from new fields, but almost all of this was sold to the new market segment of power stations, and competition to sell to industrial consumers remained limited. A review by the Office of Fair Trading led to negotiated undertakings between

BG and the OFT, with BG promising to supply no more than 40 per cent of the industrial market by 1995, releasing gas supplies to its competitors as necessary, and to set up a separate unit for transportation and storage, with regulated charges for third-party access. Negotiations over the form of this regulation broke down, however, and BG was referred to the MMC by both the Director General of Fair Trading and the Director General of Gas Supply in July 1992.[3]

The MMC (1993a, 1993b) was clear that competition in the market was not working properly, and that one reason for this was BG's control of transportation and storage. The MMC considered that an integrated BG would inevitably be at an advantage over its rivals, and recommended that the company should be forced to divest these activities by 1997. It also recommended that the threshold for supply competition should be reduced to 1,500 therms from the same date (it had been reduced to 2,500 therms in 1992). The move to full competition for every consumer, however, should only take place after 'a most careful assessment of the consequences' (MMC, 1993b, 1.9).

The report was met by a furious lobbying campaign by BG, as the government decided how to respond to it. The government effectively reversed the MMC's two main recommendations – competition for all consumers would be introduced by 1998 (with trials in parts of the country from 1996), and BG would not be broken up. There were concerns that the structural change would disrupt preparations for competition, and this was given a higher priority. Since the deadline for full competition in electricity had been set for 1998 (although this was in fact to be missed), it seemed appropriate to give the gas industry the same deadline.

In 1997, however, BG did in fact separate itself into two parts. BG plc kept transportation, exploration, and most of the company's production, while Centrica plc was given the supply business and the remaining gas fields. It is likely that this decision was due to a problem with 'stranded costs'. BG had bought large amounts of gas on long-term take-or-pay contracts with prices that were now well above the price of gas on the short-term wholesale markets. The question was who would absorb this difference. Under regulation, it would probably have been the consumers, but competition might make this impossible, as competitors' offers would be linked to the short-term prices. (In practice, BG was able to keep its prices above those of its competitors while only gradually losing market share, so that its remaining customers did bear part of the loss.) Another possibility was renegotiating the contracts, so that the gas producers and BG shared the loss. This would not be attractive for the producers, however, particularly if BG had other profit streams that might be set against its losses on the contracts. The supply business's financial position would be weakened if it was split off from the rest of BG, but this would strengthen its negotiating position against the gas producers. From the point of view of the overall group, splitting off the supply business would reduce the amount of stranded costs that it had to bear (Helm and Jenkinson, 1997; Waddams Price, 1997).

Ironically, the group would probably have been in a better position had it agreed to be broken up in 1993 – by the time the decision was taken, the problem with the contracts was becoming apparent. Since it was not legally possible for Centrica to be too weak when it was created, the company was given some of BG's production assets. Had a stand-alone supply business been created in 1993, with no production, it would have been able to drive a harder bargain when renegotiating its contracts. Other gas producers would probably have had to absorb some of the stranded costs that were in fact met by transferring production assets from BG to Centrica, reducing BG's profits.

Since 1997, Centrica has diversified into electricity supply and then into generation. Moving into electricity supply was an obvious move, and Centrica's existing customer base has made it the most effective competitor in the market – it is now the largest supplier (for domestic consumers) in the country. Similarly, the former electricity incumbents are competing in the gas market, and each is the second-largest gas supplier in its area. Selling gas and electricity together can reduce transactions costs, and most consumers who change supplier buy gas and electricity from the same company.

In 2000, BG divested its transportation business to a separate company, Lattice, which then merged with NGC in 2002. Since interruptions on the gas network can have significant impacts on the electricity industry, there are great advantages in having a single company responsible for both transmission systems. Gas storage has been split off from transmission, however, as the regulator has been keen to develop competition in this part of the industry. Most recently, in 2005, some of the regional gas distribution networks have been split off and sold to other companies.[4] This should improve the regulation of all the regional gas networks, since the regulator will now have several independent operators to compare when assessing companies' claims about their revenue needs. The gas industry has thus moved from a single monopoly to one in which there is competition – actual or comparative – in almost all of its activities.

5 Price controls in the electricity industry

While the Littlechild Report had warned that the RPI – X system would lose much of its attractiveness if it proved necessary to re-set the price control, in 1992 Professor Littlechild found himself resetting the price control for the National Grid Company's transmission revenues, as Director General of Electricity Supply. The company had been privatized with a control of RPI – 0, and in a five-page statement, the regulator affirmed his confidence in the method, confirmed that he had taken all of his legal duties into account, and proposed a new control of RPI – 3. This control was accepted by the company. In 1993, the price controls for retail supply were reset, but since these consisted mainly of cost pass-through elements, the financial stakes were low and they attracted little public attention.

This was not to be the case with the third set of price controls to be reviewed, covering the Regional Electricity Companies' distribution revenues. These covered £3.8 billion a year in revenue, or around 25 per cent of the average customer's electricity bill. The companies had proved to be extremely profitable since their privatization, even though the rest of the economy was in a recession, and Parliamentary Select Committees had twice called for the regulator to tighten the price controls before they were due to expire. The regulator resisted these calls on the basis that to react to high profits during the life of a control would significantly weaken the companies' incentive to cut costs in future. In October 1993, the regulator published a consultation paper giving some information on the companies' operating costs and characteristics, and asking opinions on some of the issues to be considered in the review. The regulator did not intend to publish any more information until he revealed his proposals the following summer, but a leak occurred in May 1994. This leak, generally blamed on one of the companies, suggested that he was considering price cuts of around 25 per cent at the start of the new price controls.

When the proposals were published, in August 1994, the initial cuts were for 'only' between 11 per cent and 17 per cent, much less than commentators had been expecting, and the regulator was criticized for his leniency. One month later, he published price controls for the two Scottish companies, with much smaller price cuts. These companies' initial price controls, set by the Scottish Office, had been less generous than those set by the Department of Energy for the English companies, leaving less slack for reductions when the controls were reset. There was still a perception that the regulator had been tougher on the Scottish companies, however, and one of them appealed to the MMC against his proposals.

In November 1994, there was a takeover bid for Northern Electric, one of the RECs. The company lobbied for the bid to be referred to the MMC (in the hope that this would kill the unwanted approach) and when the government announced that the bid would not be referred, Northern unveiled a defence strategy based on promising shareholders a package of shares and special dividends valued at £5.07 a share, plus increasing normal dividends in future. It was just over four years since the company had been sold for £2.40 a share, and this defence document caused an uproar.

The regulator happened to be in the middle of a period of formal consultation needed before his proposals could be incorporated into the companies' licences. While there had been no prior intention of using this consultation period to reopen the substantive decisions, on 7 March 1995, the regulator announced that he would be seeking views on whether he should now do so. At the end of the consultation period, he announced that the price reductions for the first year of the new controls would be implemented as previously announced, but that he would undertake a full review of the appropriate prices for the following four years. His position was that he had to respond to the new information revealed in Northern's defence document, and that it would have been worse for the companies' incentives to have continued with a price control that risked becoming unsustainable than to have taken action when he did. Legally, there was no doubt that the regulator was allowed to reopen the review in this way, but his actions had been completely unexpected and severely weakened his reputation with the companies and investors.[5]

In May 1995, the MMC published its report on Hydro-Electric, the Scottish company that had appealed against its price control (MMC, 1995). The MMC report effectively contained a formula that could be applied to calculate what it believed to be an appropriate value for the price control. This went further than the Commission's previous price control report, on British Gas, which had discussed the elements of the company's price control, but had specifically avoided giving a precise formula. The regulator was able to draw on arguments in this report to support his revisions to the RECs' price controls – even so, the reductions he announced in July were smaller than commentators had been predicting.[6]

The main lesson from this episode was learned – regulators started to release far more information during price control reviews, to minimize the risk of surprises when the final numbers were announced. Furthermore, the MMC has now adopted a similar formula-based approach in a number of reviews, so that all parties can anticipate the result of an appeal to the Commission. The Commission is not formally bound by precedent, but generally favours consistency over time. However, it has been willing to modify its approach in response to further consideration – in 1997, it changed the way it had dealt with British Gas' depreciation of capital investment. At privatization, investors had paid much less than the book value for British Gas' existing assets, and the MMC used a marked-down value when considering the appropriate value for the price control – remember that this report did not give an explicit formula. The company's depreciation charge, however, was not marked down. This was clearly inconsistent (Newbery, 1997), although it need not have produced a windfall gain to investors.[7] The second time it dealt with the matter, however, the MMC reversed its policy, adopting the consistent policy of marking down both the value of the pre-privatization assets and the depreciation charge on them. While consistency over time is useful in regulation, institutions must retain the flexibility to change their position, and the MMC had this flexibility.

If both sides can anticipate how the MMC will rule on a particular price control, we might expect that it would rarely be necessary to go to the MMC. However, one regulator was to argue that he did not have to follow the MMC's recommendations. In July 1996, the electricity regulator for Northern Ireland (which was not covered by the British regulator) published proposed revenues for Northern Ireland Electricity (NIE), and the company appealed to the MMC. In March 1997, the MMC reported firstly, that it would be against the public interest if NIE did not have a price control, and secondly, that the new control should give NIE revenues of £575 million over five years – roughly halfway between the company's and the regulator's positions. The regulator used this report to impose his original proposals!

The privatization acts had stated that the licences could not be amended without the company's agreement unless the MMC ruled that not to amend them would be against the public interest, but the Acts had not explicitly said that the amendments had to be the ones recommended by the MMC. Northern Ireland Electricity sought a Judicial Review of its regulator's actions, but lost, on the basis that the MMC had not explicitly said that its figure of £575 million should be taken as a floor. This left regulation in a very unsatisfactory position – the MMC had been put into the system to protect companies from an over-zealous regulator (or government), but the judgement seemed to imply that as long as the MMC held that some regulation was needed, then the regulator retained discretion over what formula to apply! Fortunately, the Court of Appeal decided to read the MMC report as a whole, inferred that it would be against the public interest to give NIE revenues that differed from £575 million, and over-ruled the earlier judgement.

The position was cemented in the Utilities Act 2000, under which the Commission had to approve any licence amendments made in response to its reports, giving it the final say in the process. That Act also replaced the individual regulators for gas and electricity in the UK with an Authority, with a mix of full-time and non-executive members. When regulators were individuals, the relationship between the regulator and the industry had often become personalized, creating conflict. This is less likely when the regulator is actually a group, and more recent moves to split the functions of Chair of the Authority and Chief Executive of the supporting office have further depersonalized matters. With a predictable formula, and a transparent review process, regulation has moved towards the technocratic and away from the political. It will never be possible to remove the political element entirely, but Keynes' analogy of the economist as dentist is a useful guide for regulators – they may inflict pain on their charges, but it should be predictable.

6 Electricity wholesale market rules

The final institution considered in this chapter is the wholesale market for electricity. This was created specially for the privatization – when the industry was nationalized, the Area Boards simply received power from the Central Electricity Generating Board and paid its bulk supply tariff. In the run-up to privatization, the industry was worried that the new institution of a wholesale market would jeopardize its security of supply, and ended up designing a market that replicated as many as possible of its pre-privatization procedures.

The Pool was a compulsory day-ahead auction, in which every large power station had to participate. Stations submitted almost the same information to the system operators, one day in advance, as they had when the industry was nationalized, and the system operators used almost the same procedures in deciding which units to schedule to meet the forecast demand. The key difference was that while stations had submitted cost information before privatization, they submitted up to five prices afterwards. The stations also had to inform the system operator of their forecast availability over the period, and give a range of technical operating parameters – generators were to discover that changing the values of these parameters could increase their revenues.

A linear computer program combined the operating parameters with the prices, treating the latter as if they were costs, and calculating the schedule that would minimize the 'cost' of meeting demand, just as it had before privatization. A set of algorithms then calculated the average cost of power from the most expensive station in normal operation in each half-hour, and set it to be the System Marginal Price in that half-hour. Another algorithm calculated the probability that demand would exceed the available capacity, given the capacity declared available in advance, and its past reliability. This Loss of Load Probability was multiplied by the Value of Lost Load (set administratively) to give a Capacity Payment. Other costs incurred by the system operator were recovered in an Uplift Charge. Generators received the System Marginal Price and the Capacity Payment for their scheduled output, while suppliers paid these prices, plus Uplift, for their actual demand. On each day, the sums going into and out of the Pool had to balance.

As already mentioned, the Pooling and Settlement Agreement contained elaborate procedures for its own amendment. A Pool Executive Committee, with five generator and five supplier representatives, would decide on proposals, but its decisions could be referred to votes by all member companies, and dissenters could then appeal to the regulator for a final decision. These procedures were intended to protect minority interests while still allowing change when necessary. In some areas, change was definitely foreseen, for it had not been possible to reach a final agreement before the deadline for implementing the new system.

One of these areas was transmission losses – some energy is wasted in heating up transmission wires as power flows through them. At the times of highest demand, these implied that 100 MW of extra generation in the South-West of England could be as effective in meeting a rise in demand as 110 MW in the North. It would be economically efficient to signal this by multiplying production and demand by scaling factors that reflected these marginal transmission losses. It would also lead to a large loss of income for northern generators, and a significant rise in costs for southern retailers. It is perhaps hardly surprising that it was not possible to reach agreement in the run-up to privatization.

The issue was included in a schedule listing decisions that would be required in future, and a scheme for resolving it was proposed in 1994. The quantities sold to or bought in the Pool would be scaled up (in the south) or down (in the north) by zonal transmission loss factors, reflecting the average losses incurred on power produced in each region. The use of average losses produced weaker signals than the economically efficient use of marginal losses, but it also reduced the changes in company profits. This was not enough to make it acceptable to all Pool members, however, and so the decision was appealed to the regulator. He approved the scheme, but when the Pool had to agree the programme of work to carry it out, there was another appeal. Once again, the regulator rejected the appeal, in a judgement that showed signs of impatience with what might be seen as time-wasting behaviour.[8] The losing companies then took the issue to a Judicial Review (in essence, asking a court to check that the regulator had acted within his powers and followed the correct procedures) which delayed any further progress until the decision to abolish the Pool had been taken, and the proposals were abandoned.

One reason for the abolition of the Pool was the perception, based on experiences such as the one just described, that it was incapable of changing its rules when changes were required. The Pool was blamed for high prices (it was accused of making market power easier to exercise) and for the decline of the coal industry (the high prices encouraged entry by gas-fired plant). While the Pool had been a pioneer, other electricity markets developed since had allowed bilateral trading, and a compulsory centralized market seemed outdated (Offer, 1998).

The regulator led a review which proposed the abolition of the Pool and its replacement with New Electricity Trading Arrangements (NETA) based primarily on bilateral trading, and the government provided support, including an Act of Parliament that allowed the regulator and the government to impose changes to the companies' licences. Some central coordination is essential, and a Balancing and Settlement Code was developed for this, but the development of bilateral trading was left entirely to 'the market'. Three companies announced the formation of short-term power exchanges, but only two started, and these later merged. Over-the-counter trading is managed by a number of brokers.

The lesson of the Pool's inflexibility had been learned – the procedures for amending the Balancing and Settlement Code were designed to ensure speedy decisions. Companies would propose rule changes, a panel of industry representatives would recommend whether or not to adopt them, and the regulator (now an Authority, rather than a single person) would make the decision.

These procedures have generally worked well – most decisions were taken quickly and without undue controversy. Transmission losses were one exception, however. The industry panel reviewed two proposals put forward by companies, as modified to make them more practical, and rejected both, but the regulator decided to pursue one version of zonal transmission loss factors. At this time, however, the government was leading the process to bring Scotland into the market in England and Wales, the so-called British Electricity Trading and Transmission Arrangements (BETTA). The government was aware that implementing zonal loss factors would reduce the revenues of generators in the north of Scotland, which is exactly where it was expecting a large number of renewable generators to locate, should it make progress on its targets for a significant increase in renewable generation. Reducing their revenues might jeopardize those targets, and so the government announced that transmission loss factors would not be used once BETTA took effect. The regulator initially insisted that they would be used in England and Wales for the short interval between the time that the software needed would be ready and the start of BETTA, but then backed down.

This case may have shown the need for a body that could occasionally overrule the regulator. In any case, shortly after this episode, the Competition Commission was given the task of hearing appeals against the regulator's decisions. An appeal is only allowed if the regulator has gone against the industry panel's recommendation. This is again a sensible balancing of powers, while the fact that appeals can only be made if the regulator and the panel disagree should prevent them being used as a delaying tactic against a case that happens to reduce the appellant's revenues but is otherwise straightforward.

NETA's market rules may not be an improvement on those of the Pool – while the Pool had its faults, the short-term markets in NETA are illiquid, placing smaller participants at a disadvantage, while it is also hard to trade for more than a year or two in advance. However, the market's governance is much improved – there is a clear and efficient procedure for changing the rules, with a right of appeal against controversial decisions. In this aspect at least, the institution has evolved in a helpful direction.

7 Conclusions

The institutions created at the time of the UK's energy privatizations have changed significantly over the past twenty years. A single board has replaced two individual regulators, and while the regulator has more powers, there are some additional checks and balances, and the regulators now act in a generally more transparent manner. RPI–X regulation has evolved towards rate of return regulation, driven by a formula based on a company's predicted costs, although the regulators do try to give the companies incentives to keep costs down.

The industrial structures have changed – the integrated monopoly of British Gas has evolved into a number of transportation companies, storage companies, and a competitive supply sector. Most supply companies sell both gas and electricity. Wholesale markets have been designed, and re-designed, for both commodities. With a single regulator, they share common features, but differ to take account of the physical characteristics of each product.

The process of change is best described as one of evolution – there was quite a lot of trial and error, and while a few politicians and advisers may have had a clear vision of where they wanted to go, almost no-one knew how we would eventually get there. The institutions that we have now are generally performing well, and while the experience of the past twenty years shows the dangers of making predictions, it is hard to think of major changes that could be required.

The impact of these institutions on performance is harder to assess. In some respects, the initial institutions were clearly inadequate, such as in the 'competitive' part of the gas market. Customers suffered from British Gas' pricing behaviour, and changes were needed to improve matters. The Pool's difficulties in changing its rules meant that electricity trading was less efficient than it could have been. In many other areas, however, the initial institutions were reasonably good – regulatory boards have advantages over single regulators, but we were generally fortunate in the people appointed to those positions. When the starting point is good enough, the impact of subsequent improvements is less obvious. The UK started from a set of institutions that was generally adequate, and has improved them since.

Notes

1. Some gas also comes from other areas, including a few onshore fields, and the Morecambe Bay field off the north-west coast of England.
2. The actual decision to refer a case to the MMC was generally made by a government minister at this time.
3. The DGFT referred BG under the Fair Trading Act 1973, dealing with the competitive market, while the gas regulator referred BG under the Gas Act 1986, seeking changes to the licence governing its regulated activities. The MMC accordingly produced two reports, one for each reference, although most of the evidence was published in two further common (and lengthy) volumes.
4. Some of the buyers, such as Scottish and Southern Electricity, are also gas suppliers, but the networks have to be strictly separated from the supply businesses, giving no real scope for anti-competitive actions.
5. The damage to his reputation was worsened by the fact that the announcement of the new review came 24 hours after the government had raised £3½ billion by selling shares in the two major generating companies, and their prices dropped by about 10 per cent, even though they were not formally affected by the distribution price controls.
6. The regulator's reputation suffered a further blow because of his decision to give each REC its own number 24 hours in advance of the official announcement. The numbers, or rumours about them, quickly started to circulate, and the regulator had to rush down to London to give the official announcement the afternoon before he had planned to do so.

7. As long as the regulator reduced the value of the company's assets, on which it was allowed to earn a return, by the depreciation charge that was also used in the price control calculations, the present value of the company's revenues did not depend on the depreciation charges used.
8. Such behaviour was clearly rational for northern generators – if a small amount of management time can be devoted to postponing the loss of 2 per cent or more of your income by several months (or more), it is a worth–while trade–off for the company that appeals.

References

Armstrong, M., S. Cowan and J. Vickers (1994) *Regulatory Reform: Economic Analysis and British Experience* (Cambridge, MA: MIT Press).

Helm, D.R. and T.J. Jenkinson (1997) 'The Assessment: Introducing Competition into Regulated Industries', *Oxford Review of Economic Policy*, vol. 13, no. 1, pp 1–14.

Levy, B and P. Spiller (1996) *Regulations, Institutions and Commitment: A Comparative Analysis of Telecommunications Regulation* (Cambridge: Cambridge University Press).

Littlechild, S.C. (1983) *Regulation of British Telecommunications Profitability* (London: HMSO).

Monopolies and Mergers Commission (1988) *Gas: A Report on the Matter of the Existence or Possible Existence of a Monopoly Situation in Relation to the Supply of Gas Through Pipes to Persons Other Than Tariff Customers*, Cm 500 (London: HMSO).

Monopolies and Mergers Commission (1993a) *British Gas plc: Volume 1 of Reports Under the Gas Act 1986 on the Conveyance and Storage of Gas and the Fixing of Tariffs for the Supply of Gas by British Gas plc*, Cm 2315 (London: HMSO).

Monopolies and Mergers Commission (1993b) *Gas: Volume 1 of reports under the Fair Trading Act 1973 on the Supply within Great Britain of Gas Through Pipes to Tariff and Non-tariff Customers, and the Supply within Great Britain of the Conveyance and Storage of Gas by Public Gas Suppliers*, Cm 2314 (London: HMSO).

Monopolies and Mergers Commission (1995) *Hydro-Electric plc: A Report on a Reference under Section 12 of the Electricity Act 1989* (London: HMSO).

Newbery, D.M. (1997) 'Determining the Asset Base for Utility Price Regulation', *Utilities Policy*, vol 6, no 1, pp. 1–8

Newbery, D.M. (1999) *Privatization, Restructuring and Regulation of Network Utilities* (Cambridge, MA: MIT Press).

Offer (1998) *Review of Electricity Trading Arrangements: Proposals, July 1998* (Birmingham: Office of Electricity Regulation).

Vickers, J. and G. Yarrow (1988) *Privatization: An Economic Analysis* (Cambridge, MA: MIT Press).

Waddams Price, C.M. (1997) 'Competition and Regulation in the UK Gas Industry', *Oxford Review of Economic Policy*, vol. 13, no. 1, pp. 47–63.

Index